S0-BLA-921

This Small City Will Be a Mexican Paradise

This Small City Will Be a Mexican Paradise

Exploring the Origins of Mexican Culture
in Los Angeles, 1821–1846

Michael J. González

University of New Mexico Press | Albuquerque

©2005 by the University of New Mexico Press
All rights reserved. Published 2005
Printed in the United States of America
10   09   08   07   06   05   1   2   3   4   5   6   7

LIBRARY OF CONGRESS CATALOGING-IN-PUBLICATION DATA

González, Michael, 1958–
  This small city will be a Mexican paradise : exploring the origins of Mexican
culture in Los Angeles, 1821–1846 / Michael González.
      p. cm.
  Includes bibliographical references and index.
  ISBN 0-8263-3607-8 (pbk. : alk. paper)
  1. Mexicans—California—Los Angeles—Ethnic identity.
  2. Mexicans—California—Los Angeles—Social conditions—19th century.
  3. Elite (Social sciences)—California—Los Angeles—History—19th century.
  4. Group identity—California—Los Angeles—History—19th century.
  5. Racism—California—Los Angeles—History—19th century.
  6. Indians of North America—California—Los Angeles—Social conditions—
19th century.   7. Los Angeles (Calif.)—Ethnic relations.   8. Los Angeles
(Calif.)—Race relations.   9. Los Angeles (Calif.)—Social conditions—
19th century.   I. Title.
  F869.L89M5173 2005
  305.868'72079494'09034—dc22

                              2005013447

Design and composition: Melissa Tandysh

To myself I whispered that I still had my gun, and that I was a free man—free to trace the fugitive, free to destroy my brother.

—Vladimir Nabokov, *Lolita*

Homo sum nihi humanarum ame alienum puto.
(Because I am a man, the ways of men are not strange to me)

—School primer from Los Angeles, ca. 1840

This small city is beginning to show its astral magnificence and brilliance in a manner that [when] a traveler comes . . . everybody tells him [Los Angeles] will be a Mexican paradise.

—Leonardo Cota, 1845

Contents

Acknowledgments

HEREIN IS THE STORY OF MEXICAN LOS ANGELES, and, as in the unfolding of any story where there are many characters, there are many people who have contributed to the writing of this tale. I would like to honor my colleagues Iris Engstrand and Jim Gump for bearing with me as I labored to produce this manuscript. I would also like to thank my many students who have heard me talk about "the book" for years. The book has finally come to pass, and one student in particular, Jenny Snively, contributed to its writing. Her research on marriages in Los Angeles provided a great deal of help at a critical time. The Haynes Foundation of Los Angeles also deserves my gratitude. The grant they awarded me helped lift some of the gloom that often accompanies any creative effort. My friends and colleagues at various institutions offered important insights. Raymund Paredes, when vice-chancellor at UCLA, provided me with the inspiration to begin this project. I have always valued the times I sat down to talk with him. Walter Brem at the Bancroft Library at UC Berkeley helped me locate rare items. At the Seaver Center for Western History, Janet Fireman lent valuable assistance and pointed me to some important collections. Hynda Rudd at the city clerk's office in Los Angeles offered important counsel as I tried to make sense of the municipal archives. I would be remiss not to mention Jay Jones, also of the city clerk's office, who answered my every query. Scholars in the field of Borderlands history took time out of their busy schedules to offer me advice. Michael Engh, Leonard Pitt, and Richard Griswold del Castillo read earlier incarnations of this manuscript and helped me sharpen several points. Ramón Gutiérrez offered even more aid. His critical eye pointed out some glaring weaknesses in my argument. He also provided assistance when I needed it most, and for this kindness, I can never thank him enough. David Holtby, editor-in-chief for UNM Press, was always gracious enough to address my concerns no matter how tight and burdensome his schedule. I would be well served to follow his example. Lydia Lennihan, also of the Press, showed great patience when she prepared my manuscript for publication. She, too, merits special thanks.

Family members lent me support whose value was incalculable. My brother Gregory applied a journalist's touch to one of the earlier drafts. In Texas, my in-laws Jonás and Olga Alvarez had faith in me through thick and thin. My parents, Henry and Grace González never wavered in their support, and if I turn out half as well as they, I will be a success in life. Finally, my wonderful wife Olga lent the best support of all. She read various drafts, listened to my ideas, and encouraged me to persevere. She is also the mother of Olga Belén and Lucas Gabriel, our twins who entered this life as I put the final touches on my manuscript. It is to her that I dedicate this work, and there are not enough words to describe how much I value her love and wisdom. All these individuals contributed to the story, though I take full responsibility for all missteps and errors. But, all the same, to reach this point, I have stood on the shoulders of many.

M. J. G.
San Diego, 2004

INTRODUCTION

Tongues on Fire

STOP, FOR A MOMENT, AND WONDER: What did most inhabitants of Los Angeles want between 1821 and 1846, the years Mexico governed California? Did they wish to cultivate ties with Mexico? Or did they want to escape Mexico's embrace? Some scholars argue that the residents of Los Angeles, along with their neighbors in other California settlements, preferred to be left alone. One historian explains that the province became the settlers' "patria," or nation. Mexico, on the other hand, loomed as a "foreign place," the home of "strangers."[1]

Such an argument suggests that the people of Los Angeles—like their contemporaries elsewhere in the province—found success by standing apart from Mexico. The first inhabitants came in 1781 when Spain established Los Angeles to produce food for nearby presidios, or forts.[2] The residents never exceeded three thousand people at any point during Los Angeles' first seventy years of existence, but they had sufficient numbers to apply their talents. They first cultivated grain and, over time, turned their attention to other livelihoods. After the start of the Mexican period in 1821, many grazed cattle, and once or twice a year—sometimes more—they slaughtered their herds to collect hides or tallow, the fat gleaned from the carcasses.[3] Trading the cattle products with Yankee ships anchored off the coast, a good number used the visitors' wares to embellish their rank and seek advantages over their neighbors. Prosperous families, especially those who profited in the cattle trade, ignored their Indian ancestry and insisted they had Spanish blood. Another, less successful group followed

1

behind. They, too, tried raising cattle, but if success proved elusive they cultivated farming plots or moved into town to practice a trade. A few, impressed by the pretensions of wealthy compatriots, also claimed Spanish descent. The remaining inhabitants who had experienced misfortune, or failed to develop their abilities, seemed content with their lot. As one scholar suggests, they awaited the fiesta to hoist the drinking cup and feast on beef.[4] Indians, meanwhile, rarely treated as companions or neighbors by the other inhabitants, filled the lower ranks. They worked on the cattle spreads or tilled a farmer's fields. Some, especially children and women, landed in domestic service and maintained the employer's home.

In this version of events, the prosperous residents of Los Angeles, and any who aspired for riches, often resolved their troubles without using force. By the 1830s, prominent inhabitants wanted Los Angeles to have a bigger say in provincial affairs. On two occasions, they prevailed on superiors in Mexico City, or used their own initiative, to make Los Angeles the capital of California. In Monterey, the community that usually sat as capital, the inhabitants resented the change of venue. Neither side, though, resorted to drastic action. In the first dispute, each faction relied on compromise to return the seat of government to Monterey. Or, as happened in the second case, they agreed that both settlements would share the responsibilities of governance.[5] When the residents of north and south had other disagreements, with Los Angeles again serving as a site of unrest, troops formed ranks to settle matters. But the rivals did not lay waste to one another. The side with the most men fired a few salvos to intimidate the opposition and force surrender. The Indians, in the meantime, offered residents even fewer reasons to reach for the gun or bayonet. One scholar implies that the inhabitants of southern California rarely faced the prospect of Indian war.[6] If some Indians became difficult, as would happen at times, they suffered banishment from Los Angeles or atoned for their crime by serving in a labor gang.[7] For the more recalcitrant, a public execution would quiet rebellious hearts.

Throughout these episodes, or so we may assume, the residents of Los Angeles continued to seek wealth and pleasure. They strutted and preened, played the aristocrat, or, for humbler sorts, enjoyed the weekend party. Cattle ranching remained the chief occupation, offering meat for the dinner table and providing the sums many needed to finance their pursuits. But in 1846, the end came. The Americans invaded and everything changed.

To be fair, the preceding descriptions contain some truth. Though their reliance on the cattle trade seems exaggerated and subject to romance, some inhabitants did use livestock to indulge their aristocratic fantasies. Other descriptions also prove accurate. The residents of Los Angeles, a bit too ambitious on occasion, upset compatriots in Monterey by seeking to move the site of the provincial capital. And, it is true that the disputes between north and south often took a serious turn, though without severe consequences. The residents of Los Angeles and other California settlements faced each other on the battlefield only to let displays of bravado, and not bullets, decide the contest.

But the other assessments that describe the inhabitants' thoughts about leisure or Indians, and, of course, Mexico, contain nothing more than simple, broad strokes. The fine detail or exacting point, the qualities that amount to the strivings of the mind and spirit, escape notice. Once brought to light, the humblest concern or boldest desire may suggest that the residents of Los Angeles wondered what more they could do to find fulfillment. By the nineteenth century, social upheaval had convulsed Europe and parts of North America, events that many people throughout the world noticed, even in distant California. It seems unlikely that the residents of Los Angeles would resist the call to revolution and continue deferring to the powerful. During a political dispute in 1836, one inhabitant penned an appeal entitled, *Salus Populi Suprema Lex Est*, "The Welfare of the People is the Supreme Law," a line that comes from Montesquieu's *Spirit of the Laws*.[8] To some residents, the rule of law, and not the prerogative of the wealthy, seemed a better way to direct a community's affairs. If there is reason to doubt the nature of political authority, then other questions may arise about life in Mexican Los Angeles. Would the residents of Los Angeles, living in a land isolated by the ocean on one side and desert on the other, always wish to stand apart from Mexico? Or would they, and their California compatriots, call upon Mexico to relieve the burdens of a desolate existence?

The questions bear on current events. At present, Mexican immigrants and their descendants fill California. They accounted for a third of the state's population in 2000. Within two decades, the number will increase to at least forty percent.[9] Los Angeles, in particular, best reflects the Mexican increase. Throughout the region that comprises metropolitan Los Angeles, nearly half of the population has some connection to Mexico. Aside from Mexico City, the Los Angeles area has more people of Mexican ancestry than any other place in North America.

Some state residents, to judge from letters to the editor in local newspapers, fear that Mexico is plotting to reconquer California. One writer to the *Los Angeles Times* recently warned that "Mexican officials are exacting a methodical revenge for past historical events by slowly but surely eating away at the sovereignty of the United States."[10] But those who think invaders stand poised at border may think twice after learning that Mexicans have lived in California for nearly two centuries. Such knowledge does not require any opinion about who settled California first. Indians can challenge, and refute, any claim to primacy. Still, when receiving word about Mexico's legacy in California, some critics may feel obliged to reconsider their grim scenarios.

But for the lesson to work, we must return to the nineteenth century and see how the inhabitants of Los Angeles looked at Mexico. Of course, any attempt to divine human wants and compulsions may prove a difficult task. Some *angeleños*—the residents of Los Angeles—only desired a comfortable place to rest from a day's labors.[11] A few more wanted enough rain and sunshine to bring in a bountiful crop. Yet others looked forward to a good smoke, a tasty meal, or the fancy hat and pair of shoes sitting in a shopkeeper's store. But one wish above all often dominated. If it did not, it at least occupied a prominent spot in the heart with other wishes. For in the end, most angeleños regretted their solitary life and desired a close connection to Mexico.

In these opening pages, the examination of angeleño sentiments proceeds by steps. One of the first steps addresses the reasons why the angeleños felt attracted to Mexico. Mexico held enough appeal in its own right. But it is worth wondering if something, or someone, inspired the angeleños' affections. At one more remove come examples of the angeleños' attachments to Mexico. A document serves as evidence, as will items of cloth or glass. On occasion, the angeleños preferred more intellectual offerings and welcomed particular ideas from Mexico. To some, these thoughts proved more substantial than any material item. At the last, we study how the angeleños fashioned their wishes and aspirations. The wealth or status of each angeleño, while presenting obstacles to agreement, did not always prove significant. One angeleño, two angeleños, even a handful, and not much more than that, can speak for the multitude who remained silent or occupied different ranks. But to start, oftentimes the most difficult step to accomplish, we deal with the doubt that Mexico mattered at all to the angeleños.

In all truth, Spain, too, inspired great feeling. Beginning in 1769, and ending in 1821 when Mexico won independence, Spain ruled California for more than fifty years. Spain gave California its name, from Calafia, the

Black Amazon queen from a sixteenth-century novel, or from a play on the Latin phrase, *calida fornax,* "hot furnace."[12] Spain promulgated California's first laws, laws that Mexico often saw fit to continue, named the first governors, and founded the towns that would later grow into cities. Some of California's first settlers came from Spain. Spain also promoted the growing of grapes for wine and the planting of citrus trees. It commanded settlers to plow the ground for wheat and corn, flax and hemp. Spain introduced cattle and horses. Sheep came later, as would hogs.

But beyond any item or foodstuff it brought to California, Spain received the most notice for establishing the missions. Spain built all of California's twenty-one missions, save for San Francisco Solano, the only one constructed under the Mexican regime.[13] The first mission appeared in San Diego, close to the modern-day border between California and Mexico, with the last rising northeast of San Francisco, nearly four hundred miles to the north. The rest, meanwhile, fell in between. Some sat close to the ocean or dotted valleys in the interior. A few had a civil settlement or fort close by, but others, except for neighboring Indian villages, occupied more lonely spots.

Spain's plan to construct the missions, and thus convince the Indian converts, or neophytes, to labor for God and King, invited various reactions. At times, the missions aroused anger and disappointment. From the first days of colonization, settlers and provincial administrators worried that the missions commanded too much influence. A settler who wanted to try his hand at farming often lamented that the Church claimed the most fertile stretches of territory. Great herds of livestock, usually grazing the finest pasture, filled the outer reaches of the mission estate. Closer in, nearer to the mission compound, neophytes tended fields rich with crops and fruit trees. The provincial administrators, meanwhile, complained that they had trouble exercising their authority. Franciscan priests, the order that ran the missions, had great say in California's affairs. When disputes arose with the administrators, the clerics gained the support of royal officials in Mexico City by saying that they knew best how to make California thrive. For their part, the administrators tried to present their case, but usually failed.

The missions' good fortune declined after Mexico gained independence from Spain.[14] The Mexican government, wary of the Church's influence, secularized the missions in 1834. The process, designed to last three years, freed Indian converts who met certain qualifications and awarded them with parcels of land. The mission site, meanwhile, would serve as the pueblo, or settlement, for emancipated Indians. Though secularization did not seek to benefit the provincial residents, they found ways to claim their share of mission territory. The Indians had trouble adjusting to freedom, and many lost their holdings to the settlers.[15] In other instances, the officials who ran the mission estate assigned to the provincial government distributed property to applicants who wanted to farm or raise cattle. By 1844, when secularization had run its course, a great portion of mission lands rested in the hands of settlers.

But the missions did not always receive scorn. Prior to the 1830s, and even in the years thereafter, witnesses claimed that the missions helped sustain the province. Some settlers argued that the missions opened up their granaries when drought or famine hit the province. A few more added that the mission neophytes performed necessary chores in settlements or on outlying homesteads. The settlers' delegate to the Mexican Congress, aware that some of his constituents relied on the missions for survival, worried that secularization would devastate the province. He declared in the early 1830s that the "inhabitants of California are convinced that . . . the sources of public prosperity which have given life to the country and by which it subsists are the missions."[16] Without the missions, he warned, California faced "inevitable ruin."[17]

For those who welcomed the missions, they usually lavished tribute on Spain, not Mexico. Some settlers, especially in the American era when they longed for simpler times, focused their praises on Spanish priests. A witness remembered that one priest proved so conscientious in his duties that the "people held him as a saint."[18] Another priest, who received the "love" of "everyone," used "good advice" to calm political disputes and prevent the "[shedding] of blood" that occurred in "other parts of Mexico."[19] Toward the end of the nineteenth century, Spain's legacy continued to shine. One angeleño boasted in 1874 that California's inhabitants possessed Spain's "character, features, and mental gifts . . . [making] them the true sons of that proud nation whose deeds, power and significance gave her pre-eminence over the powers of the earth."[20]

But if Spain's feats earned attention, Mexico's contributions to California life provided more reason to excite comment. Mexico's impact begins with the origins of California's settlers. Up until the American invasion in the mid-nineteenth century, many, if not most, of the people who settled California came from Mexico, or as it was known before independence in 1821, New Spain.[21] Some came as soldiers assigned to the presidios that ran along the California coast. The first troopers arrived in 1769 to protect the new mission at San Diego, and for twenty years thereafter, more detachments established the presidios at Monterey, San Francisco, and Santa Barbara. Over time, especially at the outset of the nineteenth century, different sorts headed north. For various reasons, some had fallen out of favor with the government and suffered banishment to California. Others, meanwhile, arrived on their own initiative. They took a ship to the province, or for the more intrepid, they came on horseback across mountains and desert.

Most individuals joined expeditions organized by the colonial, or later, national government to build settlements in the province. Hearing that the members of an expedition would receive land, tools, animals, seed, and other inducements once they reached their destination, a poor individual would think the trip was worth the trouble. For their part, the organizers, afraid that scoundrels would volunteer, often chose members of a family for an expedition.[22] A husband and wife, especially if they had children, would supposedly have greater desire to work and resist the temptation to loaf. Once all agreed to terms, the party, which often had between forty and two hundred members, headed north. The first expedition established San José, a town in the northern half of California, in 1777. Four years later, another group from Mexico traveled to the lower portion of the province and founded Los Angeles, some three days' ride from San Diego, the southernmost outpost in the province.[23] Finally in 1797, one last expedition established Branciforte, a settlement nearly seventy miles south of San Francisco, and now home to modern-day Santa Cruz.[24] After Mexico assumed control of the province in 1821, the national government sent one more expedition north to settle territory northeast of San Francisco. In 1834, José Híjar and José María Padrés, following the suggestions of their backers, recruited a party of teachers, craftsmen, and farmers.[25] The Híjar-Padrés colony, as the expedition came to be known, disbanded soon after arrival. The reasons for failure are far too complex to relate here, but many settlers remained in California and resided in places like Los Angeles. Other groups, which may have received the blessing but not the support of the national government, arrived throughout the years. Some parties traveled from Sonora, a state in northern Mexico.[26] A few more began their journey in New Mexico, one of Mexico's territories to the east of California, and settled in Los Angeles or moved up the coast to make their home in the northern part of the province.[27]

Once in Los Angeles, or any other provincial settlement, the migrants and residents, who were often descended from Mexicans who had come years before, set out to form some tie to Mexico. Most angeleños recognized that Mexico promised the means to succeed in a desolate land. When studying a map, or having braved the trip overland, the angeleños knew that they teetered at the edge of the nation. Enrique Krauze, a Mexican historian, explains that the residents of Mexico's northern territories, where dwelled the angeleños, "felt the values of the center with greater depth and urgency."[28] The "center," Krauze says, that point in Mexico where the country widens to the north, and to the south tapers to a funnel, provided the setting for great cities. Mexico City, Guadalajara, Guanajuato, and other cities rose among the valleys and mountains of central Mexico. Each city created the practices that people throughout the nation often imitated or altered according to their taste. As Krauze suggests, the further north the inhabitants lived, the greater the chance they would seek out, and confirm, some connection to the center.

Any attachment the angeleños nurtured and labored to maintain calls for scrutiny. If some angeleños felt compelled to emulate, even admire, Mexico, other impulses besides affection directed their sentiments. After all, as many recognized, it took some effort to adopt and follow Mexican practice. In other instances, some possibly wished to avoid the effort altogether. They might have preferred to march deeper into the interior, or move up the coast. Isolated, left alone to their own pursuits, they could construct routines more to their liking.

But because many wanted to follow some form of Mexican life, they apparently had good reason. When the angeleños scanned the mountains waiting for travelers to come overland, or waited for ships to drop anchor off the coast, some felt the pain of solitude. They, like any person left alone, took a moment to ponder their imperfections. Admittedly, few described the insecurities that darkened their dispositions. But at some point, even the most insensate and uneducated persons would have pondered their weaknesses. In time came the acknowledgment that inside their being, or in everyday practice, they missed something. Some angeleños likely fixed on the poor cut and weave of their neighbors' clothes. A few more, when listening to the words and phrases used in conversation, cringed at the brusque, vulgar terms employed by their neighbors. Others faced more disturbing possibilities. When studying their character, or examining their appearance, they made a discovery few would have liked.

This realization turned clearer when they heard about the stories circulated by the "common" residents of Mexico City. According to the tales, "barbarous Indians called Mecos" lived in California and the "savages" often made short work of any person "fool enough" to head north.[29] Mexicans who traveled to Los Angeles related the charge to provincial residents. Or, the angeleños likely learned about the claim in correspondence mailed from the interior. The more literate angeleños knew that the word Mecos came from Chichimeca, the name for Indian tribes inhabiting Mexico's northern reaches. But in the next instant, the angeleños would wonder who the Mexicans saw when mentioning the word. According to the historical record, the angeleños, as well as the other residents in California, rarely, if at all, uttered the term Mecos.[30] The Indians of California earned all sorts of names, but Mecos was not one of them. When Mexicans in the interior employed the word they did not repeat what was said in Los Angeles, but relied on their own usage. Moreover Mecos, as the angeleños knew, presented other meanings. The word described someone who was, according to one definition, "indecent . . . and obscene."[31]

It would not take the angeleños long to realize why Mecos seemed an appropriate term. When studying their dress and manner, perhaps indecent to some, they saw the people whom many Mexicans scorned. They, the angeleños, were the Mecos. Thus, when the angeleños wished to become Mexican, or claim some affinity with Mexico, they also confessed that they did not want to be Indians. If they had doubt about their choice, they looked at the California Indian to see, in human form, the life that awaited them if they spurned Mexico.[32] They would become Mecos, or wild Indians, a fate many wanted to avoid. But, to their relief, Mexicans, or at least Mexican ways, supposedly helped the angeleños escape a barbaric existence.

With the Indian close or living among them, the angeleños' regard for Mexico seemed a matter of convenience. They did not care for Mexico so much, but only wished to avoid indigenous influence. Even so, while fear, and not affection, sometimes provided greater motivation, the angeleños' attachment to Mexico seemed no less sincere. Any sort of dread or suspicion concerning Indians could, when turned around, result in feelings for Mexico equal in weight and intensity. But regardless of how or why their sentiments emerged, the angeleños summoned forth some aspect of Mexico to find comfort or security.

Some angeleños, when they wished, preferred to call themselves "Mexican." For a few, the word described an individual from one of the states in the nation's interior.[33] At other moments, the name Mexican, and its reference to Mexico, seemed a popular choice for the angeleños.[34]

If expected to explain where they lived, some said they lived in Mexico, not California. As a good number noted, they inhabited a Mexican province, Alta California, a stretch of territory that began at what is now Oregon and ran south to the present-day border with Mexico. By 1832, and the years thereafter, residents recognized that they inhabited a province that formed part of a nation. The angeleños often composed, or, if possible, signed, political appeals that opened with some variation of the line: "[To the] Mexican citizens residing in the upper territory of the Californias."[35]

Others insisted on using multiple names, but to use one or another designation would not make them any less Mexican. An individual, for instance, could boast he was an angeleño. He might add that he was an *abajeño* (from the Spanish word, *abajo*, for below), a resident who inhabited the lower region of California between San Luis Obispo and San Diego, a distance of more than three hundred miles. At times he might bristle if he was confused with those who resided in the upper half of California, the *arribeños* (derived from the Spanish word, *arriba*, meaning up or above). Then again, the individual could insist he was a *californio*, someone who inhabited any spot in the province.[36] But the various names, rather than cancel each other out, served by degrees as a set, and then subset, of the category "Mexican."

On occasion, the angeleños spoke of Mexico, or Mexicans, in the most intimate terms. Pablo Vejar, a resident of Los Angeles in the early nineteenth century, remembered that word of Mexico's beauties "swept" him off his feet.[37] Antonio María Osio, a man who lived for a spell in Los Angeles, wrote that he loved Mexico.[38] For good measure, he added that he was "Mexican to the four sides of his heart."[39] Long time inhabitant Juan Avila recalled that Romualdo Pacheco, a Mexican officer, was "well built" and "handsome."[40] Pacheco was "such a . . . gentleman," Avila sighed.[41]

In other moments, the angeleños affirmed their attachment by following Mexican habit and practice. José Arnaz, an angeleño merchant in the 1840s, suggested that some of his customers favored items manufactured in Mexico. Men desired *poblanos*, a style of hat from the Mexican state of Puebla. Other customers admired Arnaz's Mexican saddles, each one going for at least $300. If they fancied something else, they could buy Mexican brandy. The bottles went so quickly, Arnaz remembered, that he had to buy the stuff in "large lots" to keep an adequate supply. Women could select more elegant items from Mexico. They could throw a silk *rebozo*, or shawl, around their shoulders. If they wanted a lighter fabric for a hot summer night, they could try the rebozo spun from linen. For women who wanted something finer, they could wear *vestidos de charros*, Mexican dresses embroidered with gold or silver thread. On the bodice, from top to bottom, ran a row of silver and copper buttons that caught the outfit's sparkle.[42]

Mexico often held other attractions for the angeleños. Pancho Rangel, a member of an old angeleño family, remembered sitting down to feast on beans and tortillas, long a staple of the Mexican table. There was no sweeter music, Rangel claimed, than to hear "the clapping of hands of women making tortillas in the morning."[43] Mexican holidays provided the angeleños with more reason to eat well. José Joaquin Maitorena, a member of the Los Angeles *ayuntamiento*, or municipal council, in 1828 wanted his colleagues to stage a celebration for the Virgin of Guadalupe, the patroness of Mexico. Unfortunately, Los Angeles "did not have a drop" to drink, and Maitorena asked the priest at Santa Barbara Mission to sell the angeleños a barrel of wine. Apparently it was best to honor the Virgin with a full cup.[44] Eight years later, Antonio María Osio, who once sat as treasurer for Los Angeles, explained that he spent seventy-five pesos to finance the celebration for Mexican Independence Day on September 16. He did not say what he used the money for, but the cost, nearly a tenth of what the treasury collected per year, suggested that he helped pay for the celebrants' food and wine.[45]

There was more to Mexico's appeal. The angeleños applauded Mexican theater troupes that passed through town.[46] (The angeleños loved a good show.) They divided Los Angeles into four quadrants, or *manzanas*, a practice popular in Mexico where residents sliced up cities and towns into districts.[47] Following the example of compatriots in Mexico City, the angeleños formed a chapter of Los Amigos del Pais (The Friends of the Country), a literary society.[48] Other angeleños kept a book of Mexico's statutes in the home. During disputes with the ayuntamiento, they riffled through the pages to prove that the law was on their side.[49] At election time, the angeleños often selected Mexicans to sit on the ayuntamiento. Of the sixty-two men elected to the municipal council between 1822 and 1848, sixteen came from Mexico, more than a quarter of the total. In contrast, only five Americans won a seat on the ayuntamiento. And from this number, only one, Abel Stearns, gained office before 1844.[50] In other moments, the angeleños insisted that only the national government could maintain the province's peace and stability. When the residents of Monterey overthrew the provincial governor in 1836 and tossed him into jail, the angeleños held a public meeting to see if they would lend their support.

According to a witness, the angeleños did not take long to reach a decision. They denounced their northern compatriots and "declared their loyalty [to the governor] and Mexico."[51]

The Monterey episode, and any crisis that compared, made many angeleños contemplate what would happen if enemies threatened their attachment to Mexico. By 1836, news had come from Texas that Anglo-American revolutionaries, with the aid of the *tejanos*, the Spanish-speaking residents, had defeated Mexican forces and declared independence. But, as the angeleños soon discovered, the Americans, rather than share power as promised, set out to deprive the tejanos of their property rights and political privileges. The angeleños, worried about Anglo-American intentions in California, believed they too would suffer the tejanos' fate. Their fears were confirmed when they heard what Anglo-American settlers planned to do after helping the residents of Monterey imprison the Mexican governor. The "foreign adventurers," the term some angeleños used to describe the Americans, intended to unfurl a flag with the lone star of Texas and deliver the province to the United States. The angeleños rallied to keep California part of Mexico. The Los Angeles municipal council said the residents of Monterey were "hallucinated," and warned them to beware of Anglo-American lies.[52] Sometime later, a Mexican official who resided in Los Angeles continued the denunciations. In a letter to the ayuntamiento, the author complained that the rebels in Monterey wanted to "make California another Texas." He asked, "Shall we then be like the Texans, victims sacrificed to foreign ambition?"[53] The ayuntamiento, inspired by the letter and other appeals, mustered troops to fight the rebels. The angeleños suffered defeat, but the Americans never flew the Texas flag in Monterey, and California remained, for the time being, a province of Mexico.[54]

The Americans made trouble a decade later, but this time matters turned out differently. After the United States attacked in July of 1846, the angeleños could no longer avoid the prospect of American rule. In Monterey, the residents were the first to experience the agonies that afflicted their counterparts in Los Angeles. A witness noted that the inhabitants of Monterey, remembering "the nationality they held so dear," felt "sorrow" when the Anglo-Americans replaced the Mexican flag with the Stars and Stripes.[55] In time, the angeleños had their own reasons to weep. When American forces seized Los Angeles in early August, three hundred angeleños, nearly half of all the male populace, signed a call to arms that asked for volunteers to defend "the great Mexican nation." If they did not fight, the appeal warned, the angeleños risked seeing "our women violated, our innocent children beaten by the American whip, our property sacked ... [and] our temples profaned."⁵⁶ The angeleños expelled the Americans, but it was not enough. The Americans recaptured Los Angeles on January 10, 1847.

American insults only increased the angeleños' distress. One angeleño remembered that some Americans who had "solicited and obtained Mexican citizenship" chose to support the United States after war came. When news of their betrayal reached Los Angeles, explained the witness, "the people became indignant to see that these men, many of whom had married [local women] ... and made their fortunes in the shadow of the Mexican flag, now showed their ingratitude."⁵⁷ There is no room to debate if Mexico's ouster encouraged the Americans to commit outrages, but by 1856 some angeleños had tired of life under the United States. One angeleño despaired and wrote to a newspaper, "California is lost to the Hispano-Americano."⁵⁸

At this point, some readers may sit with arched eyebrows. Respect? Admiration? Sorrow even? For Mexico? Mexico seemingly had little to offer California.⁵⁹ After Mexico gained its independence in 1821, various factions engaged in bitter disputes that spread ruin and instability.⁶⁰ Monarchists wanted another king, though a few thought a sovereign would rule more wisely if guided by a strong constitution. Meanwhile, centralists, some of them conservatives who did not think Mexico needed a king, wanted to establish a strong, authoritarian government. Liberals, on the other hand, often opposed to monarchists and centralists, wanted the state to exercise more authority.

In time, many people throughout Mexico grew frustrated when the national government could not sort out its affairs. The president often received blame after things went awry. On occasion, rebels formed ranks to depose the president and install their favorite in Mexico City. When the usurper stumbled, as would happen often, a new set of rebels, or the same group from before, gathered again to put yet one more man in office. But change did not always require the formation of troops. The man in power, sensing the anger in Congress and the public, knew the moment had come to step down. The disruptions continued for years. In the period between 1821 and 1857, Mexico had sixteen presidents and thirty-three provisional national leaders, a record that would not stir patriotic feeling.⁶¹

According to some historians, the troubles convinced many inhabitants that Mexico, as a nation, did not exist.⁶² To be sure, Mexico had a capital, a legislature, and a flag, some of the things any nation would possess. Nor should it be overlooked that in the central part of the country the populace respected any symbol or institution that emphasized Mexico's legitimacy as a nation. But in more distant places, the sense of nationhood lost its appeal, and the government had trouble enforcing the law or winning the loyalty of citizens.

If they felt so inclined, the angeleños, and their californio compatriots, could question their allegiance to Mexico.[63] Mexico moved slowly to develop provincial towns and ports. At times, it provided little protection from hostile ships that prowled the coast. Mexico seemingly failed again when it could not stop other enemies. Indian raiders often descended from the mountains in the interior and seemingly roamed with impunity. Yankee adventurers also rode down the mountain trails. Some sided with Indian raiders and made off with a rancho's livestock. Other Americans only wished to trade, but their ability to move freely through the province only confirmed Mexico's weakness. When asking Mexico City to provide protection, the californios felt more frustration. A bankrupt treasury offered scant funds to finance a proper defense. Or, just as galling, intrigue in the capital diverted attention and left californio requests unfulfilled.[64]

Mexico compounded its errant ways through the years. Incompetent officers often received commands to sit as governor or occupy some office in the provincial government. To make matters worse, the responsibilities of leadership addled weak or unstable minds. In one instance, Governor Mariano Chico, a Mexican colonel, stormed into Los Angeles with an armed force and threatened to hang anyone who did not profess loyalty. (As it was no one swung from the trees.)[65] Chico continued his odd behavior when he left California in 1836 after being deposed in a coup. As he climbed into a rowboat that would take him to a ship sailing for Mexico, he embraced an Indian woman, saying she "was the best man" in the province and hoped crows would "peck out the eyes" of one of his californio rivals. Before setting off, the disgraced governor punned his name, declaring "Me voy Chico, pero volveré Grande"—roughly, "I'm leaving small but returning big."[66] Another time, the Mexican government forced prisoners into uniform and sent them to California. Once the convict soldiers arrived in California, many abandoned military discipline and returned to their criminal ways. On different occasions, Mexico City dispensed with the formality of swearing prisoners into the military and loaded them onto ships sailing north. Abandoned or destitute children, many of them orphans, also headed to California. The colonial, and later, national government, especially in the first decades of the nineteenth century, heeded the church's requests to send the unwanted youngsters to Monterey or other provincial settlements.

Some undesirables, except for bumbling governors or convict soldiers, caused little trouble, and in time, found success. But the thought that California seemed neglected, or only earned interest as a penal colony, disturbed many californios. At least twice before 1846, some provincial residents debated whether to ask Great Britain, or even the United States, to assume control of California.[67] In later years, a few californios continued to resent Mexico. Juan Bautista Alvarado, a resident of northern California, compared Mexico to a "stepmother."[68] Ygnacio Sepúlveda, a member of a prominent angeleño family, claimed that the californios "did not have the best feelings towards those who did not have the fortune of being born in the province." It was no surprise, he concluded, that some of his compatriots felt "antipathy toward the Mexicans."[69]

At this point, with word of the government's failures and settler hostility, it seems quite bold to say that the angeleños felt attached to Mexico. To support our argument, we use a wide range of materials that supposedly illustrate the angeleños' intentions. The *recuerdos*, a set of reminiscences the californios produced in the late nineteenth century, seem a treasure. Hubert Howe Bancroft, arguably the first significant scholar of the Anglo-American period, asked old californios to write about provincial life under Spain and Mexico. On other occasions, he sent his scribes to interview individuals who did not have the time or desire to put their words on paper. A few californios like Antonio María Osio wrote their own memoirs, but most testimonies involved the hand of Bancroft or one of his scribes. The recuerdos, at least eighty in number, and which now reside at the University of California, Berkeley, form the foundation of Bancroft's epic *History of California*, one more item we consult often. The seven-volume study, beginning with Juan Cabrillo's voyage along the California coast in 1542 and ending with the Gold Rush, offers details few sources can match.

Other materials, some of them rarely consulted by scholars, also appear valuable. The ayuntamiento records, the documents that preserve the proceedings of the municipal council, brim with information. The censuses from 1836 and 1844, surveys ordered by the Mexican government, contain more telling details. Many tallies and records compiled by the ayuntamiento add to the sources revealing angeleño thoughts and perspectives. The papers compiled by the Coronel, del Valle, and Sepúlveda families, a collection of letters or statements produced by the angeleños prior to 1846, contain descriptions that a municipal record would rarely preserve.

But in some instances the evidence may deceive. Bancroft's recuerdos, for instance, present details that should give readers pause.[70] Each witness sounds sincere, but the speakers, many up in years when they presented their life story, describe events that happened twenty, thirty, sometimes forty years prior. The passage of time could corrupt any memory. The rank and occupation of each speaker also invites doubt. Most of the people who worked with Bancroft or his scribes came from prominent families. Presumably few presented the perspective of the humble farmers and artisans who made up most of the californio population. Bancroft's *History*, for that matter, while rich in detail, also presents challenges. First published in the 1880s and never revised, the *History* possesses conclusions and arguments that can jar modern sensibilities.[71]

As for the ayuntamiento documents and any other angeleño source penned before 1846, more questions arise about accuracy. The number of angeleños who admired Mexico, and how deep their passion went, seems difficult to calculate. With some rare exceptions, no written document counts Mexico's supporters. As for the fervor of angeleño emotions, some letters or declarations honor Mexico, but the samplings may not confirm that most people felt inspired to offer tribute. Many who had mastered their letters knew that Mexico supported any claim to sophistication. But others who could handle a book and pen possibly held their praise. They may have harbored grudges against Mexico, or at least felt apathy. The individuals who could not read and write, a large part of the populace, give no reason to think they were more likely to admire Mexico. Perhaps some, maybe even a great number, disliked Mexico. With so much uncertainty about angeleño intentions, it seems rash to think that a few people could speak for many of their neighbors.

We require another method, perhaps a better way of judging the sources, to show that most angeleños felt attached to Mexico. Clearly, there lived some angeleños and californios who felt hostility. But to issue qualifications and words of caution may render meaningless any point we make. There is more reward, and more reason, to say that Mexico seemed quite popular with the angeleños.

To strengthen our argument and avoid mishaps, we must employ what Giambattista Vico called *fantasia*. Vico, an eighteenth-century philosopher from Italy, believed that the imagination, what he called fantasia, helped scholars see the world as did their subjects.[72] Vico challenged the idea that knowledge about nature and humanity could only come from scientific observation. He feared that the empirical method, the chief instrument of science, often degraded the study of human conduct. Faith and benevolence, even love, each feeling impossible to measure, much less prove by the scientific method, would no longer serve as motivations for a person's deeds or beliefs. Only political power, he worried, its impact easily observed and quantified, would appear as the primary force in the making of history. Even worse, Vico feared, with human yearnings failing to attract study—science, remember, cannot measure aspiration or desire—the past becomes nothing more than a tale of one group seeking to impose its will on another. If faith, or any item with emotional content, earns study, it only appears as an instrument wielded by an oppressive or dominant class.

Vico did not deny human brutality. The angeleños, as we will see, enjoyed inflicting pain and torment. He only proposed that fantasia, the use of the imagination, can improve the study of history. Vico, though, when speaking of the imagination, did not suggest that scholars invent or exaggerate detail. Rather, he implied that the joy and suffering that constitute human existence could help scholars decipher the past. To employ a simple test, think once more about Pancho Rangel and his description of an angeleño meal. In addition to tortillas, Rangel spoke of dining on "roast meat" and "cheese."[73] Though he did not mention any flavoring, it would not be wrong to say that he took bites from jalapeño peppers to spice up his dish. For us who inhabit the present, the descriptions of food can awaken the palate. The thought of roasted meat may make the mouth water, or for the more sensitive, the prospect of a chile pepper burning the tongue could make one think of tears coursing down the cheeks. If we can imagine the taste of jalapeño peppers, then other experiences from long ago may lay within the grasp of those of who employ fantasia. To expand on Vico's argument, when adopting the angeleños' perspective and imagining how they perceived their existence, we may observe things that have escaped our notice. We put out our hand, at least in the mind's eye, and touch what they touched. Their vision becomes our own and we see the sights that would have filled the eyes. Or, when turning inward and communing with our thoughts, we can sense the angeleños' hopes and fears.

This is not to say that humans in any time or place want the same things, or entertain similar desires. Rather our shared humanity serves as a portal through which we can enter. Once we acknowledge the ties that make us human, we can appreciate the perspective of another being. In the same instance, we, and the subjects we study, retain separate personalities. As a consequence, there may be thoughts or feelings that will always prove elusive. But there is no reason for the scholar to lose heart. The differences and remoteness imposed by time, however significant, do not impair understanding. The qualities we share with people in the past, more profound than any obstacle or hindrance, allow us to experience a world different from our own.[74]

The imagination functions best when working in concert with other methods. There is no reason to throw out the scientific approach. We count and measure the information buried in the ayuntamiento's tabulations, or extract figures that present, at least numerically, the things that inspired angeleño enterprise. Once the calculations sit at our disposal, they add more texture to Vico's ideas and help us evaluate the angeleños' documents.

We gather up a single document, and another, and maybe one more, each produced over the twenty-five years Mexico ruled California. Now, let loose the mind and imagine. With the imagination the veil drops, bringing into sight all that is hidden. If these documents and any others exist, no doubt more testimonials, many lost or destroyed, possessed the same sentiments. Even more, a document could be the summary of many conversations one angeleño had with another. The conversations have vanished, but the feelings or impressions they conveyed could circulate in any record.

Once before us, the document in our hands, and the others in whose place it stands, overflows with meaning. A word, and where it sits in a document, can reveal much. The date of the document, and what circumstances the author, or authors, faced, also provides information. When catching the tone of a piece, or eyeing the words, we may sense the thoughts a writer and his neighbors knew well—a good number of angeleños, like many of their compatriots throughout California, admired Mexico. Any outpouring for Mexico reflected a complexity that the angeleños expressed in various ways. Perhaps, as some admitted, Mexico could test angeleño patience. But with the Indians causing worry and suggesting an unflattering comparison, the angeleños needed to ease their distress. Mexico, however imperfect, provided the benefits and privileges that allowed the angeleños to say they did not resemble Indians.

To see angeleño sentiments unfold, we look—with the aid of fantasía— at the following petition penned in 1846:

February 19, 1846

To your Excellency the Governor [Pio Pico] we come before you the undersigned, and say that since the Indian ranchería was removed to the pueblito—a move calculated to end excesses and thefts—the aborigines . . . taking advantage of their isolation . . . steal from [neighboring orchards]. . . . [O]n Saturdays [they] celebrate and become intoxicated to an unbearable degree, thereby resulting in all manner of venereal disease, which will exterminate this race and . . . be beneficial to the city. To preserve the public health and do away with the vice of polygamy . . . [and] the excesses of prostitution [so that] the residents of Los Angeles would not be encouraged to do the same, we ask that the Indians be placed under strict police surveillance or the persons for whom the Indians work give [the Indians] quarter at the employer's rancho.

Signed:
Francisco Figueroa and Luis Vignes

Signatories:

Felipe Lugo	Ricardo Lankem (Laughlin)	—?—Villela
Juan Ramírez	Samuel Carpenter	Tomas Serrano
Januario Avila	Agustin Martin	Mariano Ruiz
José Serrano	Guillermo Wiskies (Wolfskill)	Antonio Salazar
Manuel Sepúlveda	Luis Bouchet	Casciano Carreon
Gil Ybarra	Maria Ballesteros	Maria Anta. Pollorena
Desiderio Ybarra	Francisco López	Vicente Elizalde
Miguel Pryor	Estevan López	Antonio Coronel[75]

Examine, first, what the petition seems to be. Only then, after agreeing on the apparent details, can we see more deeply, and perhaps, deeper still. At one look, the document appears simple. Two men, Francisco Figueroa and Luis Vignes, composed the petition; twenty-four of their fellow angeleños signed. The twenty-six signatories, each a member of the *gente de razón,* or the "people of reason," a group we examine in the following chapters, condemn Indian misconduct. Yet again, the petitioners say, the authorities, in this instance, the governor and his agents, must discipline the Native Californian. Current measures, they suggest, once popular, had failed to establish order. Some time before—the petitioners do not say when—the ayuntamiento had grown tired of Indian mischief and forced the Native Californians to live outside of Los Angeles. The *ranchería*, or Indian settlement, apparently sat close to the center of town, but the municipal council removed the Indians to another site, a *pueblito*, or small village, that sat some distance away. The Indians who resided on a distant cattle rancho or proved to be trusted servants in town could continue to live with the master. But all others without an employer needed to reside in the pueblito.

To the petitioners' dismay, the Indians continued to make trouble. During the weekends, the Indians supposedly staged wild celebrations inside Los Angeles or in the pueblito.[76] When drunk, if we can believe the petitioners, a few Indians apparently stole onto nearby farms to pluck fruit from orchards. If an orange or pear tree offered easy pickings, the petitioners feared for the security of other, more expensive items. A merchant, for instance, or the cattleman with a home in town, might think that their belongings would tempt the Indian reveler, who, after a few drinks, would barge into nearby homes looking for loot.

At times, the Indians preferred other delights. The petition, for instance, warns of "polygamy" and "prostitution," practices, to judge from the descriptions, which intrigued the angeleños. Pleasure, however, exacted a price. As the petition suggests, the Indians, and some gente de razón, risked contracting "venereal disease." The signatories, frustrated, their patience exhausted by the Indians' misdeeds, condemned the debauchery. They proposed new disciplines to control the Indians. "Police surveillance" held great promise, while an employer's vigilance in punishing troublemakers offered one more way to restore order.

But behind the petition's denunciations and warnings sit other meanings, all richer than we can assume. Presented to the governor on February 19, 1846, the appeal may reveal much about the angeleños' mentality. In four months, the United States would invade California. By the following January, six months after hostilities began, Mexican forces would surrender the province to the Anglo-Americans. The angeleño petition, one of the last produced in the Mexican era, presents an honest summary of what the signatories and their neighbors considered their dearest, most urgent beliefs. Of course, the angeleños had no idea that the petition would serve as their final testament. But circumstances intervened and gave the petition a stamp of finality. Any document the angeleños composed after the American conquest would reflect a faulty memory or the frustration of defeat. The petition, granted prominence by historical accident, reveals the angeleños in the midst of their labors. Different sources, from personal papers to the minutes produced by the Los Angeles ayuntamiento, remain vital, but all work best when compared with ideas within the petition. The angeleños, as represented by the petition, think, plan, and aspire for a better future, never assuming that within a matter of months, all would change.

Other elements confirm the petition's distinctive nature. The number of signatories, for instance, and who they were, suggests that a wide range of people put aside their differences to discipline the Indians. In earlier years, an author of another petition or document only sought individuals with whom he had the most in common. The ayuntamiento, for instance, more than any other group in Los Angeles, seemed quite selective in determining who could sign a document. The evidence suggests that when ayuntamiento members disliked a governor's policies, or wished to address other matters, they only invited male property holders to sign a petition.[77] Individuals who had no holdings apparently could not add their names. Women also proved lacking when ayuntamiento members looked for supporters. No woman received an invitation to pick up the pen for an ayuntamiento appeal, much less any other angeleño item that required a signature. At times, the ayuntamiento members became even more exclusive. They, and no one else, composed appeals without explaining their reasons or giving notice to the public.[78]

Occasionally, citizens who held no municipal office would produce an appeal. They did not, however, always circulate the document and urge all to sign. Only trusted friends and neighbors would read the words and, if need be, contribute their signatures. In 1835, to take one case, recent immigrants from Sonora petitioned the ayuntamiento to make Governor José María Figueroa resign from office.[79] Angeleños born in California or different parts of Mexico, or so it seemed, did not sign the document. Perhaps they received no invitation to add their signature, or, more likely, they did not even see the document. Even if they had had a chance to study the petition, few might have felt comfortable applying their names.

One year later, in 1836, an adulterous wife and her lover stood accused of killing the woman's husband. The dead man's friends and relatives, more than forty individuals, feared the murderers would escape justice, and they marched on the jail to execute the pair. During the uproar, the vigilantes defied the ayuntamiento's commands to let a judge decide the murderers' fate and signed a declaration explaining their intentions. No member of the ayuntamiento attached his signature, as had former members who sat on the municipal council in years past.[80]

The 1846 petition, however, attracted people from all walks of life. The 1836 and 1844 censuses, along with the *padrones*, or voting registers, confirm that a disparate group signed their names. Only one person, Agustín Martin, remains unknown—he appears in no civic record. Two women, María Ballesteros and María Antonia Pollorena, added their names. No other petition, as far as we know, features the name of any woman. When we turn to the two dozen men the diversity increases. Some could have been rivals who had sided with the vigilantes or the ayuntamiento in 1836. Of the men who voted to execute the couple, and possibly formed the firing squad, five signed the 1846 petition: Juan Avila, Ricardo Lankem (Richard Laughlin), Guillermo Wiskies (William Wolfskill), Juan Vignes, and Luis Bouchet. One man who sat on the ayuntamiento during the episode, Felipe Lugo, added his name in 1846.[81] Directly below Lugo's signature appeared that of Juan Ramírez, who, in 1836, received an appointment by the ayuntamiento to sit as *juez de campo*, or judge of the fields.[82] Perhaps Ramírez, like his patrons on the council, lamented the vigilantes' actions and harbored misgivings, but he signed in 1836, nonetheless. Other men who served on the ayuntamiento before 1836, Januario Avila, Gil Ybarra, and his father Desiderio Ybarra, may have resented the vigilantes' deeds, but they, too, signed alongside Ramírez.[83]

Some of the signatories lived in different parts of Los Angeles. The padrones of 1835 and 1838, though composed a decade before the petition, suggest that several signatories lived on opposite sides of the settlement.[84] Each padrón, for instance, noted who lived in each of the four districts, or *manzanas,* of Los Angeles. Desiderio Ybarra and José Serrano lived in manzana two; manzana three was home to Antonio Coronel, Felipe Lugo, and Juan Ramírez; in manzana four lived Estevan López and Guillermo Wolfskill. (The evidence suggests that no signatory lived in manzana one.) The diversity involved more than place of residence. A good number of petitioners came from elsewhere. Six had emigrated from Mexico. Three Americans, along with two Frenchmen were also signatories. A single New Mexican added his name. The biggest group came from California, with fourteen signing the petition.

The occupation of the petitioners, though in less striking terms, also featured some variety. Seventeen claimed farming as their livelihood. Two cowboys who grazed livestock on their own property or common pasture added their names. A carpenter and a shoemaker rounded out the petition, along with a lone merchant. Four performed occupations not recorded, and of these, among them the women, they probably owned a store or some other business.[85]

Though such variety would suggest that people with different means and occupations might refuse to cooperate, there is little sense that the angeleños always stood at odds with one another. Los Angeles never totaled more than a few thousand people during the Mexican era, a living arrangement that invited more intimacy and fellowship than we might suppose. They often had no cause, as could happen in a larger more populated community, to set and organize individuals according to rank.

Nonetheless, the angeleños, while more generous about evaluating income or status, used a different approach to identify, and value, each individual's worth. The angeleños did not use the idea of class to divide society into rich and poor sectors, with a middling group in between. Instead, they employed designations that described an individual's attempts to succeed at some business or livelihood.

How the angeleños measured effort, and in which endeavors, needs some explanation. In 1836, when recounting the rise of the vigilantes, Victor Prudon, one of the leaders, said the "most useful and moral part of the city's population" took up arms to execute "the two murderers."[86] As one would expect, "fathers of respectable families and honest citizens" joined. But of greater interest, Prudon said that "reputable property owners, merchants of integrity, and industrious workmen" assembled to defend the angeleño "families and [their] possessions."[87] The 1836 and 1844 censuses describe the men who fit Prudon's description. In 1836, 132 farmers, merchants, or craftsmen lived in Los Angeles. Eight years later, the number had jumped to 287.[88] All these individuals comprised, to use Prudon's term, the most "useful and moral part of the population."

If a responsible occupation and property ownership bestowed recognition during a vigilante episode, in later years the same standard would continue to determine an individual's worth. By relying on the term "useful," the angeleños employed a more flexible sense of how one person would rank above another. They rarely, if at all, used the categories "rich," "elite," or "wealthy."[89] The descriptions of "middle class," or "bourgeois," never appear in the record. All these terms, each a marker we use in modern times to arrange and identify social classes, did not accord with angeleño thinking. Wealth mattered, of course, as would the aristocratic bearing the more successful angeleños cultivated. Nevertheless, wealth alone offered poor proof of angeleño diligence. To the angeleños, productivity, that is, the effort an individual put forth in some craft or business to find profit, seemed the best measure.[90] Still, hard work on its own did not always suffice. If so, an Indian sweating for an angeleño master could count as an example of productivity. What mattered more was the skill one used to develop or procure a bit of property, an opportunity Indians did not always possess.

Many individuals, if productive, or to use the angeleño term, "useful," could receive praise regardless of their occupation. If an individual worked hard and prospered, he deserved tribute for having profited from his efforts. But the evidence suggests that the person who failed to prosper, despite every effort, would not necessarily lose favor. All signs of diligence, and attempts to grow crops or run a business, still testified to his productivity.

Meanwhile, the person who was not useful would fail to win respect. The angeleños, however, did not always speak of a "lower class" when expressing their scorn. As the 1846 petition reveals, they spoke of "intoxication" or "venereal disease," terms that suggest that an individual occupied the lower ranks when failing to show appropriate conduct. If a person dwelled in poverty, his laziness, or pursuit of pleasure, had brought him to ruin. The Indians, for instance, at least to the angeleños, lacked the character to apply their talents and thus deserved little respect. On occasion, an angeleño could sink to the lowest tier. When tempted by alcohol, or other delights, he hardly seemed "useful" and deserved ridicule.

A wealthy angeleño, though a person of means, could even possess the moral weakness that cursed Indians and impoverished compatriots. It is worthy to note that the cattlemen who owned vast tracts of land sometimes failed to win notice from their neighbors. They did not earn mention in Prudon's piece. The cattlemen could be "property owners," one of the words Prudon employed, but the term lacks specificity and most likely described farmers and entrepreneurs. Nor did the cattlemen receive an invitation to sign the 1846 petition. Cowboys added their names to the document, but no cattlemen. Perhaps, by having others work for them—in most cases, Indians—the cattlemen did not display the enterprise that won the attention of other angeleños. The cattlemen, at least in the opinion of their neighbors, performed little work and lived off the toil of others.

With effort, and a plot of land or a business, serving as signs of distinction, the angeleños defined rank and privilege in different ways. The idea of an elite class, which can describe a small, unique group, took on a more expansive meaning. The sense of who reclined at the top, and who did not, often depended on the diligence one used to develop a business or piece of property. Any individual who worked at some craft or profession dwelled in the upper ranks, while the more slothful sat below. How many people filled the higher echelons seems difficult to estimate. We have already discussed the 132, and later the 287 enterprising individuals who appeared in the censuses. The first figure from 1836 (132) suggests that of the 603 men who lived in Los Angeles, at least one out of four pursued a productive occupation. By 1844, with 627 men inhabiting Los Angeles, the 287 property owners accounted for nearly one in two men. As the censuses suggest, in any given year, a quarter to at least half of all angeleño men devoted themselves to some worthwhile enterprise.[91] The figures hardly add up to a majority, but all the same, the requirements to sit in the upper tier seemed accessible for many individuals, including, at times, women.

Thus, the signatories of the 1846 petition, or any other document we review, were not a select few who had enough education to record their thoughts. Rather, by representing industrious neighbors who lamented the Indians' conduct, the twenty-six signatories used the petition to speak for a multitude. After church, at market, or during a fiesta, the angeleños had any number of venues to exchange their thoughts. The man or woman who could read and write and sign the petition expressed the concerns of illiterate neighbors. That was not all. Foreigners, Mexicans from the interior, people with different occupations, and living in different parts of Los Angeles, could also find their thoughts expressed in the petition. This diverse populace sometimes found unity in family or social ties. But, as the 1846 petition suggests, those who wished to promote, and defend, their enterprise enjoyed a bond whose shape could emerge in any document. The number of productive people does not account for a majority of angeleños, but there is no reason to think that we concentrate on the concerns of a select few.

Of course, the urge to diminish social distinctions could obscure, but not remove, the tensions that separated one angeleño from another. During times of trouble, especially when Indians threatened to attack, the angeleños' worries and concerns rushed forth. If fear gained a hold, as we will see much later, the angeleños blamed compatriots for making trouble. The strange newcomer or the struggling tradesman who once enjoyed acceptance now fell under suspicion. Perhaps like the Indian, they, too, contemplated malicious and subversive thoughts. Despite the uncertainty, calm would prevail. The prominent and humble angeleños knew that together, rather than apart, they could better handle the Indian menace. Thrown together by a common foe, each group had the same concerns, thereby confirming that the person who took up the pen was qualified to speak for his neighbors.

When the petitioners and their compatriots complained about Indians, other topics, some perhaps just as sensitive, arose during the conversations.

The topics of discussion no longer survive, but within the petition, the vehicle of angeleño sentiments, the vestiges of each thought and utterance remain. Thus, the petition, when read carefully, can reveal how the angeleños acquired, and applied, any idea about Mexico. For instance, the petitioners complained that the Indians "encouraged" the angeleño populace to abandon good sense and indulge the body's appetites. In this word, "to encourage," we see an unspoken question: If not the Indians, then who should "encourage" angeleño conduct? To seek encouragement would suggest that the petitioners sought, and wished to imitate, certain individuals. Mexico, we would think, as might Mexicans and Mexican ways, could have supplied the examples that most angeleños wanted to emulate. It may not matter that references to Mexico do not always appear in the evidence. But with fantasia, and sensing what kind of principles and ideas the angeleños used to structure their lives, we can imagine how the angeleños wished to know who they were, and how they wanted others to know them.[92] The elements that lent purpose to their lives came from Mexico. Without Mexico, or Mexicans, to "encourage" appropriate conduct, the angeleños would become Indians, and few could think of a worse fate.

If "encourage" contains many meanings, other words would likewise convey a great many hopes and aspirations. When the petitioners wrote the words "Indian," (and "work"), "excess," "the same," "beneficial," or "exterminate," each term could express more than we think. So rich is the petition, that one of the words highlighted in the sentence above will open each of the following chapters. When examining the word's contents, we can see that the angeleños' desire to take on Mexican habits followed a progression. They moved from stage to stage, until, at the finish, they claimed a tie to Mexico. "Excess" suggests that the Indian and angeleño struggle presented challenges that needed to be overcome. The terms "same" and "beneficial" reveal why the angeleños punished and, at times, killed Indians. They wished to remove the Indians from close contact, forgetting that in some instances they too were Indians, or had Indian ancestry. "Exterminate" represents the culmination of angeleño ambitions. With the Indian gone, they could fashion a Mexican personality and inform men, women, and children of their responsibilities. "Indian" and "work," meanwhile, the terms that open the following chapter, say more about the angeleño attraction to Mexico. By defining what kind of qualities made any person or thing "Mexican," they identified the traits that marked one as an "Indian." To discover how the angeleños determined who was Mexican and who was an Indian, we turn to the pursuit of pleasure.

February 19, 1846

To your excellency the Governor [Pio Pico] we come before you the undersigned, and say that since the **Indian** ranchería was removed to the pueblito—a move calculated to end excesses and thefts—the **aborigines** . . . taking advantage of their isolation . . . steal from [neighboring orchards]. . . . [O]n Saturdays [they] celebrate and become intoxicated to an unbearable degree, thereby resulting in all manner of venereal disease, which will exterminate this race and . . . be beneficial to the city. To preserve the public health and do away with the vice of polygamy . . . [and] the excesses of prostitution [so that] the residents of Los Angeles would not be encouraged to do the same, we ask that the **Indians** be placed under strict police surveillance or the persons for whom the **Indians work** give [the **Indians**] quarter at the employer's rancho.

Signed:
Francisco Figueroa and Luis Vignes

Signatories:

Felipe Lugo	Ricardo Lankem (Laughlin)	—?—Villela
Juan Ramírez	Samuel Carpenter	Tomas Serrano
Januario Avila	Agustin Martin	Mariano Ruiz
José Serrano	Guillermo Wiskies (Wolfskill)	Antonio Salazar
Manuel Sepúlveda	Luis Bouchet	Casciano Carreon
Gil Ybarra	Maria Ballesteros	Maria Anta. Pollorena
Desiderio Ybarra	Francisco López	Vicente Elizalde
Miguel Pryor	Estevan López	Antonio Coronel

CHAPTER ONE

"Indians" and "Work"

Indians and the *Angeleño* Choice
Between Pleasure and Toil

TO BEGIN OUR STORY, we show how the Indians' image and ideas about work contained all the elements that attracted or repulsed the angeleños. ("Indians," or its variant, "aborigines," appears four times in the petition, "work" only once, toward the conclusion.) The term "Indian," and who or what the petitioners envisioned when using the word, reveals the angeleños' motives for choosing Mexican ways. Even more, the Indians' conduct, often distorted by the angeleño imagination, marked the difference between rogues and responsible citizens. A passion for drink, the wish for a prostitute's company, theft, and the destruction of property stood as testaments to Indian depravity. In contrast appeared diligence and responsibility, qualities possessed by individuals devoted to work. At the same time, the virtuous habits revealed the appeal of liberal thought, a set of ideas that had acquired a great following throughout nineteenth-century Mexico. The idea of work, and any of its attributes, would often assume different shape. But in the end, many angeleños knew that diligence involved every manner of worthwhile effort.

By condemning the Indians and lamenting their corruption, the angeleños showed that allegiance to Mexico offered great reward. The choice, however, presented greater challenges than we suppose. Many angeleños recognized that the grind and toil of productive effort promised no respite. But when looking at the Indian fiesta, the weekly celebration that impelled the twenty-six signatories to compose their complaint, some saw an escape from their responsibilities. The drink and music, that moment of abandon when all cares evaporated, offered temptations that some found hard to resist. The fiesta, filled with so many delights, added one more dimension to the choices faced by the angeleños. As we will see, work and responsibility needed to balance, even equal, the pleasures the angeleños desired, and, in some cases, dared to enjoy.

The Indian Bacchanal

The Indians abounded in sufficient numbers to test the angeleños' will. To be sure, the Indians threatened the angeleños in any number of ways, but their motives for causing disruption rarely appear in the historical record. A few sources, from court testimonies to church documents, express the Indians' opinion, but they often speak under duress. In many instances, they have no comments or ideas other than the thoughts attributed to them by angeleño commentators. Nonetheless, even when robbed of words the Indians' deeds or their very presence reveal a people the angeleños found impossible to ignore. At any point during the Mexican period, the Indians, people we may also call Native Californians, accounted for at least a quarter of the total population in the Los Angeles area. The proportion of Indians may have been higher. Witnesses from the period, especially when counting Indians, sometimes erred or did not care if they recorded an accurate figure. Still, the number of Indians proved significant. In 1836, the year of the first Mexican census for Los Angeles, the gente de razón, individuals who claimed to be non-Indian, totaled 1,675 people. Meanwhile, 555 individuals made up the Indian populace.[1] Eight years later, in the 1844 census, the figures show slight changes. The gente de razón, who, for our purposes, would be another name for the angeleños, accounted for 1,847 individuals, an increase of nearly two hundred people. Meanwhile, the Indians added about one hundred persons, reaching a total of 650.[2]

Far from being a monolith in which all dissolved into one figure "the Indian," the Mexican censuses of 1836 and 1844 suggest that the Native Californians possessed great variety.[3] Many lived in the ranchería, the Indian village that sat to the east of Los Angeles, at least when the angeleños did not raze or burn it to the ground.[4] A few more lived with gente de razón families in town, while others resided near or on nearby ranchos, the cattle spreads that sat outside Los Angeles. Still further out, a good number lived close to the mountains that bordered Los Angeles to the east. The Indians' differences multiplied in other ways. Some Indians professed Christianity, but the censuses did not always record who had, or had not, converted.[5]

Even so, a good number of Indians seemed to be gentiles, or non-Christian Indians, from areas surrounding Los Angeles. The gentiles alone confirmed the diverse nature of the Indian population. In the view of one scholar, the gentiles of Los Angeles and points beyond spoke up to twenty-one languages, a number that would increase if we add the tongues spoken in San Diego and surrounding areas.[6]

If feeling diligent, the census takers identified the group affiliation of each Indian. A few Apaches from Sonora appear in the censuses, as do Paiutes, Indians who usually made their home in the territory of New Mexico. But most Indian groups in Los Angeles came from southern California. Serranos, who lived in the mountains and inland valleys to the east, often settled in Los Angeles to find work. Next to them resided the Cahuillas, originally the inhabitants of an area fifty miles to the southeast.[7] Indians from Baja California, though the census taker did not record the name of their group, also called Los Angeles home. The census taker also identified Indians whose origin is now a mystery. The unknown Cayego or Caniego, make the list, as do individuals who bear the title "Agua Caliente," the name of a place or a group that has escaped description.[8] If the census taker knew nothing about an Indian, save for his or her name, he merely entered "gentil" in the space marked for an individual's place of origin.

Other Indian groups require more explanation. The Gabrielinos, or Gabrieleños, for instance, one of the Indian groups who lived in the area before the Spaniards established Los Angeles, do not appear at all. This is no surprise, however. By 1836, most had converted, or felt compelled to convert, and entered the rolls of San Gabriel, the mission east of Los Angeles that gave the Gabrielinos their name. When they appeared in the censuses, the surveyor simply wrote "San Gabriel," their mission affiliation. Admittedly, Indians from other areas would have lived at San Gabriel Mission, but we can suppose most belonged to the Gabrielinos. No Fernandenos, meanwhile, or as sometimes spelled, Fernandeños, earned mention in any census. Some residents of San Fernando Mission northeast of Los Angeles probably escaped the surveyor's notice, but it seems most moved out of the area. Indians from missions far to the south also made their way to Los Angeles. The census taker noted that Indians from "San Juan" and "San Luis," the shortened names, respectively, for the missions of San Juan Capistrano and San Luis Rey, found work on local ranchos.[9]

The Indians, great in number and spread throughout Los Angeles and its environs, seemed well-placed to intrude on every part of angeleño life. Even if some played an unwitting role in the process, the Indians provided most angeleños with the reasons to take on Mexican habits. Nearly one in four people in the region, the Indians would have seemed all around— in the home, outside the home, walking in the streets, living in the ranchería, and perhaps even farther out, on horseback, a gun in hand, waiting to strike. But the suggestion of ubiquity, with the Indians in all spots, could easily suggest that they would appear in places where they otherwise would not be. As some angeleños feared, the Indians would erase, and eliminate, any boundary that kept them at a distance. Soon enough, some angeleño witnesses suggested, when looking at the Indian, and then at themselves, they would see no difference.

As the 1846 petition implies, the celebration on Saturday evenings, or at any other time, confirmed that some angeleños had begun to resemble Indians. But what this resemblance constituted and how it came about needs some definition. Admittedly, the petition says nothing about the two groups sharing the same appearance. Such an admission may not matter, however. Many angeleños, as would the inhabitants of other provincial settlements, had Indian forbears, and, for some observers, it might take some effort to distinguish one group from the other. In other instances, and perhaps of greater concern, the resemblance between the two groups could also suggest that the angeleños had begun to behave like Indians. When observers watched the fiesta, or heard reports about what transpired on Saturday night, they found evidence that Indian practices had found favor with some gente de razón. The image of the fiesta, with the thought of different people pressed together during the celebration, brought forth suggestions of intimacy and passion, feelings, in the view of some observers, that emerged as references to sex. Angeleño witnesses, though, did not think of sex as a loving exchange between partners. Rather, sex, or at least sex with Indians, conveyed a sense of menace. In many accounts about gente de razón dalliances with Indians, observers condemned what they saw. In 1846, for instance, the petitioners worried about friends and compatriots who sought the company of Indian prostitutes.[10] That same year, in another appeal, an angeleño bemoaned the Indian "bacchanalia and its evils."[11] It would not take much to see that after the descriptions about intimacy or exchanges of affection, the writers posed the thought that the weekend celebration threatened to transform gente de razón participants into Indians. When referring to any kiss or embrace the angeleños shared with their indigenous companions, witnesses implied that friends and neighbors had lost all reason. Their rationality gone, all sensibility aflame with emotion, the gente de razón seemed no different than Indians, and soon enough, in some form or manner, they would become Indians.

Although many angeleños witnessed the parties, none described the offerings that proved so tempting. It could be that some witnessed traditional dances or rituals. The festivities, if practiced up through the mid-nineteenth century, could draw curious angeleños, a possibility that displeased witnesses who wanted the gente de razón to stay away from Indians. An Indian ceremony, though, would not necessarily degenerate into a revel. The participants, among them gente de razón, may have consumed food and drink, but it seems unlikely that anything more scandalous would occur. Still, the angeleños witnessed, or attended, more spirited celebrations that had nothing to do with Indian traditions. Many gente de razón could confuse one event with one another, but, to be sure, some witnessed proceedings that could prove alarming.

One example from 1855, nearly ten years after the American conquest, demonstrates what the Indian "bacchanalia" might have looked like.[12] Manuel Clemente Rojo, a journalist for *La Estrella*, a bilingual newspaper that began publishing in Los Angeles sometime around 1853, explained that during a stroll on Sunday morning he entered the central plaza and "saw scenes more disgraceful than anyone can imagine." There, before his eyes, gathered all the *canalla*, the members of the lower class. They, all of them "bums and scoundrels," fouled the "atmosphere with obscene words." More alarming, considering that the day was Sunday, the celebrants also "corrupted the Christians" who walked by on their way to Mass. Men and women, presumably drunk, rolled about the ground pulling at each other's hair. Meanwhile, the "beautiful sex," perhaps a euphemism for prostitutes, paraded about baring, "for all to see, their primitive state." Outraged, Rojo concludes, "Here, Bacchus reigns supreme."

Rojo, though he was not explicit, described the cavorting of Indians and gente de razón. He mentioned Indians once, and used, or referred to, the less specific term of canalla at least three times. If only Indians appeared at the celebration, Rojo might have belabored the point. Instead, he spoke of the canalla, or lower class, a more vague term that could include the gente de razón.

Lest there be any thought that only poor or shiftless angeleños favored the Indians' company, Rojo suggested why he and more respectable individuals would consider joining the celebration. As a journalist, Rojo probably had a decent education, a degree of cultivation that would impress any angeleño who claimed, or wished to claim, the same background.

At the beginning of his essay, Rojo said, "last Sunday we were carried . . . [to the celebration] by shouting and an infernal noise." Rojo, however, who had lived in Los Angeles for some time, would have known what transpired during the parties. When saying that the noise "carried" him off, as if lured by a siren's song, Rojo could not resist the urge to take a peek. He knew quite well that the participants swilled strong drink. And the prostitutes, revealing their forms beneath loose fitting dresses, possibly invited Rojo to contemplate more intimate thoughts.

If Rojo experienced temptation, other individuals who shared his background would likewise cast covetous glances at the Indians. Of course, some individuals would not want to risk their reputations by joining the Indian fiesta. But the bacchanal, which in its simplest form supposedly promised participants sex and drink, could assume different shape for some gente de razón. The man who valued discretion could entertain an Indian companion in his home. Or, he might retire to a local tavern, where, still out of sight from curious eyes, he could enjoy the house specialty and try his hand at monte, a card game popular with Indian gamblers. The bold angeleño who fancied the Native Californian's company might think that his social position would shield him from condemnation. On one occasion, witnesses complained about gente de razón landowners who allowed Indians to hold celebrations on the family property.[13] As evidence that some prominent angeleños consorted with Indians, witnesses complained that the celebrants risked contracting the affliction that punished those who indulged a bit too much. In words Rojo could have written, one angeleño worried that Indian prostitutes exposed their angeleño customers, a few, apparently, who seemed quite comfortable in their circumstances, "to all manner of venereal disease."[14]

With all sorts of individuals joining the fun in 1855, a decade earlier it was likely that angeleños from different backgrounds welcomed the chance to befriend their Indian companions. For most celebrants, Saturday night remained the best time to meet. The "president" of the ayuntamiento, responding to concerns about excessive drinking in the ranchería, proposed in 1833 that "a citizen" supervise the "conduct of Indians."[15] He did not need to add that the watchman would also keep an eye on the gente de razón who went to the ranchería. Eleven years later, some angeleños shook their heads that tavern keepers contributed to the Indians' "scandalous drinking" by selling *aguardiente*, a potent concoction brewed from grape stems. The concerned citizens convinced the ayuntamiento to ban the sale of alcohol on "feast days" and fine any proprietor who ignored the decree.[16] Nothing, though, stopped the party. Some angeleños complained in 1846 that the Indians continued to meet on "Saturday [in the ranchería or the plaza in the center of town] to get drunk, gamble, [and] commit crimes."[17] Presumably, if one looked hard enough, one would also see a few gente de razón enjoying the festivities.

The celebration remained popular into the American era. In 1847, the ayuntamiento grew impatient with the celebrations and once again ordered a guard to watch the ranchería. Only Indians, and no gente de razón, the municipal council declared, could enter for any reason.[18] But as time progressed, the gente de razón continued to attend the celebrations. The ayuntamiento, tired of the mischief, tried to stiffen the penalty for socializing with Indians. It decreed in 1850 that any non-Indian who went to the ranchería risked "a twenty peso fine and ten days in the presidio (the fort which served as a prison)."[19]

The ayuntamiento members, or any other person who complained, did not exaggerate their concerns. The evidence suggests that angeleño merrymakers sometimes outnumbered the Indians. At one ranchería event in 1847, a witness claimed, "two-thirds of the participants were gente de razón."[20] By using the 1844 census—there is no reliable survey for 1847—we can estimate how many angeleños, at least in this instance, went to the celebration. To arrive at a reasonable figure, we first have to calculate how many Indians attended. Only then, after estimating the number of Indians, can we count the angeleños. The 1844 census says that 650 Indians lived in the Los Angeles area. Of these, say some authorities, 377, lived "in town," with another one hundred or so residing in the home of their employers.[21] As for the remainder, 173 in number, they most likely lived in the ranchería.

From the figure of 173, perhaps around a quarter, approximately forty-three Indians, attended the celebration. A smaller number could have come, but the tone of angeleño complaints suggests that quite a crowd liked to unwind on Saturday night. We may even be too conservative in our reasoning. Indians who lived in surrounding areas most likely joined the party in the ranchería. Meanwhile, the Indian servant who resided with an angeleño employer would also think it a good idea to spend an evening downing a glass or two with friends.

Remember, though, that "two-thirds" of the participants were angeleños, most of them probably men, a point we address in another chapter.[22] If forty-three Indians attended the festivities, then eighty-six angeleño men comprised two-thirds of the celebrants. In 1844, 627 gente de razón men lived in Los Angeles. When considering the number eighty-six, we find that nearly one in seven gente de razón men joined the celebration. Some participants may have been drifters or criminals, but troublemakers cannot bear all the blame. Among the eighty-six men, a good chance existed that respectable citizens also knew the way to the ranchería. Rojo's description, after all, contained enough clues to suggest that reputable angeleños attended the weekend festivities. That being said, the witness who came up with the figure of "two-thirds" could have miscounted or exaggerated his calculations, but the point remains that many angeleños favored the Indians' company. It must have been quite a party.[23]

The Indian celebration, with all its attractions, could emphasize the inadequacy of angeleño life. Outside Los Angeles, or even within, at the doorstep of the family home, the Indians supposedly enjoyed liberties that the most adventurous gente de razón would not imitate. Even if the Indians, especially after conversion to Christianity, grew more modest, or had acquired an unfair reputation for performing deeds only a few pursued, they alarmed and amazed the angeleños. The Indians tattooed their bodies, or prayed to unfamiliar deities. At times, an Indian mother killed her first-born child, believing that if she did not, she would grow old quickly. Or, if a little one had a defect, the parents abandoned the infant to the elements, hoping that death would come quickly. Other Indians married, divorced, and married again, or they married when married to someone else. One never knew what else they did, and in gente de razón homes, Indian habits no doubt acquired a more horrific cast as family members repeated, and exaggerated with each telling, what they had heard about the Native Californians.[24]

But any mention of liberty does not mean the Indians only performed deeds that the angeleños found scandalous. In californio settlements, or when in operation inside the missions, the Indians revealed one more part of their personality. Many Native Californians, the men especially, became expert artisans. In mission churches Indians painted glorious images of the Virgin Mary, her gown and visage reflecting a careful hand. Some, with equal care, delicately rendered Christ. At times, above a door, Indian artists produced the unblinking eye of Providence. Along the borders of the church interior, they painted floral designs and other decorative motifs, putting a shaft of light in one spot, or in another, swirling lines of color. The ceilings, too, featured ornate designs. Images of angels fluttered above the altar. Elsewhere on the ceiling, twining grapevines or trees laden with fruit ran along the length of the church. The Indians did not confine their talents to Catholic themes. Some artists, if feeling defiant, adorned the interior with indigenous symbols or figures.[25]

Outside the church, in the mission yard or in an artisan's shop, Indians displayed more of their gifts. Indian carpenters brought forth beautiful shapes from a block of wood. Iron, once subjected to the flame and bellows, yielded to the supple hands of an Indian blacksmith. An Indian weaver, often a woman, spun wool into cloth. Afterward, she used the material to make a blanket or garment.

The Indians' aptitude reached into other realms. One californio remembered that "two or three" Indian boys entered a seminary in Rome to study for the priesthood. During their formation, the boys learned Greek, Latin, and, perhaps, Hebrew, languages few, if any, californios mastered.[26] At least one Indian survived the experience and became a priest. As far as is known, no gente de razón received holy orders, or went on to prepare for a life of the cloth.

Some commentators noted that many Indians learned the European style of music in the missions. A fair number nimbly handled violins and trumpets, some of the many instruments Indians played. Others had learned to sing in the Baroque manner, their voices scaling the notes with ease. Possessing great ability, Indian musicians often played the music written by mission priests.[27] On other occasions, the Indians performed the works of more accomplished artists. The music historian Craig Russell says that beginning in the eighteenth century the Indian musicians and singers of California's missions played the music of Mexican composers. One composer, Ignacio de Jerúsalem, the Chapel Master of Mexico City's cathedral from 1713 to 1738, produced works that, at least for the standards of the era, put Mexico at the forefront of "modern" musical styles. The Indians at San Fernando Mission, for instance, often performed Jerúsalem's *Polychoral Mass in D*.[28]

Even after secularization, Jerúsalem's *Mass* possibly remained a popular selection for Indian musicians. In 1837, to celebrate the signing of the *Siete Partidas*, the document that superseded the Mexican Constitution of 1824, an observer explained that the angeleños attended Mass "where was sung a solemn Te Deum." The witness mentioned nothing about the choice of music, nor did he describe the performers who played at the Mass. But when the priest celebrated a "Te Deum," which was another way of describing a High Mass, the most solemn and elaborate ceremony of the Roman Catholic rite, he might think that Jerúsalem's work provided the most appropriate music.[29] If true, only Indians had the training to master the sophisticated score.[30]

The exasperation that emerges in angeleño writings suggests that the Native Californians presented a challenge that required resolution. The Indians, without trying to, mocked the angeleño effort to maintain a sober, moderate life. Many Native Californians created, with tender, skillful hands, impressive pieces of art. Others sang beautifully, or coaxed the most wonderful sounds from a stringed instrument or woodwind. A few showed great talent in the classroom and learned ancient languages. At another turn, though, Indians sported tattoos or worshipped strange deities. The angeleños' consternation might have increased if they thought the same Indian flitted back and forth between the two ways of life. One moment he applied himself to chores, but the next, off he went to indulge some unknown urge. Few, if any, Indians followed every desire to take on different habits. But, most angeleños had no interest in correcting misperceptions. When they saw an Indian supposedly eager to shift shape, they glimpsed their own frustrated longings. Some no doubt thought it took great effort to ignore the body's appetites and pursue a life of moderation. As we have already seen, nearly one in seven angeleño men went to the ranchería each Saturday night. As for the other angeleños who remained at home, a few likely stood suspended between sin and virtue when wondering if they should attend the celebration.

But to look at an Indian, easily stepping between one world and the next, some angeleños felt envy. They too wanted the same freedom. If the Indians performed the pious or brazen act with equal agility, they enjoyed other pleasures without remorse. They drank deep from the bottle, issued the war cry from the top of their lungs, or kissed and stroked partner after partner. Meanwhile in Los Angeles, to the angeleños' chagrin, the priest and magistrate offered, what? Laws to regulate conduct? The expectation that work, and nothing else, should be the sum of human activity? A Catholic rite that condemned the body's appetites and threatened the wayward with hellfire?

Thus, we can imagine what kind of wishes churned within the angeleño man, sometimes the woman, but more the man, who witnessed the Indian celebrations.[31] The angeleños knew that to follow the Indian would discredit the religion and way of life they held sacred. But, when attending ranchería celebrations or seeking the love of Indian companions, a good number wanted to experience the liberty that the Native Californian supposedly relished. At a crossroads, the angeleños reconciled competing urges by mistreating Indians. Of course, cause and effect, that sequence of logic that dictates how to reach a conclusion, may not apply here. The gente de razón in Los Angeles, and elsewhere in California, do not say explicitly that they calmed their fears and insecurities by making Indians suffer. We only have a correlation, the weight of evidence on one side, the conclusion on the other, and a spare, simple strand providing a connection. But a correlation, while lacking specificity, provides the best way to understand why the gente de razón delivered blow after blow. Gente de razón ferocity, often expressed without remorse or constraint, suggests that some drew Indian blood to experience, and dispel, the thrill of the Indian bacchanalia.

Nonetheless, it can be argued that the gente de razón had many reasons to feel rage. As will soon be clear, after 1821 liberal ideas from Mexico emphasized racial equality, a development that did not please the gente de razón. The Indians, formerly dwelling in the lower ranks of society, now could claim the same rights and privileges as any other citizen in the nation. If entitled to the benefits of citizenship, the Indians could expect, and, in theory, even demand, fair treatment from gente de razón employers. Yet, as the record shows, the gente de razón continued their harsh practices. A glance at the 1836 census for Los Angeles suggests that angeleño proprietors had no trouble pressing Indians into service. One cattle spread, Rancho Santa Ana, had sixty-eight Indian workers. True enough, the census says nothing about the labor arrangement, but it was not uncommon for a cattleman to round up the Indians from a nearby ranchería and force them to work.[32]

Perhaps, then, the secularization of the missions stoked gente de razón anger. When the national government secularized the missions in 1834, some emancipated neophytes received title to church property, choice bits of land often coveted by the gente de razón. But, in most instances, the Indians' right to mission land offered little protection. From Monterey to Los Angeles, few gente de razón had trouble prying plots of land away from their Indian owners.

Or, it could be that when looking at the Indians, the angeleños saw an unflattering image of themselves. Already we have emphasized, and will show repeatedly, how the angeleños and Indians resembled one another. But any resemblance, and the way the angeleños perceived the similarities, requires more explanation. It would be tempting to conclude that the destitute Indian reminded some angeleños of their own miseries and say nothing more. By the 1840s, the time when the petitioners presented their appeal, many Indians had suffered great tribulation. A good number had lost the parcels of land they received after secularization. To survive, they toiled at menial tasks and received a pittance for their labors. A few found solace in alcohol, and if angeleño observers can be believed, Indian drinkers soon ruined mind and body. No doubt some angeleños looked as dissipated as the Indians, a bit of knowledge that probably failed to improve the gente de razón mood. But even if some angeleños looked as impoverished as the Indians, others did not. Any angeleño who experienced the Indians' predicament could prove disturbing, but another provocation seemed better suited to stir the furies regardless of rank or occupation. It is more likely that the Indians excited passions that made the angeleños feel good. When they cocked their firearms or unsheathed knives, they meant to kill the Indian, and, at the same time, kill their desire for Indian ways.

The gente de razón enthusiasm to punish Indians may suggest little else. When traveling to Santa Fe in 1839, Miguel Blanco, or Michael White, an English sailor who settled in Los Angeles, remembered that his angeleño and New Mexican companions decided to attack a Paiute village to avenge some supposed outrage. Blanco protested, even threatening to shoot anyone who joined the raid, but his rifle misfired. Unimpressed by Blanco's pleas, his companions responded, "Que no es pecado matar esos indios gentiles"—"It is not a sin to kill pagan Indians."[33] To the gente de razón, the Indians' faith, or the lack of faith, rarely mattered. Around the same time, José María Amador, a resident of northern California, pursued Indian horse thieves and meted out treatment that his angeleño contemporaries would understand. When he and his men caught the culprits, Amador discovered that at least one hundred had converted to Christianity. Amador did not care, however. He executed each convert with two arrows to the back and two arrows to the front. The ones who "refused to die immediately" earned a spear through the side.[34] Cruelty, though, did not always appear during a spectacular slaughter. In the privacy of the home, or outside among the herds or crops, the gente de razón could bring more torment. They beat, kicked, and whipped the Indians. Some yelled a curse, delivering a string of words as sharp as any blade. Other gente de razón, especially men, could concoct different tortures. They drew a woman or child close, and resisted any entreaty to stop their thrusting and grabbing.[35]

When brandishing a weapon, or imposing their will, the angeleños performed a paradox. They found pleasure by eliminating the pleasure supposedly enjoyed by Indians. Within the violent moment, the mercy required by religion or scruple vanished. What mattered was compulsion and desire.[36] In one sense, the brutal conduct captured the freedom of the Indian celebration. Again, the sweep and whirl of the Indian festivities reflected angeleño imaginings. The Indians, if they could utter a defense, might say the Saturday night events rarely reached the scandalous proportions that horrified observers. But angeleño opinions mattered more. During the party, the participants supposedly did as they wished. In like fashion, the angeleños who punished Indians also sought freedom. Yet, they did not drink or dance; instead the freedom they desired revolved around violence. In that one instant of abandon, when they brought down the rifle butt or gave Indians the back of the hand, the gente de razón erased all restriction and found joy not in drink, but in destruction.

But to live in perpetual conflict, seeking at every turn some way to discipline and punish Indians could become tiresome. It would be easier, as a former angeleño said in 1851, "to create." Antonio María Osio, the author of the remark, presents the phrase in a mournful passage describing California's fall to the United States. "Everything they [the californios] worked so hard to create," Osio uttered, "would now be gone."[37] Osio, though he referred to the American victory, no doubt drew on his experiences with Indians to recognize what devastation war could bring.[38] He had fought neophytes who had escaped from the missions or joined punitive expeditions hunting Indian raiders. Aware that war often spared no one, Osio recognized that "everything" the Americans threatened to trample had long sat in danger during conflicts with Indians.

Therefore war, and its threat of destruction, prepared the angeleños to seek more beneficial pursuits. In one sense, war brought uncertainty and made them vulnerable to attack. They may have enjoyed victory, but in the next moment the angeleños faced retaliation from their Indian antagonists, or, by 1846, formed ranks to meet the American invaders. The perpetual state of conflict left them in a perilous condition in which they suffered, or pursued, conquest. With war bearing reminders that violence and revenge brought limited reward, the angeleños wanted something more. They welcomed another type of existence, or as they would have said, they wished to "create" some connection with Mexico.

Mexico and the Promise of Work

To fulfill their wish, the angeleños needed a stimulus. One angeleño, who had emigrated from Mexico City as a youngster, claimed that in the 1830s Mexicans had brought "enlightenment" to California.[39] With enlightenment, the angeleños acquired, as did their californio compatriots, the ideas that would surpass the pleasures promised by the Indian celebration. Enlightenment, after all, suggests an awakening. At some point, an individual sat in darkness or he favored activities that clouded the mind. Later, once his sensibilities and mind lay open to new experiences, he could realize every talent. Of all the Mexican principles and ideas that could qualify as enlightenment, only one, liberal thought, seemed best suited to transform the angeleños' nature. Conservative opinions from Mexico circulated as well. But the conservative insistence on maintaining the authority of the king, or, after independence, placing a powerful president in office, did not always resonate in southern California. Liberal ideas, with their implicit promise of enlightenment, enjoyed greater popularity.

But in Mexico, as some angeleños knew, "liberalism," or "liberal," presented many meanings.[40] Liberals often believed in racial equality. Others wanted political power invested in the states, not the central government. A few more wanted to restrict the political activities of priests, or, as was the case in California, limit their influence by secularizing the missions. Some wanted to seize landed estates and distribute the property to the most impoverished citizens. A liberal could believe in one of these causes or all of them, but at times consensus could prove elusive. Still, at least to the angeleños, a liberal spoke of improving humanity and removing the impediments that prevented the individual from intellectual or economic achievement.

Of all the liberal ideas that pleased the angeleños, work seemed the virtue many prized the most. We have already discussed diligence and productivity, two aspects of work, but the concept of worthy toil involved other qualities. In a broader sense, the individual at his labors, when joined by others equally devoted to their duties, contributed to the welfare of the nation. Jean Franco, a Mexican historian, explains that liberals wanted the populace to make use of all their talents and deliver Mexico from its backward ways.[41]

At the same time, Franco suggests, the productive citizen cultivated his spirit and purged noxious habits.[42] Through work, men from all backgrounds—women often lacked the same opportunities—could liberate themselves from the colonial custom of relying on social position, and nothing else, to prove their worth. Before independence in Mexico, and to a certain extent in California, law and custom determined each individual's rank or privileges. Priests or military officers, when accused of crimes, would sit in judgment before their peers rather than go to civil court, a privilege the king sometimes altered, but never banned. Opportunities increased if one was a *peninsular*, an individual who came directly from Spain. The Crown appointed peninsulares to the most powerful posts in the colonial government or Church hierarchy. Next in prestige came *criollos*, or any white person born in Mexico. They often received the positions directly below the peninsulares. *Castas*, meanwhile, or people of mixed blood, had less advantage, especially in the early years of Spain's settlement of Mexico. For example, the *mestizos*, castas who had Spanish and Indian ancestry, often could not attend university or join worker's guilds. The Indians, though, usually received the least consideration. Some served as village elders and a small number joined the priesthood, but most had no chance to improve their circumstances.[43]

After independence, the liberals passed laws that tried to remove the advantages bestowed by blood or social position. If all citizens resided on the same plane, at least as envisioned by the liberals, work, merely the product of talent and drive, and nothing else, would determine the individual's place in society. When a person labored hard, he would advance. But to slacken, and not work, meant that failure would come, and soon after, poverty. The historian Franco concludes that work, at least as conceived by liberals, established a new rhythm in Mexican life.[44] The citizen alone, and no other person or entity, marked life's progress. He relied on his efforts to determine how far he advanced, or, if his zeal proved wanting, he remained in one spot.

Work, as defined in Mexico or California, fulfilled the term "create." Creation, above all, seemed the point of work. When attending to his labors, an individual provided for the household. In another way, though, work gave an individual the chance to make himself anew. As the Mexican liberals, and their angeleño admirers argued, work could transform the most scandalous individuals into industrious citizens. Indeed, by 1833, California seemed one of the places where a citizen could reap all sorts of riches. During an address to the Mexican Congress, the Minister of Relations declared that the province's fertile soil and abundant resources blessed any person willing to labor. "California," he declared, "rewards the man who works hard."[45]

The evidence suggests that liberals from Mexico's interior instructed the angeleños in the virtues of work. True enough, the angeleños did not need lessons to know that the person who failed to work risked starvation. But at the same time, some needed to know why work enriched the spirit. For those angeleños interested in acquiring lessons, they could seek out any number of liberals. So many came by the early nineteenth century that Valentín Gómez Farías, Mexico's vice-president in the mid-1830s, and one of the organizers of the Híjar-Padrés expedition, wished he could join the migration north. A strong liberal, Gómez-Farías had grown weary of the capital's machinations, and, in the words of one friend, "wished to retire to California."[46] A bit later, when hosting the farewell ball for the Híjar-Padrés expedition, Gómez-Farías supposedly told the celebrants that California would become "a haven for liberals when they could no longer remain in Mexico."[47] He never left Mexico, but he perhaps knew what kind of welcome he would receive from compatriots in the north.

Some liberals in California seemed to be exiles. At times, individuals deemed too revolutionary in their opinion and conduct risked banishment to the north. Vicente Gómez, for instance, famed as El Capador, "The Castrator," for his treatment of priests and Spaniards in the recent struggle for independence, refused to cease his marauding and soon earned a trip to California.[48]

The liberals who belonged to a Masonic lodge also received the boot. The *yorkinos*, individuals who followed the York rite, often espoused liberal opinions. (The *escoces*, or those who belonged to the Scottish set, tended to be conservative.) Often junior officers, petty advocates, and artisans, the yorkinos ran afoul of the conservative regimes that rose to power in the early nineteenth century.[49] One did not need to be a yorkino to make trouble, but the lodge's reputation for liberal sympathies made members likely suspects when the authorities hunted down dissenters. Soon after becoming head of state in 1830, General Anastacio Bustamante, a conservative, ordered the arrest of liberal pamphleteers who criticized the government. Some writers landed in jail. Others, meanwhile, a few in chains, went to California. In July 1830, a brig packed with fifty felons landed in Monterey.[50] The prisoners' crimes escaped explanation, but circumstances suggest that with the rise of Bustamante and other conservative leaders, some convicts, perhaps a bit too avid with liberal opinions, traveled north to pay for their offenses. The expulsions continued. Four years later, General Antonio López de Santa Anna, a man who often sided with conservatives, closed congress.[51] The move caused outrage, especially among yorkinos. A few proved so disruptive that they soon received the penalty of banishment. The Híjar-Padrés expedition, for example, when it departed Mexico City in 1834, had two political exiles in its ranks, Gumisendo Flores and Nicanor Estrada.[52] It is not known if they were necessarily liberals, much less yorkinos. But given the climate of the times, the two men, and possibly others, suffered the consequences for spreading liberal opinions.

Exiles were not the only ones to come north. Before the 1840s, army officers with liberal sympathies often held positions of authority in California's government. The literary critic Rosaura Sánchez says that José María Echeandía and José María Padrés, two yorkinos who held the rank of lieutenant colonel, had each served as governor prior to 1837.[53] Angustias de la Ord, a resident of Santa Barbara, remembered that when Echeandía served as governor, he seemed aflame with new thoughts. He was a "man of advanced ideas, enthusiastic, and [a believer in] republican liberty."[54] Padrés, one of the two men after whom the 1834 expedition was named, left a bigger mark. He possessed "liberal ideas that could be called ultraradical." De la Ord explained he was a teacher who "imbued" his pupils with the "principles of the federal system in Mexico."[55]

Individuals who were neither exiles nor in the military also thought California a good place to apply liberal principles. Some, especially those who settled in Los Angeles, could have impressed compatriots. Francisco Figueroa, one of the authors of the 1846 petition, would have no trouble attracting attention. In all truth, not much is known about the man. But a rough approximation of his nature may be found by looking at his brother, José María Figueroa, the Mexican governor who supervised the secularization of the missions and about whom more is known. José María read Jeremy Bentham, the English philosopher popular with Mexican liberals.[56] Ancient Greek and Roman philosophers also made his reading list, as did French thinkers like Voltaire.[57] Francisco, who no doubt had many chances to talk to his brother, or sample books resting on José María's shelf, likely found opportunities to put his knowledge to use in Los Angeles. Luis Vignes, the other author of the petition, received different instruction in liberal habits. Vignes, born in France, recognized that bloodshed and the taking up of arms served as a way to abolish the evils that oppressed humanity.[58] Ten years old when the French Revolution broke out, Vignes came of age during a turbulent time. He was from Bordeaux, a city in southeastern France famous for its revolutionary orators. We do not know what he heard, but any denunciation against the Church and monarchy would not slip easily from the mind.[59]

Alongside Figueroa and Vignes stood others who could be just as avid in their liberal beliefs. For the moment, we exclude women and talk about the men. According to the 1836 census for Los Angeles, fifty-four men, out of 603 total, originated in states noted for liberal politics. Forty-six came from Sonora, with six and two, respectively, claiming Sinaloa and Vera Cruz as their birthplace. Some of these men could have been apolitical. A few certainly seemed down on their luck. Ten men carried "N," for *ninguno*, meaning no employment, next to their names. For the remainder, who appeared honorable, and presumably had formed political opinions, there was a good chance they possessed liberal notions. With the conservative movement gaining strength in Mexico—remember that by 1834 Santa Anna had closed Congress—they likely thought it best to live elsewhere. Eight years later, in the 1844 census, of the 627 men in Los Angeles and its environs, thirty-seven had once lived in states with liberal sympathies. Twenty-seven came from Sonora, twelve from Sinaloa, and one each from Chihuahua and Yucatan. Only one bore the "N" after his name. If any of these men professed liberal opinions, they did not think Los Angeles a bad place to call home.[60]

The liberals, yorkino or otherwise, who resided in Los Angeles brought items that emphasized the necessity of work. It seems likely that a few expatriates hummed songs that inspired diligence. One tune from the early 1830s, "Canción sobre el amor del trabajo" ("Song on the Love of Work") called out, "Work is wealth . . . [and] is before pleasure."[61] Admittedly, there is no way to confirm if the song found its way to Los Angeles, but a Mexican play, bound in the form of a pamphlet, certainly made the trip. The drama, which came to Los Angeles sometime in the 1830s, featured a soldier and a farmer discussing ways to find success. In the prologue, the playwright explained that he wanted to teach "the parents of families" how "to inspire [a] love of work in their sons."[62]

At times, the angeleños' descriptions of work suggest that they employed words and images imported from Mexico. José María Váldez, an angeleño who went before the ayuntamiento in 1837 to ask for a farming plot, offers evidence (an expatriate's words perhaps? a song? a play?) that he had received instruction in work's rewards. He explained that a bit of farmland would help him "reach greater advances in his work and facilitate the advancement of his family."[63] Other angeleños seemed equally proficient in applying their lessons. A member of the ayuntamiento in 1840 praised an angeleño who had "developed and cultivated the land." The plot of land now was more "beneficial" than before.[64] During the same period, the ayuntamiento believed that work helped transform malcontents. Francisco Duarte, a vagabond, had several days to find employment and prove "he is working for someone."[65] If he failed to comply, the ayuntamiento threatened to arrest Duarte. Another man who had defaulted on a loan repaid his debt by laboring "on public works."[66] Sometimes the ayuntamiento decreed that a debtor had to work for the person who had made the loan. Juan Elizalde, unable to make good on a loan of forty-eight pesos, worked for Nemesio Domínguez until the debt was paid.[67]

Over time, liberal attitudes about work remained popular. Francisco Ramírez, an angeleño journalist, told his readers in 1857 "to work, work and be independent."[68] Others who had recorded their impressions in the late nineteenth century used imagery that first surfaced in the 1830s. José del Carmen Lugo remembered that angeleño families went to bed at eight o'clock in the evening and rose the next morning at three. After praying, "the women attended to the kitchen and the men went to the field."[69] In some instances, the Americans commented on the angeleño devotion to labor and employed descriptions that a Mexican liberal would appreciate. Horace Bell, who had come to Los Angeles in the 1850s, marveled in his old age that the "californios were not lazy." "With the morning star," he explained, "all men had to be in the saddle and on the go."[70]

Angeleño diligence brought forth riches. There are accounts that speak about the quantity of cowhides, but as we know, and will see again, any mention of the cattleman's efforts is suspect. Of greater interest would be the bushels of grain or any other item the angeleños produced, but these goods often escaped precise tabulation. All we have is some brief note or reminiscence that offers glimpses of angeleño enterprise. The secretary for the Los Angeles ayuntamiento reported in 1843 that local farmers and entrepreneurs produced many items for export. He saw workers fill the hold of one Yankee ship with figs and other types of fruit. They then loaded, said the secretary, 112 cheeses, sixteen hams, and one barrel of angelica, a natural laxative pharmacists mixed into potions.[71] In later years, witnesses commented on the angeleños' efforts to make the land productive. Juan Bandini, a resident of San Diego, remembered that in the 1840s, "cotton, sugar cane, and flax" grew on the lands surrounding Los Angeles.[72] He saw other items roll out of the angeleño cornucopia. Bandini praised the "peaches, figs, pears, apples, and diverse others [which ripened] from May to October."[73] Henry Delano Fitch, a Yankee merchant who also lived in San Diego, noted that farmers cultivated other crops that went to market. He recalled that traders in Hawaii coveted the "mustard seed and beans" of southern California.[74]

At the close, we can see why, and for what purpose, the angeleños worked. Responsibility, diligence, the need to measure effort through application, in sum, the qualities one earned through worthwhile toil, helped the angeleños reject the fiesta's temptations. It was not only drink and sex that offended. Rather, the Indians' pursuits resembled a life without limits. With all sense of limit and propriety gone, the angeleños feared that disorder, and then ruin, would come. Mexico, already far away, would seem more remote. And the angeleños, cut off, or at best, maintaining some tenuous, fraying tie to the nation's interior, turned to face their troubles—alone.

As proof that work, and not pleasure, inspired their conduct, some angeleños complained about Indians who failed to put their shoulder to a task. A member of the Los Angeles ayuntamiento lamented in 1844 that when the Indians drank, they refused to work and "hurt their employers."[75] Two years later, several angeleños worried that the Indians committed all sorts of "excesses and robberies" rather than prepare for the next day's labors.[76] By refusing to work, or so the angeleños insisted, the Indians earned no consideration and deserved harsh treatment. The angeleños, meanwhile, believed they chose a different destiny. With work, and any of its disciplines, they became more accomplished and escaped the Indian's influence. There was no mistake, the angeleños declared; they deserved to stand with any other person in the nation.

If they wished, the angeleños could summarize what they had created. They feared the Indian celebration and to subdue temptation, they used violence. The violent moment provided the angeleños with the thrill of abandon, the chief attraction of the Indian fiesta, but shooting and killing, in themselves, promised limited satisfaction. Only liberal principles from Mexico, especially as expressed by work, offered the benefit the angeleños sought. Even more, by celebrating the idea of work they resolved their troubles. They fashioned a tie to Mexico and stood apart from Indians. But the conflict with Indians, so central to the gente de razón experience in California, did not go away. The struggle persisted and penetrated to the core of provincial life. How the conflict touched the angeleños' existence and shaped their every endeavor suggests that the Indian, even if subdued, continued to command great influence.

February 19, 1846

To your excellency the Governor [Pio Pico] we come before you the undersigned, and say that since the Indian ranchería was removed to the pueblito—a move calculated to end **excesses** and thefts—the aborigines . . . taking advantage of their isolation . . . steal from [neighboring orchards]. . . . [O]n Saturdays [they] celebrate and become intoxicated to an unbearable degree, thereby resulting in all manner of venereal disease, which will exterminate this race and . . . be beneficial to the city. To preserve the public health and do away with the vice of polygamy . . . [and] the **excesses** of prostitution [so that] the residents of Los Angeles would not be encouraged to do the same, we ask that the Indians be placed under strict police surveillance or the persons for whom the Indians work give [the Indians] quarter at the employer's rancho.

Signed:
Francisco Figueroa and Luis Vignes

Signatories:

Felipe Lugo	Ricardo Lankem (Laughlin)	—?—Villela
Juan Ramírez	Samuel Carpenter	Tomas Serrano
Januario Avila	Agustin Martin	Mariano Ruiz
José Serrano	Guillermo Wiskies (Wolfskill)	Antonio Salazar
Manuel Sepúlveda	Luis Bouchet	Casciano Carreon
Gil Ybarra	Maria Ballesteros	Maria Anta. Pollorena
Desiderio Ybarra	Francisco López	Vicente Elizalde
Miguel Pryor	Estevan López	Antonio Coronel

CHAPTER TWO

"Excesses"

The *Angeleños* and Their World

THROUGHOUT THIS CHAPTER we will study the word "excesses." The term may ring with outrage and scandal, the strains of the Indian bacchanal. "Excesses," after all, spoke of the angeleños' concern that the Saturday night fiesta severed their bond with Mexico. But the fear of "excesses," and its reference to troublesome Indians, could seep into other areas of angeleño life. When sounding the word again, we can hear the angeleños talk about Indian ancestors, nature, the quality of town life, a sense of time, and religion. But before addressing the substance of their discussions, we must first understand excesses as perceived by the petitioners and their contemporaries. The word, appearing twice in the appeal, once in line three and again three lines later, suggests an abundance of feeling. Pain, agony, pleasure, each brimming with sensation, could overwhelm an individual's propriety. Left weak and exhausted, with decorum erased, the angeleño man or woman was helpless before a caress or a blow with a fist.

Most angeleños, suspicious of excess, labored to strike a temperate, discreet pose. Antonio Coronel, for instance, one of the petitioners in 1846, remembered that during the Mexican period angeleño men adopted courtly airs and addressed each other formally. Women, meanwhile, dressed with great reserve. Many, wishing to obscure their shape, draped their upper bodies with shawls and kerchiefs. If shy about the patch of skin peeking out beneath the skirt and shoe tops, some sheathed their legs in stockings. To the observer, said Coronel, only the woman's face and hands appeared visible. Exposing any other part of the body would be "immodest."[1] The sense of propriety extended to family relations. Married men or women, despite their age and obligations to each other, still yielded to the authority of their parents. The father, though, seemed the most demanding and any child who turned defiant risked his wrath. Coronel suggested that curses, maybe accompanied by some quick punches, seemed the father's favorite way of exacting obedience. And, as some commentators imply, pity the poor son who, without thinking, dared smoke in his father's presence without asking permission.[2] In daily life, it is hard to say how many angeleños took on moderate habits. Most citizens could have been coarse and ill mannered, but at least punctilious conduct, the cordial, almost stiff, bearing one person should show another, seemed the ideal form of behavior.

Excesses, then, violated the modest, formal habits many angeleños hoped to cultivate. But again, excess may contain other meanings. For deeply set in the mind, so deep that they sat beyond expression, different thoughts mingled with talk of excesses. In one way, excesses described tumults in the angeleños' nature. Emotions and the body's senses, for example, ever bubbling, forever on the brink of arousal, called for regulation. Men treated each other formally. Otherwise, a boastful man, vain, impetuous, and a bit indiscreet, might stir envy, then a sense of revenge in another male. A woman cloaked herself in ample clothing. Any hint of the woman's shape might be too much for an admirer's eyes. The naked ankle, for instance, if bared to public view, presumably would overwhelm the man's senses. Children, however old, deferred to parents. When a child, even if mature and graying, challenged father or mother, who knew what would transpire next? With authority usurped, nothing would stop an inquisitive, tempestuous spirit from defying the government, then the Church.

Talk of excesses, though, while prominent, could draw notice from other elements. Alongside references to excess in the appeal, come descriptions of restraint. The petitioners wanted to "preserve" public health and "do away" with the "vice of polygamy." One more line down we see the warning that the gente de razón should turn away from sinful habits. (They should not behave like Indians, the petition commands.) Finally, at the end, the petitioners claimed that "police surveillance" would help keep the peace. For Indians too fascinated with sensual ways, the gente de razón master, the "employer" says the petition, emerged as the best person to impose discipline.

Excess and restraint, each opposed, but bound to the other, present one more way to describe the Indian and gente de razón confrontation. As shown before, the gente de razón, at turns attracted to, and repulsed by, Indians, seem transfixed, even obsessed by their antagonists. The tension they had with Indians, for some the greatest cause of concern, would flex and expand in the mind. Soon enough, when the angeleños discussed Indians, or referred to themselves as members of the gente de razón, they invoked images of excess and restraint. In many documents, including the 1846 petition, the writers assumed that Indians always succumbed to the body's desires. The gente de razón, on the other hand, seemed more modest and restrained in their appetites. If any gente de razón faltered, it is because they drew too close to the Indian. Thus, in most accounts, not only the 1846 petition, when Indians earn mention, next comes talk of excess. A similar process repeats for the gente de razón. When gente de razón writers described their temperament or conduct, they often presented images of restraint.

At all moments, the qualities of excess and restraint, and the persons on whom they rest, depend more on perception than fact. It could be that most Native Californians did not prefer wild amusements. Perhaps calmer activities brought satisfaction. As for the gente de razón, it was they, not the Indians, who spurned discipline. Sin and the indulgent moment, not the satisfaction of worthwhile labor, gave them the greatest pleasure. Nonetheless, at least to the gente de razón, it did not really matter who really welcomed or rejected discipline. What seemed more important was how a belief or impression, even if lacking proof, acquired validity. The perception, and its association with any individual, merged, and, at least to observers, became inseparable. To think of Indians was to imagine excess. Excess, meanwhile, whatever its form, often invited comparisons to Indians. As for the gente de razón, they merge with images of restraint. And any discussion of restraint emphasized the austere nature of the gente de razón. All the more, the impressions the gente de razón had of themselves, and the Indians, sat at the core of all judgments about provincial life. The thought of Indians and excesses, or the gente de razón and restraint, soon became the lens many angeleños used to measure their experience.

Attitudes on Race

On occasion, the references to excess and restraint shaped perceptions of race. Excess may suggest the fate of being overwhelmed, erased, maybe in some ways, swallowed. In its immolation of boundaries and categories, excess leaves nothing intact. The angeleños who denounced the frivolous moment would, when touched by a surfeit of gaiety or debauchery, lose their austere nature. In the same instant, the Indian, at once the symbol and practitioner of excess, also possessed the talent to erase or obliterate. Some gente de razón, for example, remembered, or so they claimed, that during wartime the Indians ate their prisoners. The residents of northern California discussed this concern more fully than their compatriots in Los Angeles. Salvador Vallejo, whose family resided north of San Francisco, recalled that some "natives were cannibalistic."[3] José Palomares, a resident of San José, remembered that Indians roasted soldiers alive and later dined on their charred limbs.[4] Of course, tales of Indian cannibalism proved false. We do not know for sure, but the californios might have confused the Native Californians with Plains Indians, who sometimes ate the hearts of dead enemies. (Aztecs, too, with their commitment to human sacrifice, could have crept into the imagination.) Or, the gente de razón misunderstood the Native Californians' habit of taking scalps. Shamans cured the hanks of hair as they did sides of venison and later put the hairy trophies on display. In any event, the Indians did not feed on californio flesh.[5]

But, as a nightmare distorts a dreamer's doubts and worries, a feast of gente de razón haunches and ribs, however untrue, captured, in grotesque form, the fear of excess' workings. The experience of erasure or obliteration, the end, seemingly, of the Saturday bacchanal, would differ little from the fate of the gente de razón roasting before Indian foes. The Indian celebration and the cannibal feast, each excessive, swallowed the gente de razón. The music and tumult of the Indian fiesta drew the individual into the crowd. Soon one celebrant was like any other. The process repeated when the gente de razón victims supposedly turned on the spit. They became the main course at dinner and, in time, the meal and Indian diner became one.

With excess follows restraint. The gente de razón, as tied to restraint as the Indian was to excess, supposedly favored diligent, moderate habits. For some gente de razón, especially those in Los Angeles, the wish to take on Mexican ways offered the best means to hold off the Indians' influence. But even more, restraint promised rewards far richer than behaving with abandon. In restraint, meaning at times to have or hold, the opposite of excess' wide and ample reach, the angeleños found the distinctions that removed them from Indians.

As members of the gente de razón, many angeleños boasted of privileges that they did not have to share with Indians. A good number believed that they possessed razón—reason—the gift they supposedly had in abundance. But for some gente de razón, with the debauched Indian so close, intelligence, a desire to work, the quick tongue, a mind good with figures, all a sign of reason, might not have been enough to draw distinctions between the two groups. Some gente de razón certainly knew that their features and appearance could qualify them as Indians. A few noted, as stated earlier, that Mexicans in the interior often claimed that "Mecos," or wild Indians, lived in California, a possible reference to the gente de razón.[6] Others, when they wished to remember, knew that a relative or spouse was an Indian from Mexico or California.[7]

The problem of determining whom was who could multiply in other ways. One could say the Indians drank, but so did the gente de razón. More troubling, at least to conscientious individuals, a few gente de razón in Los Angeles made a decent profit running the saloons and taverns the Indians frequented.[8] Another person might claim that the Indians lived in huts. But as we will see later, a few gente de razón, especially those out on ranchos, lived in dwellings no grander than an Indian's *jacal*, a structure of branches and grass. Some, though, could insist that Indians, and no one else, wore ragged clothing. Perhaps so, but Antonio Coronel admitted that the poor gente de razón wore clothes of "a cheaper material."[9] If unfortunate angeleños looked a bit down and out, they would resemble the poorest Indians.

With each population occupying the same locale, even at times mixing together when at work or play, the gente de razón set themselves apart by claiming they possessed white skin. But the question then arises over the gente de razón's understanding of pigmentation. The angeleños' insistence on fair skin obscures a complexity that many ignored or refused to address. Some californios, though not all, looked like Indians. Others, of course, resembled Spaniards. White and dark, the gente de razón were not all of one color, or of the other. Various shades blessed their form. But when called to describe their appearance, many claimed to possess a light hue.

The era often determined how the gente de razón perceived the color white. When they spoke of white skin in the early nineteenth century, they did not necessarily mean pigmentation. The gente de razón, following practices popular in Mexico, possibly described whiteness, that set of attributes many associated with white skin. Beauty, education, a refined touch, any sign of wealth affirming heaven's favor, would "whiten" a black or brown person, even anyone who bore a mixture of shades.[10] For example, up through the eighteenth century in Mexico, the king granted a

Cédula de Gracias al Sacar, a certificate of whiteness, to claimants who could afford the fee.[11] As time passed, the crown distributed fewer certificates. Nonetheless, the individual who regretted his appearance knew he could still use some asset to lighten his complexion. To be sure, the person with dark skin, no matter how talented or wealthy, would still encounter hostility from the more exalted corners of Mexican society. But, despite lingering prejudice, the individual who possessed the necessary qualities (and cash) could claim some of the prestige often accorded someone born with white skin.[12]

At times, the location of one's residence would influence any attempt to change status or rank. Within Mexico, the opportunity to claim whiteness cheered people who had black or Indian ancestors. But most dark Mexicans, if they remained in the nation's interior, often could not acquire the education or expertise to improve their position. Their agony increased when some suffered slights because of their African or indigenous roots. Even today in Mexico, the insult, "no seas indio,"—"do not be an Indian"— can cut and slash the spirit. If the taunts ring out in modern times, there is no reason to think that the abuse would have been any more sparing two centuries earlier. When the opportunity came during the colonial period, and the years thereafter, some impoverished men and women in Mexico braved a trip to the northern territories. Once there, amid other outcasts and pariahs, the newcomers could more easily grant one another the prestige, if not the attributes, they most coveted.

The 1818 census of Los Angeles suggests how a dark citizen could use a particular advantage to claim, or better, assume in the eyes of others, a creamy or rosy hue. When the census taker counted 326 people, he identified every resident by the color of his or her skin, or what he *thought* was the color of each person's complexion.[13] Indio, usually a racial category, appeared as a hue. *Rosado,* commonly red or pink, became, in the parlance of the surveyor, the color distinguishing the offspring of whites and Indians. *Trigueño,* akin to the color of wheat, seemed another common shade that suggested racial mixture. For variety, the surveyor sometimes used the designation *mestizo* to describe someone with a Spanish and Indian heritage. *Prieto,* denoting a dark color, even black, offered one more view of gente de razón skin tones. Finally, the color *blanco,* or white, described citizens with fairer complexions. To tabulate the figures, 133 were blanco, by far the biggest category. Fifty-three persons fit into the category of rosado, the second biggest set. Prieto followed next, with thirty-two people. A smattering of colors graced the form of the remaining populace.

Precision could prove elusive. In the survey, Desiderio Ybarra, prieto, and his wife, María de Jesús Baleriana Lorenzana, blanco, produced three children, each one, in the census taker's view, white.[14] Later in the count, however, Antonio Briones, prieto, and his spouse Domilaria Ramírez, blanco, the same hues as the previous couple, had two children, both mestizo, or individuals with Spanish and Indian blood. The census taker, of course, could have recorded, if not fully understood, the working of genetics. In one instance, Ybarra, a prieto, and, Lorenzana, a blanco, produced white children. In another case though, biology supplies a twist, and the parents, the black Briones, and the white Ramírez, brought forth mestizos, suggesting children with dark complexions.

But it could be that the surveyor let the parents' wealth or prestige shade his perceptions. The dark Desiderio Ybarra, for example, seemed an important figure. He won election to the ayuntamiento on three separate occasions, each time sitting as regidor, or alderman. He gained his first seat in 1827, but by 1818 he could already have established his reputation as a man of influence. Perhaps Ybarra, a farmer, had made a profit growing crops or tending cattle. Impressed compatriots, the census taker among them, therefore thought that Ybarra, despite his dark skin, possessed gifts others would attribute to a white person. Ybarra, though, perhaps a bit too dark to earn the title of blanco, would at least have enough status to confer light, creamy tones on his children.

Briones, however, who never held office and seemed a person of modest means, lacked the gifts to impress the census taker.[15] He and Domilaria Ramírez, his wife, both poor, maybe a bit scruffy in appearance, could not lighten the complexion of their mestizo children. To speculate some more, the children could certainly have been white. But the parents, desperate, pressed for luck, could have struck onlookers, the census taker especially, as so poor that the children lived in circumstances more befitting Indians than Europeans.

Nonetheless, to the disappointment of some gente de razón, whiteness seemed a prize any person could achieve. Some gente de razón surely recognized that the way they defined success, or determined one's rank in society, would benefit the Indians. As we already know, a few Indians, especially those who dwelled in the missions, could match, maybe exceed, the talents of the gente de razón. Some Indians could read and write. Others could perform Baroque music, play an instrument, or carve an implement with great care and love, perhaps shaming the skills of the californios. The Indians who toiled as farmers or ranchers, a scant number to be sure, but still worthy of note, could prove the equals of the gente de razón in business sense or skill. The very means to lighten one's skin tone seemed so accessible, at least in theory, that Indians could soon claim the advantages that the gente de razón cherished. The gente de razón, however, anxious to preserve their rank, might not wish to share any privilege. A sense of hierarchy would disappear, as would the gente de razón's authority to command or punish the Native Californians. The dark gente de razón, in particular, craving whiteness, likely grumbled that they had to share their prestige with Indians.

The Indian's opportunities to claim whiteness, no matter how illusory, improved over time. After Mexico's independence in 1821, the new government abolished the caste distinctions that had persisted since the Spanish conquest. All whites, blacks, Indians, and mixed bloods now enjoyed equal rights as citizens of the nation.[16] No doubt, day-to-day, the person with a fair complexion, as well as a wealthy person of mixed blood, might still win favor or receive great respect. But independence, and its promise of equality, weakened the idea that an individual could use some stroke of good fortune to claim the privileges of whiteness. Every citizen, or so went the thinking, deserved the same consideration under the law.

With talk of equality, many californios possibly worried. When all residents possessed the same rights and privileges as any other, the bacchanal, the climactic moment of Indians and excess, soon appeared. The californios and Indians, made equal by the law, though in some ways, regular custom and practice would be slow to change, would seem indistinguishable. If abiding on the same plane, the Indian, as the incarnation of excess, stood poised to obliterate or swallow whole the gente de razón.

Dreading excess and ravenous Indians, the californios labored to preserve their advantages. Earlier, we discussed how the idea of work, at least in Los Angeles, granted the gente de razón some authority over Indians. But in time, when precisely we do not know, the angeleños found one more method to create distinctions. In the years after Mexico's independence, the gente de razón, hoping to distinguish themselves from Indians, claimed they had white skin.

We do not speak of whiteness, the rank or status one could reach on merit. Rather we mean white as some register revealing how much, or how little, pigmentation one has. When called to describe their appearance, the gente de razón declared that every person within their ranks shared white skin. It mattered little if one was wealthy or humble. Even if it was fantasy (and it was), the insistence on white skin could bolster the spirit. The gente de razón had found a trait the Indians would never possess. The Native Californian, equal in rights and privileges, at least theoretically, dissolved all distinction. But the californios, when insisting on a fair complexion, pushed the Indian away. If bound together by the claim of white skin, the gente de razón found comfort and protection, elements that amounted to restraint.

By 1831, the new classifications had begun to set. Juan Bandini of San Diego, appointed by the Mexican government to describe the people and resources of Alta California, spoke in terms that we now know as excess and restraint. Using images that reflected the bacchanal's outrages, Bandini explained that the Indians, especially those who did not live in the missions, seemed "careless and lazy." They had many vices, with "robbery" and "telling lies" being the most "dominant passions."[17] Meanwhile, a fair complexion, synonymous with restraint and its virtues, graced the gente de razón. Bandini noted that the gente de razón, or "los blancos"—the whites—were "robust, healthy, and presentable."[18] (He added that the Mexican government should do a better job of educating the "whites."[19])

During wartime, the distinctions became sharper. In 1837, Gil Ybarra, a member of the Los Angeles ayuntamiento, suggested how white skin gave the angeleños reason to band together.[20] Hearing that Indian warriors approached Los Angeles, Ybarra warned that the native attackers wanted to kill, "all the white people [gente blanca]."[21] As we saw before, war, which once afforded the gente de razón some release, now threatened to consume them. With thoughts of an enemy on the march, Ybarra might see in graphic bloody form the result of equality. The Indian, if the same as the gente de razón, would know no hindrance. As the fiesta eliminated distinctions, war used violence to achieve similar results. All who attended a bacchanal or went into battle mixed together. When the participants hoisted the glass or prepared to bring down the deathblow, nothing could check the emotions or the body's appetites. But, at the same moment, with Ybarra speaking of war, and by implication, excess, he suggested that the gente de razón, as "white people," could rally together and contain, indeed restrain, disorder.

Some thirteen years later, in 1850, with the United States now the sovereign power in Los Angeles, the struggle between excess and restraint persisted. The municipal council, worrying as ever about the Indian fiesta, feared that the celebration would swallow the gente de razón, and maybe a few Anglo Americans. The members decreed that "all whites [todo blanco] cannot mix with the native Californians."[22] Around the same time,

Antonio Coronel, a teacher in a Los Angeles school, wished to enlighten his gente de razón and Indian charges about the distinctions that many parents knew so well. During a class assignment, the little ones wrote, with Coronel supervising, "padre, madre, hijo, hija, gente blanca, indio [father, mother, son, daughter, white people, Indian]."[23] Perhaps, we only see a spelling exercise, each word chosen randomly. But in view of excess and restraint, with man before woman, boy ahead of girl, then whites and Native Californians, the assignment's logic implies that even in the classroom the youngsters learned who commanded and who did not.

By the late nineteenth century, the distinctions separating the gente de razón and the Indians took firmer shape. Some californios claimed that physical attributes distinguished them from Indians. A few californios believed that the Indians' eyes and brown, almost yellow complexions revealed their Asian origins. One californio, for instance, theorized that "in a very remote epoch California was invaded by [the] Chinese or Japanese."[24] He could not decide, but he concluded that most Native Californians had Japanese ancestors.[25] When describing the Indians as people from another land who had different features, the commentator implied, as would some of his contemporaries, that the gente de razón did not share a common ancestry with the Indians. After all, he suggested, no gente de razón looked Japanese or Chinese. With the Indians removed, the European thus loomed as the ancestor from whom the californios could claim descent. Ygnacio Sepúlveda, born in Los Angeles during the Mexican period, remembered in 1874 that when young, he marveled at the grace and bearing of the californio families who carried "the sangre azul [blue blood] of Spain."[26] The same year, José de Jesús Vallejo, a resident of northern California, recalled that the gente de razón "were the descendants of the Europeans or Mexicans who were white."[27]

Ygnacio Sepúlveda and José de Jesús Vallejo, like many of their compatriots, knew about the racial conceits of the United States and possibly thought that they would receive better treatment if they emphasized that they had white skin like the Anglo Americans.[28] But the two commentators, though they apparently responded to jibes about the californios' ancestry, drew on ideas that had appeared in California years before the Anglo-American conquest. Even when most Indians had disappeared from California—few would survive into the 1870s—the bacchanal, and all it suggested, continued to darken the californio imagination. White skin, as a set of qualities or pigmentation, restrained the Indians and kept them away.

Nature and Other Nasty Things

The Indian and the gente de razón confrontation, especially as reflected in the opposition between excess and restraint, also influenced the way commentators observed the natural world. In fairness, the spread of illness, the destruction wrought by severe weather, or the marauding of wild animals would occur regardless of the words chosen by witnesses. Nevertheless, when seeking to describe disruption and stability, the gente de razón relied on the images of excess and restraint. In a hostile, tumultuous world, as provincial California seemed to be, the sweep and whirl of the Indian bacchanal gave observers the vocabulary to relate their experiences. But, when wishing to speak of order, the gente de razón referred to restraint and all its associations.

As fate would have it, with disaster and death often threatening California, order, and all it suggested, did not seem a popular image when commentators sought to describe the workings of nature. If worried about disease, the gente de razón conveyed their distress by speaking of Indians and excess. When word came in 1837 that a smallpox epidemic might spread from northern California, a member of the Los Angeles ayuntamiento warned his colleagues that the "destructive force of the Almighty destroys not only kingdom[s], cities, and towns, but goes forth with an exterminating hand and preys upon science and art."[29] The comment, with the dropping of the term "Almighty," and the insertion of the word "Indian," could summarize gente de razón sentiments. By the early nineteenth century, many angeleños had concluded that the Native Californians spread disease. At Mission Santa Cruz in 1825, more than two hundred miles north of Los Angeles, the rector reported that most Indian converts "were afflicted with chronic ailments, and the rest mostly venereal virus."[30] Six years later, Governor Manuel Victoria wrote his superiors in Mexico City that "among the neophytes venereal disease [was] devouring them horribly."[31] Around the same time, the neophytes who escaped from coastal missions carried infections into distant valleys and mountain foothills. By 1833, typhus or cholera had swept through the San Joaquin Valley killing at least forty-five hundred people.[32] Later, in 1837, 1844, and 1846, reports reached Los Angeles that smallpox-infected Indians in the north. In the first outbreak three thousand died, but in the periods thereafter, there was no way to tell how many Indians met their end.[33]

All the more, disease and images of excess intersected at the Indian's body. Pestilence, reflecting the abandon of the bacchanal, brought forth ruin and corruption. The Indians, in parallel form, would seem withered from disease after one too many nights at the celebration. A mournful eye, the trembling hand, the face worn by the drinking cup (and laboring for a stern employer), all supposedly caused by the weekly party, resembled the ravages left by some affliction.

If Indians and disease compared, the angeleños employed quarantines to limit the damage each could cause. In 1845, a member of the Los Angeles ayuntamiento, afraid that the Indians harbored all sorts of ills, designated "a separate place from which the Indians can hear Mass." Being a "dirty and filthy people, [they] . . . dirty the clothes . . . [of] the gente de razón . . . and do not let them hear Mass."[34] The 1846 petition, in a manner of speaking, also speaks of quarantines. After listing the evils performed each Saturday night, the appeal called for the confinement of Indians to the master's "rancho."

Smallpox, meanwhile, almost the mirror image of the Indian menace, saw similar attempts to contain and limit its spread. In 1838, after news came that smallpox infected the area north of San Francisco, citizens in Los Angeles complained to the ayuntamiento that the pestilence could brew in stagnant water. Apparently, the disease floated off fetid pools "to corrupt the air."[35] In a petition, residents asked municipal leaders to repair the zanjas, the irrigation and drainage canals cutting through town, and ensure that nothing interrupted the water's flow. Six years later, a courier from Santa Barbara warned that smallpox had sickened a sailor in port. Fearing an epidemic, the ayuntamiento moved quickly to close possible paths of infection. Municipal leaders ordered residents not to relieve themselves in the zanjas. Cattle could not wander through open-air markets, possibly because many angeleños suspected that the animals' urine and droppings would spread the disease.[36] Lest the pestilence breed in drunks or unwashed people, the ayuntamiento ordered constables to arrest anyone who drank too much or failed to bathe.[37] Though the civic leaders did not identify the individuals with slovenly habits, given the attitudes of the day, they no doubt referred to Indians.

At other times, when no reference to Indians and excess seems apparent, a writer's description of disease drew on images of the bacchanal. We may stretch the point, but in a time when Indians always seemed on the mind, there is no telling to what lengths californio fears would go. The Native Californian, pestilence, and a good time at the bacchanal, each violating decorum, could have shaped any perception on how individuals, no matter how innocent, failed to meet the standards of appropriate conduct. A member of the gente de razón, for example, when ill, might forsake his duties, departing, as it were, from the propriety expected from all citizens. If otherwise occupied, even for a legitimate reason, he might have compared with someone who seemed distracted by the Indian celebration. In 1832, the secretary of the Los Angeles ayuntamiento recorded that an unknown ailment, possibly a respiratory virus, sickened a great many people. With so many in their beds, the ayuntamiento decided to postpone elections until everyone recovered.[38] On other occasions, various angeleños fell ill and lacked the strength to serve on the ayuntamiento. Tomás Yorba, explaining in 1837 why he could not hold office, lamented that "pulmonary disease and rheumatism" disabled him.[39] A year later, Vicente Sánchez asked for a release from his duties, saying that he suffered from "rheumatoid gout" and was scarcely "able to move."[40] Around the same time, Francisco Pantoja requested a leave of absence. He explained that he had "ruptured his right side" and saw his "intestines hanging out."[41]

As the limbs and head erupted in fever or pain, nature's elements could also turn riotous. From the sky poured down rain, a welcome arrival in southern California, but when water saturated mountain valleys or filled streams, the excess could leap channels and spread across the Los Angeles basin. The deluge, however, could take some time to reach town. Blas Aguilar said that in 1821 a flood roared down on Los Angeles after storm clouds soaked nearby mountains.[42] Four years later, another torrent hit the settlement with no rain cloud in sight. José del Carmen Lugo, describing the catastrophe, recalled that when he was twelve, he heard a "great noise." His father took young José to investigate the sound and they discovered a "great sea of water overflowing vegetable gardens, fences, trees, and whatever was before it."[43] Flowing past, sputtering and kicking, came horses and cows, many of which "perished in the flood."[44]

At times, the sky presented nothing but the unblinking sun. Throughout 1820 and 1821, a drought scorched California.[45] Another dry spell apparently returned six years later when the rector at Mission San Juan Capistrano, south of Los Angeles, reported that the Indians had no "fat . . . corn, or beans" to eat.[46] The priest said nothing about the weather, but only hot temperatures could wither the crops people and animals needed to survive. Another rainless period browned southern California in 1840 when streams slowed to a trickle and hills offered scrub to thinning cattle.[47]

Other troubles descended from the firmament, though they were often more spectacular than deadly. In 1821, a comet, "muy feo," or "very ugly," said a witness, streaked above Mission Santa Ynez, seventy miles north of Los Angeles.[48] Clouds of flies gathered above horses and cattle. The swarm thickened when workers slaughtered cattle and threw fat into heaps. One witness remembered that when flies settled on the greasy piles, Indians and gente de razón smashed as many pests as they could into the fat. The workers later tossed the buzzing mixture into kettles to make tallow.[49] Other creatures skirted the sky. In 1836, a plague of crows descended on Los Angeles. The flock feasted on groves and vineyards. Worried about the crops, the ayuntamiento hired hunters to slaughter the birds.[50]

Some pests collected on the ground. Mustard plants, their seeds spread throughout the area by floods, grew so thick that they choked crops and provided hiding places for stray cattle.[51] Amid the foliage skittered rats and squirrels that eyed angeleño granaries.[52] Alongside the smaller animals loped larger and more dangerous beasts. From San Diego, some one hundred and twenty miles to the south, angeleños possibly heard of the bull that clambered atop a church (!) and tossed tiles in different directions. A resident, either trying to corral the monster, or escape the rampage, nearly died after being stomped and gored.[53] In Los Angeles, citizens complained in January 1836 that "animals" threatened the orchards and vineyards. The record does not identify the creatures, but whether deer, wolves, bears, or some other beasts, they seemed so large and ravenous that property owners wanted permission to fire weapons at the trespassers.[54] A week later, animals again caused worry when residents heard that rabid dogs ran through the streets. The ayuntamiento, while not saying anything about the animals already infected, decreed that residents could only own two dogs. Any other canine in the household would have to be destroyed. To spare owners the agony of shooting their pets, the municipal body offered any city resident poison to dispatch the family hound without spilling blood.[55]

The City and the Rancho

With nature rampant, or excessive, the diseased and mischievous Indian close by, the gente de razón cherished restraint. But moderation and temperate behavior, the qualities often associated with restraint, would mean little if they remained an abstraction. Many gente de razón valued more substantive, definite displays. To some, a wall might represent the security they sought. Indeed such a structure, probably composed of adobe bricks and high enough to discourage attackers, once enclosed Los Angeles up through the early nineteenth century.[56] It is unclear when the wall disappeared. A map drawn by the American E.O.C. Ord in 1847, the first complete rendering of Los Angeles executed in the nineteenth century, does not present a configuration resembling a wall.[57] Yet in 1846, when the petitioners wrote their appeal, perhaps some vestige of the structure remained visible. Or, if the elements eroded the wall completely, residents might recall that some sort of edifice once girded Los Angeles.

Thus, in popular memory, the traditions and perceptions of history most residents would share, many envisioned a wall. The stark, plain face on the outside kept out Indian attackers and beasts. Inside, the residents might feel sheltered, perhaps assured that no intruder would disturb their life's pursuits, at least until the party started on Saturday night. In daily practice, through the performance of routines or rituals, the gente de razón employed measures that imitated the wall's purpose. A custom, a form of conduct, a particular belief, all revered by their practitioners, would restrain the passions. Within the boundaries of a steady habit or familiar pastime, citizens found certainty. But opposite appeared those who spurned familiar rites: individuals who, in a sense, languished outside the walls and flirted with excess.

With these descriptions in mind, we consider on what side of the divide the gente de razón placed their most creative and intimate pursuits. To start, the town of Los Angeles and the rancho, at times a spacious property teeming with cattle, might abide by the distinctions angeleños used to measure excess and restraint. But there was some question about which of the two inspired the wildest or gentlest habits. To the angeleños' chagrin, some observers in the nineteenth century claimed that the town of Los Angeles encouraged the worst behavior. Don Cosme Peña, secretary to the provincial governor in 1837, sneered that political dissidents had turned Los Angeles into "Los Diablos."[58] Five years later, Captain George Simpson, an English naval officer who visited California during a trip around the world, reported that Los Angeles was the "noted abode of the lowest drunkards and gamblers of the country."[59]

The rancho, on the other hand, often earned lavish tribute from commentators. Anglo-American travelers in particular marveled at the generosity of rancho proprietors. A weary traveler presumably could knock on a ranchero's door and, without having to offer an explanation, receive a warm welcome. The visitor felt helpful hands guide him to an honored place at the table. Tasty food, usually steaming slabs of beef spiced with chiles, awaited. Indian servants supposedly bustled about, moving quickly as the host demanded that the visitor not suffer one moment of neglect. When done, all retired to more comfortable quarters where they passed the evening in conversation or heard a family member perform with a guitar.[60]

The eagerness to share might suggest that the cattlemen had made enough money to stock a full pantry and build a home spacious enough to receive guests. The best estimates surmise that cowhides were worth two dollars apiece. Tallow, meanwhile, came in twenty-five gallon bags or barrels. Whatever its container, the tallow usually commanded the price of a dollar, sometimes a dollar and a half.[61] Yankee ships cruised the coast and using money, or offering to exchange items like clothes and shoes, they purchased the products the cattlemen harvested from slaughtered cows.

The cattle trade produced great sums. Eugene Duflot de Mofras, the French explorer and diplomat, estimated that in 1842 the cattlemen exported $210,000 worth of hides. At the same time, tallow valued at $55,000 also sailed out of California ports, while otter skins and other goods rounded out the rest of the province's goods.[62] As the years passed, business grew more lucrative. Dr. John Marsh, an American physician who practiced medicine in Los Angeles before moving to Monterey, calculated the growing riches of the cattle trade. Marsh reasoned that in 1846 the californios slaughtered 100,000 cattle. He estimated that the herds that fell under the knife were worth $800,000, and when he added the value of the hides, he said the entire enterprise "amounted to $1,000,000."[63]

Some cattlemen, amassing great wealth, could offer any number of luxuries to visitors. Though eyewitnesses did not always describe a home's interior, angeleño wills suggest that a living room, the bedchamber, and at times the kitchen, would be well appointed. Unfortunately, the ranchero families in Los Angeles did not always leave a will, or if they did leave a final testament, it has not survived.[64] Of the ones we do examine, none of them, as far as we know, came from families that profited greatly from the cattle trade. But if angeleños from modest or middling backgrounds could accumulate precious items, then the rancheros might have purchased goods of greater worth.

The most intriguing and informative wills often came from women. It seems that women, especially those who had to work about the house, took great care listing the items that constituted their sphere. Men, who could avoid domestic duty, rarely felt compelled to tabulate each dish or article of clothing in their possession. Gabriela Pollerena, for instance, granted her sister tables and chairs. She capped her bequest with forty-seven pieces of china.[65] Another angeleño woman, Victoria Reid, left "one fine chest of drawers [and] seven fancy trunks" to her heirs.[66] Joaquina Machado bequeathed an impressive estate. Among many splendid things, she left "two gold necklaces, six muslin dresses, and one pair of silk shoes."

Machado did more than will her finery, however. She also left a brandy still to her heirs.[67]

Any account about the rancho or Los Angeles, and what each site supposedly represented to the gente de razón, has influenced the interpretations of scholars. Some historians conclude that the term "seigneurial," from the French word *seigneur*, a feudal lord, best describes the cattlemen's prosperity.[68] As a lord, or seigneur, the rancheros possessed a huge estate, owned livestock, and called upon workers, in this case Indians, to exploit the land's riches. Los Angeles, though, reclined beyond the realm of decency. One scholar says that during the day, "pigs, chickens, [and] stray dogs" wandered through Los Angeles and fed "upon rotting refuse." Apparently, the weekly fiesta with Indians did not provide enough entertainment. Come nightfall, the angeleños visited saloons and bordellos "off the plaza" and filled the air "with the sounds of banjo music, curses and gunfire."[69]

But we take another approach. For the most part, visitors to Los Angeles have spoken and commanded the attention of scholars. Now consider matters from the angeleño point of view. Perhaps it was Los Angeles, not the rancho, that most held in high regard. If true, we have to imagine which place best reflected the qualities of excess and restraint. Leonardo Cota, for instance, a member of the ayuntamiento in 1845, suggested that the settlement encouraged the better part of the angeleños' nature. "This small city," he announced, "is beginning to show its astral magnificence and brilliance in a manner that [when] a traveler comes . . . everybody tells him it will be a Mexican paradise."[70]

We break the statement apart. Cota called Los Angeles a *ciudad* or "city." In Spanish and Mexican law, a municipality could hold three distinctions: villa, pueblo, and city. According to records left by the angeleños, the highest rank, city, seemed highly coveted. But a settlement such as Los Angeles, which upon its founding in 1781 was only a pueblo, could become a city if, among other things, it had served as a provincial capital.[71] In time, fate helped Los Angeles improve its rank. In 1835, José Carrillo, a southern Californian who wanted Los Angeles to enjoy greater prestige than Monterey, the provincial capital to the north, proposed changes when he sat in the Mexican Congress as California's delegate. He convinced Mexico's president to make Los Angeles the capital of Alta California and, in the same instance, turn it into a city. The residents of Monterey protested, and by the end of the year the seat of the government returned north. But Los Angeles retained the rank of city.[72] For nearly a decade, up until the American takeover, many angeleños used the term "city" in all public correspondence. When petitioners described Los Angeles, as did the individuals who wrote the 1846 appeal, they used the term "this city" or "the city." (The petitioners said that the Indians' death would be "beneficial to the city.") A decree produced by the ayuntamiento would bear the words "from the city of Los Angeles." Or when a citizen addressed the ayuntamiento, he or she would invariably say, "I, as a resident of this city."[73]

We may think that hubris or insecurity compelled residents to describe Los Angeles as a city. The settlement hardly compared with any metropolis. The dirt roads and structures with roofs slathered in tar would not strike the eye as cosmopolitan.[74] Some residents, when they spoke of cities, may not have known what they were saying. Few had ever visited a city. Leonardo Cota, for instance, the man speaking of "astral magnificence," never set foot outside of southern California. Baja California, the Mexican peninsula that was his birthplace, and Alta California, where he made his home, seemed the extent of his travels.

At the same time, however, Los Angeles often attracted urbane and sophisticated settlers. Some newcomers to be sure lacked talent or drive, but more respectable sorts made the journey north. The censuses of 1836 and 1844 help us determine who came from where; though, to be fair, they sometimes list someone's home state in Mexico and say nothing more. The *diligencias*, the marriage petitions a couple filed with the priest, provide more help by identifying the birthplace of each person asked to witness the ceremony. Other documents contain snatches of information that describe a settler's point of origin. Though the sources do not supply us with precise figures, it seems that a good number of people came from cities that sat in the center of Mexico. Ignacio Coronel and his son Antonio, both of whom made their mark as teachers in Los Angeles, came from Mexico City. The Frenchman Victor Prudon, one more schoolteacher who lived in Los Angeles for a short time, remembered he had "spent the florid years of [his] youth in Mexico City."[75] José Zenon Fernández, possibly one more resident of the Mexican capital, likewise lived for a spell in Los Angeles.[76] Individuals from other Mexican cities made their home in Los Angeles. Francisco Bazo came from Puebla. José Acosta, a native of Querétaro, also chose to live in Los Angeles, as did Juan Patricio Contreras, born and raised in Guanajuato.[77]

Many of these cities often impressed observers with their architecture and beauty. Mexico City, for instance, a metropolis of 150,000 people in 1800, the last year with the most reliable count, took the name "city of palaces."[78] When the inhabitants of Mexico's cities came to Los Angeles, a few no doubt reminisced about the attractions left behind. Some thought of broad avenues and the baroque facade of a cathedral. A night out at the theater or opera sweetened the recollection. The memory of a walk in a park, the chance to sip coffee in a café, no doubt brought one more smile to the face. The opportunity to read a Mexican newspaper filled with the latest news or peruse a political pamphlet amounted to another missed pleasure.

When the newcomers told tales of their travels, some angeleños would not care to hear of luxuries they would never experience. But an equal number might sit at rapt attention. After a fine repast, the candles burning low, drinks set before the remaining guests of a dinner party, the individuals from Mexico City or Guanajuato would praise their native home. The angeleños in attendance, perhaps amazed by what they heard, listened to each speaker. Leonardo Cota, for instance, could have sat among the eager crowd. When, to take another line from his speech, Cota spoke of Los Angeles "beginning to show its astral magnificence," he could have repeated one of the glorious descriptions he heard from the Mexican immigrants.

But Cota seemed quite aware that Los Angeles, though considered a city, had not achieved great distinction. He said that Los Angeles "was beginning to show" some sort of promise. What Los Angeles currently offered the viewer was not pleasant. Cota, it must be said, warned his ayuntamiento colleagues that garbage and the remains of slaughtered cattle cluttered the streets. Apparently, he spoke well. The ayuntamiento passed laws ordering residents to collect their refuse.

Cota, though, wanted more than clean streets. He spoke of astral magnificence—"magnificencia astral"—as inflated a phrase as one can imagine. We take Cota at his word, however. Perhaps he laid out a prescription for restraint. "Astral" and "magnificent" emphasize bright, shining qualities, suggesting that light was the essence of Cota's ideas. But we move beyond the radiance of fire or the sun. Cota could have thought in more descriptive terms. In another view, light means clarity. The mind, lit by the imagination and knowledge, can perceive the workings of creation. When the light is gone, stupidity, ignorance, the worst of custom and tradition, eclipses all sensibility. A dirty and polluted city would block the shining qualities Cota and others wished to create.

To save Los Angeles from rot and corruption, or to put it another way, restrain the grime, some angeleños tried fulfilling the promises of astral magnificence. Light and its properties, as in a shining beacon, reveal all. If obvious and noticeable to observers, beauty, not ugliness, should be clear.

Beauty, though, does not always suggest a complicated, delicately rendered form. Rather, clarity, sharpness, anything that was straight and true, each a feature of beauty as any elaborate, ornate shape, would share, or rather, reflect the attributes of light.

The relation of the two, beauty and light, and what the words meant to an angeleño, might remain a puzzle. The urban historian Daniel Garr suggests that some angeleños, honoring the traditions left them by their Spanish ancestors, followed the ideas of the Italian renaissance. In the seventeenth and eighteenth centuries, during the colonization of the Americas, Spanish administrators and priests studied the Italian ideas of beauty in which organization, the rigorous, almost Spartan approach to construction, seemed the ideal. The populace, as the government and Church hoped, would benefit from a world where the straight and true prevailed. The neat shape and precise angle would supposedly direct the citizen to more exalted pursuits. Out went the vicious, low habit. In its place would come mercy and love, followed by respect for law and religion.[79]

After the Spaniards had departed California, Italian influences, though ancient, and at times distorted, persisted in Los Angeles. Some angeleños, under the spell of renaissance thought, agreed that beauty celebrated precision and organization. The straightforward features rendered in orderly shapes and forms would invite citizens to lead a regulated, disciplined life. When an individual gazed upon the linear forms surrounding him, he saw in the design the regularity and organization he should apply to his own life. Virtue, then, the responsible and austere habits citizens should adopt, was to behavior what beauty, or light, was to architecture.

The angeleño call for a clean, beautiful city may bear more meaning than we suppose. Angeleños like Leonardo Cota did not present beauty as some abstract quality. Beauty seemed the equal of symmetry and precision, thereby providing one more way of discovering restraint. Ignacio Coronel, commissioner of city streets in 1836, and who, we remember, came from Mexico City, told the ayuntamiento that the streets of Los Angeles needed more space. The thoroughfares, he scolded, "offended the sense of the beautiful that should prevail in this city."[80] More than a decade later, Antonio Coronel, Ignacio's son, also from the national capital, complained about the streets' ugliness. The road to the cemetery, he noted, "is not well proportioned," nor did it offer the most "beautiful view of the city."[81] Cota, too, in the conclusion of his remarks, lectured his colleagues that "the leaders . . . need to lend themselves to the beauty of the city."[82]

When an observer studied the city from a distance, some angeleños believed, straight lines should greet the eye. Beauty and light, both, in a manner of speaking, free from obscurity or the intrusion of a stray wall or building, should seem evident. In 1832, for instance, the ayuntamiento "was determined," wrote the secretary, "to divide this population into four manzanas [blocks]." At the church's portals, the heart of the city, four imaginary lines would emerge, each heading in a cardinal direction. Along the severe, direct tangents, would follow city streets, each one sharp and symmetrical.[83] (The plan never came to pass, but the ayuntamiento still assigned residents to a manzana.)

When Cota invoked images of light and beauty, he merely summarized the thoughts entertained by many of his compatriots. Light, then beauty, each set against ugliness, would be, in a small way, one more expression of excess and restraint. If true, other pairings would follow the same pattern. The city would rise up as a sign of restraint, and nearby, representing excess, stood the rancho.

Cota, by making no comment on ranchos, may have referred to the contrast that many angeleños recognized. In all his other presentations to ayuntamiento colleagues, which did not amount to much, Cota avoided the matter of raising cattle.[84] The oversight may mean nothing. Cota might have thought the cattle spread raised few concerns. Dirty streets, on the other hand, demanded more attention. But the omission deserves a bit more investigation. In no testimonial or public document composed before 1850 did angeleños hail the rancho. The city, to judge from a slim and spare record, received more praise.

To suggest that the rancho did not win the gente de razón's full devotion may come as news. Many angeleños reared cattle, with a few reaping a fortune. But to the angeleños, the promise of wealth, though attractive, often could not offset other impressions. The word rancho presented all sorts of connotations. According to the dictionary of the Royal Academy in Spain, rancho can describe a common meal taken by prisoners or soldiers. At other times, the word can mean any place far from a town or city where people gathered to conduct trade. The term can also describe a hut or hovel occupied by poor people. Ranchería, for example, a collection of huts, seemed a fitting term to describe Indian villages when Spanish explorers and missionaries first sighted the grass dwellings of Native Californians. In Andalucia, a province in the south of Spain, rancho approximates the meaning used in the Americas, but the word, at best, describes property developed as the owner saw fit. Crops, just as much as livestock, could be the inspiration for a proprietor's ambitions.[85]

Only in Mexico did rancho suggest a cattle spread, but once more the word carries different meanings. Certainly a rancho could mean a great hacienda, the landed domain of a wealthy family. At the same time, however, rancho could describe a smaller, less pretentious place. Francisco Santamaría, a Mexican scholar who compiled a dictionary of Mexicanisms, explains that it would be appropriate to call a rancho a "modest . . . humble site."[86]

Other words or terms derived from rancho could convey unpleasant meanings. According to Santamaría, the ranchero, a person who dwelled on a rancho, could signify a person of "simple, even uneducated habits, a campesino."[87] Even today, in modern Mexico, some senses of rancho still suggest backwardness. To say that a person does something *a rancho* means performing habits more suitable to the country, in short, behaving like a bumpkin. Any deed sloppily done, or a gaudy or garish item, can be considered *a ranchera*.[88]

If these negative associations gained their first hearing in the nineteenth century, then some gente de razón had the means to express any misgivings about the cattle business and its practitioners. The commentators did not directly condemn the cattleman in a speech or private letter, but they confessed their ambivalence in subtler, more telling ways. Sometimes, when speakers wished to describe a moment's gravity or warn of an impending crisis, they spoke of agriculture to convey their serious intent. Any discussion of agriculture may include cattle ranching, but, to read the remarks closely, cultivation often receives more emphasis. In contrast, ranching earns little, if any, direct comment. One might say that the florid style popular in the nineteenth century would give meanings we now misread. When speakers described an enemy plundering or ruining the land, they exaggerated for dramatic effect. But again, if cattle raising truly ranked high in an angeleño's esteem, the speaker might think a rancho in peril, not the farm, would be the more appropriate image. Apparently, a reference to cultivation had a better chance to catch the listener's attention.

To suffer an injury to agriculture, if only a figure a speech, could reveal which industry mattered most to the californios. Ranching remained vital, but cultivation more so. When Governor José María Figueroa died in 1835, his secretary, Juan Bautista Alvarado, used agrarian images to commemorate the loss. Alvarado mourned that the governor was "one who planted the olive branch of peace and cultivated it in all manner of virtues which are progressively unfolding in the loyal breasts of these inhabitants; he to whom our agriculture owes its security and our commerce its protection."[89] After news came that smallpox threatened Los Angeles in 1844, citizens José Carrillo and José Mora warned the ayuntamiento that if an epidemic hit, "it would decimate the population of laborers who work in agriculture—the only industry in the country."[90] At the same time another angeleño worried that the scourge was a "destructive power . . . that . . . preys upon agriculture."[91]

In other instances, the offhand remarks angeleños made about the rancheros suggest that life on the cattle spread did not always grant sophistication or comfort. Many of Bancroft's informants noted that Nasario (sometimes spelled Nemesio) Domínguez of Rancho San Pedro grew rich trading livestock. But as an aside, some added that he was a "wild fellow."[92] Antonio Coronel implied that in the early nineteenth century the cattle business did nothing to improve life in California. After the arrival of "educated and intelligent people" from Mexico, Coronel concluded, the provincial inhabitants presumably turned away from raising cattle to try more productive pursuits.[93] José del Carmen Lugo, who grew up on a rancho, suggested that the cattle trade promised practitioners a dreary, sometimes grinding existence. Most people in the cattle business lived in humble quarters, a far cry from the great dwelling one might associate with successful rancheros. "The house on a little rancho," explained Lugo, was of "rough timber roofed with tules [reeds]." The home "rarely had more than two rooms. . . . [o]ne served as the entry and the living room, the other as a sleeping room." Most inhabitants had little reason to secure their home with a door. In most cases, Lugo remembered, the family had "nothing worth taking."[94]

Other bits of evidence confirm our suspicion about the cattlemen and their reputation. Every year, the male property owners of Los Angeles gathered to elect two alcaldes, the chief magistrates of the municipality, four to six regidores, what we would call aldermen, and one sindico, a sort of city prosecutor and treasurer. Of the sixty-two men elected to office between 1822 and 1848, fifteen had some connection to the cattle business, almost one-fourth of the sixty-two individuals who sat on the municipal council.[95] From this group of fifteen, eight claimed ranching as their primary occupation, but none of them held title to a cattle spread. Another two men reported that they were *campistas*, individuals who grew crops or grazed cattle on a substantial but still small plot of land, hardly the great estate the word rancho may imply in modern times. Of the remainder, only five held title to a cattle spread. The fifteen individuals represent a significant proportion, but in a place and time in which the cattle business was supposedly prominent, the number, far from high, may surprise.

Other details deserve mention. Each seat on the ayuntamiento had different obligations and responsibilities. An alcalde would often head the municipality. He would supervise city affairs, but also sit as judge. A sindico kept the city's accounts. At times, he would bring charges against individuals who stood accused of breaking the law or refused to pay their share of fees and taxes. A regidor, meanwhile, represented a district and fielded the concerns of constituents.

From what we can gather, the more demanding the post, the less likely voters would choose one of the fifteen rancheros for office. (For the sake of simplicity, we use the term ranchero to describe anyone who worked with cattle. As we will see, some angeleños did not always welcome the title of ranchero.) Four rancheros sat as alcalde. Another four won races to serve as sindico. Both offices apparently required occupants who possessed a quick mind or special skill, talents that voters may not have associated with cattlemen. The rest, seven in number, won seats as regidores. Voters apparently thought that rancheros would have no trouble with a regidor's responsibilities.[96] Of course, we may be too quick to judge. The cattlemen could have turned down invitations to run for a seat. On the other hand, the rancheros could have felt little need to compete for office. Some, by marriage or blood, would be related to members of the ayuntamiento, and they exerted influence behind the scenes. But all the same, some rancheros suspected that they did not impress compatriots and did not stand for election.

As the rancheros apparently knew, the men who pursued other livelihoods often proved more popular with voters. In all truth, the sources yield confusing results when any attempt is made to discover each officeholder's occupation. Despite the uncertainty, there is enough reason to see why some individuals earned more respect than the cattlemen. Recall the image of the wall girding Los Angeles. Inside the wall, where sat Los Angeles, we may see examples of restraint. Most of the men elected to the ayuntamiento displayed attributes that tied them to the city, and thus supposedly more sober and abstemious ways. Of the sixty-two men who held office, twenty-nine claimed farming as their primary occupation. If the angeleños followed Spanish or Mexican tradition, the farmer lived in the settlement. Each day, or when necessary, he visited his parcel that sat close to Los Angeles. A few no doubt grazed a small herd to put meat on the dinner table, but the bulk of their talents went to the plot sprouting with fruits and vegetables. It is worthy to note that the five rancho proprietors who sat on the ayuntamiento—that is, the individuals who held title to a cattle spread—did not claim cattleman as their occupation. According to the censuses, four said they were farmers—labradores proprietarios. The other, José Sepúlveda of Rancho San Joaquin, claimed in the 1844 survey he was a campista.

The remaining ayuntamiento members pursued other occupations. Twelve men cultivated a plot of land and worked as merchants or tradesmen. They too, after tending to their business within Los Angeles, rode out to the family plot. The last six presumably did not till the land, but worked at some business or craft, still more evidence that a good number of residents plied their trade in the city.

The man who had little or no involvement in the cattle business seemingly possessed talents that the electorate appreciated. When an individual handled money or worked a trade, he exercised some sort of discipline. He might invest wisely, or acquire a reputation as a shrewd entrepreneur. If he proved adept at his calling, fellow angeleños might think him a diligent worker who, when elected to office, would bring prosperity to all citizens.

But beyond the city outside the wall, any person who lived on a cattle spread faced a grimmer, and at times, more troubling existence. In some aspects remote and distant, the rancho could dwell far beyond the reach of genteel influence. According to the tabulations kept by the angeleños, there were few ranchos to begin with. The 1836 census counted seventeen ranchos in the Los Angeles area. By 1844, the year of the next survey, the number of ranchos dropped to sixteen.[97] Apparently, most individuals preferred to reside in the city.[98] The 1836 census, for instance, reveals that eleven hundred gente de razón dwelled in Los Angeles. But outside the city, 575 gente de razón lived on ranchos or in communities dotting the deserts or mountain approaches. The next survey, eight years later, counted 1,382 gente de razón in the city. Meanwhile, beyond Los Angeles, the gente de razón populace dwindled to 460 residents.

Alone, miles from Los Angeles, a rancho's inhabitants would not necessarily make their city cousins envious. The historian Antonio Rios-Bustamante says the great cattle spreads that amazed the Anglo-Americans did not emerge until the mid-1840s. In prior years, particularly after secularization, when claimants desired a share of mission property, a new rancho often featured crude dwellings, while the cattle herds, modest in number at the outset, would take some time to reach the thousands.[99]

In the meantime, some proprietors did not necessarily think that a rancho offered security or comfort. The individuals who lived near the mountains often feared that Indian raiders would spring out of hideaways to torch buildings or run off with cattle. It was equally likely that the proprietors who wanted to avoid attack preferred to leave the rancho vacant until all danger had passed. For those who insisted on developing the property, they left the rancho's chores to a work crew and found refuge in Los Angeles. If the property sat closer to the coast, far from Indian attackers, the angeleños would have no trouble grazing cattle, but the lonely sweeps and vistas could prove quite dull. In any event, no matter where the rancho appeared, in the interior or along the coast, few angeleños would see the great cattle spread many historians now imagine.

Perhaps now, with the image of the city wall in mind, and its suggestions of excess and restraint, the comments of Coronel, Lugo and Nasario Domínguez's neighbors, seem appropriate. Coronel, when honoring "educated and intelligent" settlers from Mexico, did not think the cattlemen deserved great praise. Lugo, providing the evidence that Coronel neglected to present, might have been accurate when he described impoverished rancheros. When speaking about the simple hovel, with furnishings so meager that "they had nothing worth taking," Lugo suggested that for most people, raising cattle did not always lead to prosperity. Meanwhile, the ranchero Nasario Domínguez, who resembled a "wild fellow" to contemporaries, possibly saw his occupation, not temperament, damage his name. Abel Stearns, a Yankee who came to Los Angeles before 1846, called Domínguez a "smart man." Domínguez, who owned 3,000 cattle in 1843, had only 300 head a decade before.[100] Domínguez, if indeed wild, would not have had the business sense to develop his holdings. Still, Domínguez, who, according to the 1844 census, was a ranchero, had no luck changing the opinion of observers. As a person who worked with cattle, and who possibly spent a good deal of time on his rancho, he could only be wild, and nothing else.

With rancheros leading lives some found wanting, few angeleños saw fit to honor individuals in the cattle business. Nonetheless, we must acknowledge witnesses in the nineteenth century who said that the ranchos resembled landed estates. The observers did not err—they knew what they saw—but their remarks deserve some context. Most cattlemen, at least in the Los Angeles area, did not acquire influence until the last years of Mexican rule. Their ascent accelerated in the 1850s, when miners in the gold fields needed meat for food and hides for leather goods. Meanwhile, Anglo-American chroniclers in the latter part of the nineteenth century, looking at the wealthy rancheros around them, assumed that the cattle trade had always brought prosperity. They argued that the cattlemen had commanded wealth and power since the 1830s. Modern historians, when reading the evidence, reach the same conclusion. They claim that the word seigneurial, or any other term emphasizing lordly rank, best described the rancheros' life and habits throughout the Mexican period. But the angeleños, it appears, knew better.

Time

The city, as we have noted, offered refuge. But in the same moment, other activities and habits conferred the same sense of protection. These routines, when performed, or at least observed, by the populace, brought to mind restraint and the need to contain excess. Inside the limits and boundaries of a revered habit, as within the confines of the city, the angeleños found comfort. Nothing foreign or hostile would take root, and the angeleños could continue their labors without interruption. Among the many rituals and practices they followed, a respect for time, the calculations needed to record each moment's passing, granted the angeleños one of the best ways to measure restraint. If they ignored the clock or calendar, some angeleños detected the image of excess and the intemperate Indian amid the blur of days and hours. The gente de razón would not rise and report for work. Few would answer the bell sounding for Mass. The trumpet blast mustering the militia would go unheeded. Sensation, pleasure, the selfish wish to seek one's satisfaction first—all other obligations be damned—would reign and leave the settlement in a desperate condition.

In daily practice or in a reminiscence, the gente de razón revealed their devotion to precision and punctuality. In the 1846 petition, two signatories, Miguel Pryor and Antonio Coronel, represented the gente de razón's wish to honor time. Pryor, a watchmaker from Kentucky, tended to the chimes and springs of angeleño timepieces.[101] Meanwhile, Coronel kept a calendar that had printed, down to the minute, the time the sun set, and rose, each day of the year.[102] On occasion, the sources make mention of clocks and watches cropping up in gente de razón homes. Coronel, for instance, remembered seeing clocks in angeleño homes.[103] José del Carmen Lugo implied that some angeleños used clocks or watches to rise early in the morning.[104] Or, even if few timepieces existed, the angeleños could use other means to keep track of the hours. A church bell, the sound possibly reaching for miles, could mark the time. An individual's voice would serve the same purpose. The ayuntamiento records speak of town criers spreading information throughout the area. Perhaps the man on his rounds would think it was his duty to announce the time for the benefit of residents.[105]

The gente de razón in Los Angeles and other settlements used the sweep of the minute hand to establish the rhythm of californio life. When military men took to the field, they used time to measure distance. In 1824, Lieutenant José María Estudillo, a native of San Diego, received orders to open a route to the Colorado River in the east. He knew that his men, astride their horses and carrying their supplies, would move at a certain pace. To calculate their rate of progress, Estudillo consulted his timepiece to measure how far they traveled. On January 6, he wrote, "we left at 7:45 in the morning and by 12:50 [we had gone] four leagues." The men rested, but at "2:30 in the afternoon" the march resumed, and "we went [another] two leagues."[106]

During campaigns against Indians, time proved even more precious. The diarists who described events took care to record each moment precisely. Any delay could mean death. To spring a surprise, speed and execution, the very essence of punctuality, brought victory. In 1829, Corporal Joaquin Piña described attacks against Indians along the Stanislaus River, three hundred miles north of Los Angeles.[107] On May 28, he wrote, "we arrived . . . at 8:07 in the morning." After a break, the soldiers marched again until "5:04 in the afternoon." They rested for the evening and the next morning "at 6:30" they continued searching for the enemy. Nearly three hours later, "at 9:07" explained Piña, scouts observed Indian "rebels leading horses."[108] Ensign Mariano Vallejo, in a report to his superiors, related the same events described by Piña. After word came that the enemy was nearby, Vallejo explained, the troops attacked at "5:00 in the afternoon." The Indians retreated, with the californios right behind them, hot on the trail. "The following day at 9:00" in the morning, Vallejo wrote, the battle continued. The enemy ran again and the troops gave chase through the night until they caught some stragglers "at 4:00 o'clock in the morning."[109]

In Los Angeles and other settlements, the inhabitants, like the military men, appreciated the precision afforded by the clock. Their punctual nature, if we may call it that, contrasted with the expanse that swept around them. To the east, sitting across the horizon, cut the San Gabriel

Mountains. A little to the north, practically running from east to west, loomed a smaller range, the Santa Monicas, and to the southeast ran one more set of mountains, the San Bernardinos. The peaks, seemingly placid, even beautiful, on days free of haze, often hid many dangers. Indian raiders, who caused so much consternation, sat in the mountains surveying all activity in the valleys below. On other occasions, a mountain pass would disgorge a flood that would sweep all before it. Behind the angeleños, to the south and west, stretched flat, marshy ground. A marsh may not seem a problem, but in the winter, rain sometimes raised the water level, making travel by horse and wagon difficult. When the angeleños observed the vast landscape, they would not necessarily want any mystery attending their daily affairs. The clock, with its purpose clear to all, each moment, if need be, measured exactly, dispelled uncertainty.

The ticking timepiece set and organized the angeleños' day. Antonio Coronel remembered that nothing superseded the time to pray. At balls or dances when eight o'clock struck, "the father of the family stopped the music and said the rosary with all the guests."[110] When finished, the music resumed and the celebrants again kicked up their heels. The ayuntamiento met each Tuesday and Wednesday, or so claimed the secretary, at ten o'clock in the morning.[111] At other moments, time's toll could be punitive. The ayuntamiento decreed in 1833 that on "feast days . . . liquor . . . can be sold only . . . between 800 and 1100 and 1600 to 2000."[112]

Respect for the clock may have encouraged angeleños to develop meticulous habits. In 1841, for instance, the prefect of Los Angeles rejected a land petition. Apparently the citizen used his own paper, not the official variety embossed with the national seal, and left the document dirty with ink stains. Tell "the individual person," the prefect ordered a magistrate, "to add the corresponding paper and [exercise] greater neatness."[113] A year later, the prefect granted a judge time to recover from an eye injury. But "when you have recovered," he lectured, "you will resume your duties."[114]

When applying for farming plots, the angeleños found one more way to express their precise and exacting nature. Within the city limits, an area of six square miles, residents measured a prospective plot down to the last *vara* (a vara measured little less than a yard).[115] In 1836, Francisco Alvarado and his brother Nepomuceno surveyed a bit of property with a tripod and plumb. They desired a parcel that ran "five hundred and five varas in a northerly direction, and 40 degrees east." The lot then ran "eighty-eight varas in a northerly direction, 57 degrees west." Thereafter, the measurement proceeded "in a southerly direction, 30 degrees west, three hundred and sixty-five varas," before going "in a southerly direction 35 degrees east . . . for six hundred and sixty-four varas."[116]

To be fair, only two other petitions carry compass readings.[117] Possibly, for a humble petitioner, the money to rent, maybe buy, the necessary implements would seem extreme. But if most applicants could not use a compass, they dispensed with the readings and used some other means to measure the length and breadth of their property. As an example, we follow the tracks of Crecencio Váldez. When he sounded off each vara— perhaps he used his own stride, or a stick and chain marked for the purpose—he performed a rite others repeated until the American arrival. Beginning at the boundary of Don Rafael Guirado's land, Váldez marked off a line running four hundred and fifteen varas to the east. Looking north, Váldez then measured a line for two hundred and eighty varas. He went another three hundred and fifty varas to the west, before moving south one hundred and fifty-two varas.[118] At each step, with or without a compass, Váldez suggested that the angeleños followed, and welcomed, the steady, relentless pace of the clock. Excess, as it would appear when one did not honor time's demands, promised a wide range of peril. But restraint, especially when represented by the clock or another apparatus that reduced uncertainty, provided the reassurance that the angeleños could establish some sense of order.

Religion

Religion, or more specifically Roman Catholicism, the faith many people followed in Mexican California, seemed another way to express restraint.[119] In one sense, the very meaning of religion encompassed the angeleños' wish to seek, and hold, a strict, regimented pose. To some scholars, the word "religion" comes from the Latin *religare*, meaning to bind or bring together. *Re*, the prefix suggesting repetition, combines with the verb *ligare*, meaning to tie, thus suggesting a reunion between the mortal and divine.[120] The etymology may not have come to the angeleños' notice, but when listening to a priest's sermons or gleaning what they could from Scripture, they learned how to find divine favor. The angeleños knew that the path to heaven's glory, a route that stretched from birth to old age, involved various strictures and obligations. Baptism began the journey and washed away original sin, the primal iniquity that cursed all people. Other sacraments, each one showering the soul with grace, kept believers focused on paradise. In the meantime, the faithful prayed or performed the loving deed, every act putting one closer to their eternal reward. Upon death, as many hoped, believers again rested in God's bosom, both tied together, as it were, once more.

But religion, perhaps more than any other element in angeleño life, always seemed challenged by excess, or what the faithful would call sin. We imagine an individual gente de razón or Indian believer preparing for his devotions. The ethnicity matters not. At times, the Native Californian— perhaps to the gente de razón's dismay—seemed as reverent as any Mexican newcomer or californio settler. Enter the sanctuary and kneel beside the believer. Hear the prayers. Peer into the heart where wrestled the demands of faith and temptation. Perhaps, in the believer's ear hell's counsel would hiss enticements. Just consider, went the advice, how recklessness, the thrill of abandon, the satisfaction of quivering flesh would bring joy no divine blessing would ever grant. But in contrast, as if perched on the other shoulder, heavenly pronouncements seized the heart. Catholic ritual, the priest's incantations, story after story, from the Bible to folklore, threatening the unrepentant with damnation, might remind believers that, in the end, paradise awaited those who disciplined the appetites.

At times, the spiritual conflict marked life's last moments. As the angeleños aged and composed their wills, some worried that at the end sin and temptation would finally prevail. Dreading a moral lapse when at death's door, they reminded the Almighty that save for the stumble in life's waning moments, they had always kept the faith. Don Vicente Ortega asked heaven to remember that he had long "lived and professed" the teachings of "Our Catholic, Apostolic Roman Mother Church."[121] Others sounded more emphatic. José Gaspar Valenzuela declared, "I have always believed and confessed in the mystery of the Holy Trinity."[122] For some testators, uncertainty seemed difficult to shake. Anastacio Avila, "being fearful of death," hoped that Christ would "forgive my sins and take me to enjoy his presence."[123]

But in some instances, religion confused all distinctions between excess and restraint. The believer who insisted he behaved with restraint would seem, to others, blind to his own excesses. To put it another way, during a moment of religious fervor, when excess seemingly consumed the senses, some believers thought they exercised restraint.

The priests, more than anyone else, distorted or even erased the categories the gente de razón used to measure conduct. At first glance, the priests apparently lacked the numbers to wield any influence, much less challenge the distinctions between excess and restraint. The Franciscans, the order that ran the missions up through secularization, and, in some instances, into the years beyond, never had more than fifty priests at any one time to minister a province that covered nearly 159,000 square miles.[124] Before 1834, the year secularization began, at least two Franciscans, sometimes only one, lived at each of the twenty-one missions in the province.[125] After secularization, the number of priests diminished some more. Many clerics sailed home to retirement in Mexico or Spain. Some remained in California, their ranks, on occasion, supplemented by priests from different orders.

By the late 1830s, few clerics served in California. Los Angeles in particular did not have a priest for long stretches of time. The 1836 and 1844 censuses, for instance, suggest that no cleric lived in the area. The surveyor could have overlooked the priests—they sometimes resided at the secularized missions—but even so, when they did appear, no more than one or two served the angeleños and Indian converts.[126]

Despite their paltry numbers, the priests seemed quite capable of making their presence felt. Some provided worthy examples of restraint. The priests, as one admirer explained in 1831, went through "indescribable sacrifice" to spread the faith in California.[127] Another supporter agreed and remembered late in life that the priests endured great suffering when tending to their congregation.[128] At times, especially in the early years of California's settlement, the priests toiled at more worldly tasks. The missionaries, anxious to turn Indians into responsible citizens, provided instruction in farming or craftsmanship.[129] In other instances, the priests looked after the welfare of the gente de razón. Before secularization in 1834, when supplies ran low, provincial governors and military commanders asked the missionaries to contribute food and goods to the californios, a request that would be difficult to refuse.[130] As payment, the missionaries would receive a draft, or letter of credit, that they could redeem in Mexico City. To digress a bit, the drafts often proved worthless. By 1820, says one authority, the provincial government owed the priests nearly half a million dollars, a debt that did not sit well with either side.[131] Nonetheless, the tension arising from business transactions did not deter priests from serving as a bulwark against all sorts of trouble. They kept believers from sin and, when needed, rescued them from poverty.

But, to some observers, the priests could represent excess. On occasion, the clerics stirred comment when they did not heed their vows of poverty. Prior to secularization, many missionaries controlled the province's richest land.[132] In the priests' quarters, the mission's bounty presented a grand table.

The American trapper Jedediah Smith remembered that Father José Bernardo Sánchez of Mission San Gabriel welcomed him with a wonderful dinner. The meal, noted Smith, "consisted principally of meats and an abundance of wine." Afterward, the dinner party relaxed by puffing on cigars.[133]

The gente de razón who had received an invitation to attend a dinner party, or had heard of a priest's rich tastes, might think that the missions, with much property and brimming larders, would be too abundant. In 1836, one angeleño condemned the priests for pursuing luxury. He spoke when secularization was in full swing and some of the priests' comforts had vanished, but apparently a few continued to live quite well. The angeleño declared that the priests "consecrate themselves to softness and licentiousness, concealing beneath the austerity of their humble sackcloth the *excesses* [my emphasis] of a worldly life."[134]

A sated priest, perhaps fat and content, would demonstrate how comfort, the occasional good time—shall we say excess?—wrecked the mind, allowing whim and caprice to rush forth. A Franciscan, though, if able to read our words, would counter that running a mission offered few pleasures. The greatest reward waited in heaven, but on earth, agony and pain would be the priest's lot. Any cleric who behaved inappropriately would have succumbed to the tests and trials of his calling.

Still, with excess and restraint providing the means to describe their existence, some gente de razón found a way to evaluate a priest's conduct. In Los Angeles, or elsewhere in the province, the citizens possibly exchanged knowing glances when they observed the priests' unusual habits or foul tempers.[135] José María Zalvidea, the rector of San Gabriel in the 1830s, a mission famed for its harvests and great herds, could qualify as a priest ruined by comfort. At dinner he would mix wine, dessert, salad, and presumably the main course into a bowl and devour the contents. When he walked about the mission garden, Zalvidea murmured to himself. At times, he exploded in a flurry of gestures, crying, "Satan I've caught you and I'm going to give you such a whipping," before resuming his journey.[136] Father Francisco Suñer, meanwhile, made few friends during his time in California. When posted at Mission Santa Barbara, one of the five missions he supervised, Suñer displayed a "violent character." Children in particular, one witness remembered, did not warm to the "brusque" and "self-important" priest.[137] Father Francisco Xavier Concepción Uria, assigned at various times to Missions La Purísima and San Fernando, also behaved oddly. He amused himself by annoying "large cats" and thumping the heads of Indian boys with a stick.[138]

The grumbling grew louder when a priest's odd habits caused more inconvenience for the gente de razón. Around 1820, Ramón Sotelo stood accused of expressing ideas not even a "Protestant would entertain." The Inquisition, far from the ferocious tribunals in Mexico or Spain, but still formidable, summoned Sotelo to Monterey and demanded an explanation. Sotelo dared argue with the friars, and his inquiries, their substance now lost, challenged Catholic doctrine. The Inquisition found Sotelo's explanation wanting and convicted him of impiety. He received a punishment to serve in a chain gang with daily lessons in Catholic belief and practice.[139] Around the same time, soldiers in Los Angeles complained that the priests from San Gabriel rarely visited town to say Mass. The Franciscans pleaded that age and frailty left them incapable of negotiating the eighteen-mile round-trip to and from Los Angeles. Several soldiers replied, perhaps sarcastically to judge from the tenor of their remarks, that the "convenience of the padres" did not dispose them to make sacrifices.[140]

A bit later, the Church elicited as much bemusement as anger when the bishop in Sonora forbade the "very scandalous dance called the waltz."[141] Bancroft reports that when the edict reached Monterey, the governor ignored the ban and gave a ball "at which the waltz was a popular feature."[142] The priests handed down other prohibitions. In 1826, Father Vicente Francisco Sarria, Prefect, or assistant to the President of the Missions, wanted to limit access to the Bible. No one, save for priests, argued Sarria, should have a copy of Scripture.[143] Few californios, at least those who could read, paid any heed to the command.

The gente de razón, however, did not lose faith. They still wanted priests to nurture the spirit. Any believer had expectations that he, or she, wanted met. Knowing that religion functioned as a form of restraint, he might wish that a priest would offer blessings and, when need be, the counsel required to reach heaven. When no priest lived in Los Angeles, especially toward the middle of the nineteenth century, the gente de razón worried about their spiritual welfare. The ayuntamiento complained in 1833 that a priest had not resided in Los Angeles for some time. The body voted "that the entire population be summoned to contribute to the priest's maintenance."[144] Four years later, with the rectory again vacant, the municipal council asked the Father President in Santa Barbara to assign a priest to Los Angeles.[145] When priests did live in or near Los Angeles, they received all sorts of appeals to consecrate significant events. Before executing the two adulterers in 1836, vigilantes summoned a priest to confess the doomed lovers.[146] (He refused.) A year later, José Carrillo, new governor of

California, took the oath of office in Los Angeles and afterward invited a priest to bless the occasion by saying a *Te Deum*, a High Mass.[147]

At other times, the priests offered examples in how to worship the Almighty. The Franciscans, for instance, emphasized the sacrifice of Christ. Of course, other religious orders in Mexico commemorated the Redeemer's death and resurrection. But some Franciscans practiced a more demanding faith. The flesh, weak and sensitive to the touch, impeded their progress to connect with the divine. To discipline the spirit, the Franciscans resorted to flagellation, the application of a scourge to the back, to tame the body's appetites. There is no telling how many priests wielded the scourge, but few would think it odd to find grace through pain. Father Zalvidea, the eccentric Franciscan who wrestled with demons, seemed especially enthusiastic about the whip. Indian servants reported that in the morning they would find the priest unconscious by his bed, his back caked with blood, the encrusted lash nearby.[148]

In the Franciscans' suffering, we find restraint. The cat-o'-nine-tails, a scourge forged from iron, seemed the preferred instrument to turn the flagellant from the pleasure of excess. Any person, the flagellant included, may wish for some delight or sweet comfort. But when surrendering to the whip, the flagellant abolished selfishness. Luxury, desire, the pursuit of satisfaction, fell away. Restraint had triumphed. The soul, no longer entangled with the flesh, awaited the divine will.[149] Even more, the practice of flagellation recalls the purpose of religion. Any ritual or practice, such as the lash, helped guide the believer to God's grace. Each stroke, perhaps keeping time with Christ's march to Calvary, sounded off the flagellant's spiritual journey. When drawing blood, the penitent awakened the spirit, and, senses ablaze with glory, the soul moved on to embrace the Almighty.[150]

Some angeleños tried to imitate the priests' devotions. The exact number is unknown, but enough apparently welcomed the lash. Others throughout nineteenth-century Mexico took to the whip with no trouble. In Mexico City, for instance, believers applied the scourge during Holy Week.[151] An angeleño penitent, like his compatriots elsewhere in Mexico, would seem no different in wishing to taste the cup Christ drank. Hugo Reid, a Scotsman who came to Los Angeles in the 1830s, described the trip of "San Joaquin" to "St. Gabriel," the mission east of Los Angeles. The year of the visit, let alone the month, is not clear, but circumstances suggest the time to be Holy Week. San Joaquin said that he entered the Church and saw "sixteen culprits flogging themselves on their knees." He asked a friend to explain, and San Joaquin learned that he was mistaken. "The persons therein . . . [were not culprits]," the friend answered, but "were performing penance to prepare for the Passion as was according to their creed."[152]

When the faithful picked up the whip, perhaps they followed the pace and beat of a particular ritual. An angeleño poem composed by Francisco Avila in the late 1830s illustrates how believers could imitate Christ when He bore the lash or the crown of thorns pushed onto the brow. If the penitent used a whip he could follow the cadence set by the poem. Another person, though, perhaps a bit reluctant about drawing blood, would prefer to imagine Christ's Passion, rather than experience His suffering. Whatever approach they desired, the penitents used the poem to express their devotion.

The persons who recited the words, or wished to tattoo them on their backs, knew that the mere mention of torture and pain was not enough. They wanted the verses to emphasize the blows and gashes. Only then, with the lines insisting on painful detail, would the faithful appreciate Christ's sacrifice. "Know my beloved," the devotion begins, "that of the soldiers who seized me there were 2,001." Of these, "25 struck me in the mouth 30 times." But there was more punishment. Later, "two soldiers . . . gave me eight blows in the mouth, 150 in the chest, [and] 1,670 lashes when I was tied to the post." When the poem described Christ's approach to Calvary, the faithful sensed the final moments drawing near. "I fell three times with the Holy Cross," the last lines read, and "the blood which poured out [amounted] to 300,670 drops."[153]

The specter of flagellation possibly influenced many forms of worship. A cleric's sermon, for instance, could compare with the swinging whip, (but not cause as much pain) when the faithful learned they needed to renounce bodily pleasure and focus the mind heaven's blessings. Prayer sometimes accomplished the same ends. To fall on one's knees at an appointed time, even when inconvenient, seemed one more way of subduing the spirit. Don Pancho Rangel, an old angeleño, recalled that during the Mexican era, residents prayed four times a day. Before daybreak, they rose early, and offered up an *alabado*, or religious hymn. The Angelus, a set of prayers dedicated to the Virgin, came at noon. Around six in the evening—Rangel is not sure—the *oraciones*, more devotions, sent thoughts winging toward the heavens. Two hours later, at the stroke of eight, residents would pray the rosary.[154] Other witnesses do not describe the need to pray four times a day, but they explain that the angeleños had no trouble falling to their knees. José del Carmen Lugo remembered late in life that some families rose before dawn to greet the day with prayers.[155] Nor must we forget Coronel's claim that at eight o'clock, all residents, even if dancing, would kneel to say the rosary.[156]

With each stab of pain, and talk of divine union, we have come full circle. The angeleños, fearing excess, welcomed restraint. Racial categories, conceptions of nature or the city, the need for time and religion, reminded all that control and precision, not abandon, brought greater satisfaction. But, when putting aside the images of excess and restraint, remaining, at the center, we see Indians and the gente de razón. The conflict between the two, rarely reaching resolution, often presented other dangers. What these dangers were, as we will see, presented the angeleños with a new set of worries.

February 19, 1846

To your excellency the Governor [Pio Pico] we come before you the undersigned, and say that since the Indian ranchería was removed to the pueblito—a move calculated to end excesses and thefts—the aborigines . . . taking advantage of their isolation . . . steal from [neighboring orchards]. . . . [O]n Saturdays [they] celebrate and become intoxicated to an unbearable degree, thereby resulting in all manner of venereal disease, which will exterminate this race and . . . be beneficial to the city. To preserve the public health and do away with the vice of polygamy . . . [and] the excesses of prostitution [so that] the residents of Los Angeles would not be encouraged to do the **same**, we ask that the Indians be placed under strict police surveillance or the persons for whom the Indians work give [the Indians] quarter at the employer's rancho.

Signed:
Francisco Figueroa and Luis Vignes

Signatories:

Felipe Lugo	Ricardo Lankem (Laughlin)	—?—Villela
Juan Ramírez	Samuel Carpenter	Tomas Serrano
Januario Avila	Agustin Martin	Mariano Ruiz
José Serrano	Guillermo Wiskies (Wolfskill)	Antonio Salazar
Manuel Sepúlveda	Luis Bouchet	Casciano Carreon
Gil Ybarra	Maria Ballesteros	Maria Anta. Pollorena
Desiderio Ybarra	Francisco López	Vicente Elizalde
Miguel Pryor	Estevan López	Antonio Coronel

CHAPTER THREE

"The Same"

The Indians and the *Gente de Razón*
Make Love and War

IN THIS CHAPTER, we say more about the gente de razón's dislike for Indians. To the dismay of many gente de razón, the Native Californians frustrated any wish to take on liberal habits from Mexico. The angeleño farmers or merchants who aspired to work, and thus embrace one element of Mexican liberalism, complained about Indian distractions. When the Native Californians inside Los Angeles whooped and hollered, or put a bottle to the lips, some angeleños grumbled that some compatriots would feel tempted to join the celebration. Indians who lived farther out could arouse more ill will. The Native Californians, at work on a distant farm or rancho, might prove sloppy—the faster they finished, the sooner the fun could begin. Or they might take the chores too lightly, leaving the tasks undone. And as we will see, in the morning or late in the afternoon when all would be at rest, a creaking gate, the crunch of soil underfoot, the soft whinny of a horse could be—surprise!—the prelude to a raid. Leaping to their feet, the gente de razón might glimpse Indian marauders running off with the herd or setting fire to buildings.

Distressed at how the Indians offended sensibilities by committing crimes or offering forbidden delights, the petitioners insisted that the gente de razón should not behave "the same" as Indians. The word "same"—the term sits three lines from the bottom of the petition—is intriguing. What precisely did "same" mean? The term, comprising the better part of the phrase that the gente de razón should "not be encouraged to [behave] the same" as Indians, condemns criminal and perverse conduct. By referring to defiance and passion, behaviors often associated with the Saturday night revel, the word "same" suggests that the fiesta's participants violated the disciplined habits favored by the gente de razón. But the term "same" may hold other meanings. In this moment of violation, with Indians and gente de razón joining together to challenge decorum, the word hints at war. We seek the reasons for war and learn why, and against whom, the angeleños prepared for combat.

Crime and Passion

At the start, we sort out the various meanings of the term "same." The word may imply that the petitioners worried about the gente de razón falling into league with Indian criminals who supposedly slunk about the city. The fear had some foundation, but not for the reasons we may think. In most instances, the evidence suggests that observers often exaggerated Indian misdeeds. The Indians who dwelled inside Los Angeles, already subject to all manner of punishment and discipline, thought it wise to avoid any legal problem that would worsen their troubles. According to the angeleño court records, documents that cover the period between 1830 and 1850, city constables brought charges against Indians only thirty-six times. The figure is significant, but the gente de razón faced more accusations. They went to trial 138 times for murder, robbery, and other misdeeds.[1] In matters of law and justice, it was the gente de razón who could take the blame for inspiring Indian felons, not the other way around. Indian criminals, even if a small number, still worried the angeleños, but "same," at least as the petitioners used the term, pointed to other concerns.

As for the prospect of Indians and gente de razón exchanging a kiss or embrace, the term "same" does not always suggest disapproval and condemnation. Few angeleños would dare admit that they enjoyed pleasure in all its forms, but talk of sex with Indians emphasized the nature of Mexican life. Up through the nineteenth century—and even into the present—many people throughout Mexico welcomed the mixing of different races and traditions. The Spanish spoken in Mexico often featured many Indian terms and expressions, a practice the gente de razón in California repeated when they adopted words from the indigenous population in nearby settlements.[2] In eating habits, with the exception of a few who claimed they kept a European table, the Mexican populace dined on food that reflected diverse origins. Prior to independence, visitors to the Zocalo, the great plaza in Mexico City, would see merchants selling snakes, dogs, ant eggs, chickens, pigs, and corn fungus for the family kitchen. In one of his works, the novelist Gabriel García Márquez says that Simon Bolivar, South America's liberator, went to Mexico City in his youth and marveled that the Mexicans would eat anything.[3] The angeleños proved as omnivorous as their compatriots in the nation's center. They learned from local Indians which herbs and plants to put on the household menu, or how to cultivate the delicacies taking root on the family plot.

Love and intimacy, though, remained the best way to achieve mixture. Save for well-born families in the interior who insisted they had no Indian or African blood, Mexicans of different hues and shades had mingled for years. The gente de razón in Los Angeles, following national custom, seemed no less enthusiastic about taking Indian partners. With the passionate embrace in mind, we see how often, and in what ways, the Indians and gente de razón pursued each other's affections. The intimacy each group shared, though at times coerced, and sometimes belittled by gente de razón partners, involved many individuals. In some instances, a gente de razón woman would receive, or encourage, the attention of an Indian man. But on most occasions, the evidence focuses on Indian women and gente de razón men, categories we keep throughout. The passionate or tender moment they shared with Indians only raised concern when the angeleños, meaning, in this case, angeleño men, lost their dominant role. In one sense, the thought of angeleño men losing their composure suggested why the Indian fiesta often caused great concern. When drinking or gambling on Saturday night, the angeleño man seemed no better than his Indian companions. But if the man retained his superior position, and dictated terms to his Indian partner, then reasons for worry would decline.

The angeleño pursuit of Indian women often involved marriage, an arrangement noted in the diligencias when priests, or someone else, identified the members of the wedding party.[4] The example of a few allows us to imagine that the angeleños had at one time or another mixed with Indians. When Bernardo Ramírez wed María Francisca Soto in 1820, the priest noted that the bride's mother was María Vicente, an "india de la mision de San Miguel en la antigua California [Baja California]"[5] Four years later, Juan Pollorena went to the altar. His mother, her heritage carefully presented in the diligencia, was Mariana Lorenzana, an Indian orphan from Mexico City.[6] After José Alfredo Rayales married in 1834, the priest recorded that the groom's father, Tomás de la Cruz Rayales, was an "indio de rio Yaqui."[7]

Prior to 1821 the two groups apparently married in great numbers, but by the beginning of the Mexican period, fewer gente de razón and Indian couples made their way to the altar. We do not know why the weddings between the two groups declined. As we recall from an earlier chapter, by 1830 the gente de razón wished to maintain their status a "white people," and apparently refused to honor any connection to Indians. Many mixed couples could have continued walking down the aisle. But the priests or church sextons who compiled the diligencias had ceased to identify the background of the wedding party. After Mexico achieved independence from Spain, the 1824 Constitution outlawed the caste designations that once determined an individual's black or Indian heritage. If any church official honored the decree, he would not always think it appropriate to comment on what sort of blood flowed through the veins of the bride and groom or their attendants.[8]

Nevertheless, no matter how confusing or incomplete, the evidence still provides important details. Between 1821 and 1848, of all the weddings at the Plaza church in the center of Los Angeles or the Missions San Gabriel and San Fernando, a total of nearly 210 ceremonies, only twenty-two featured a member of the gente de razón taking the hand of an Indian. True, more than one in ten marriages involved someone from each group, but considering that Indians could account for almost a quarter of the populace in Los Angeles, the number seems low. Among these weddings, five at San Gabriel, with one possibly at the Plaza church, Indian men stood at the altar with a gente de razón bride.[9] Another two, one at San Gabriel, and one other at the Plaza church, saw a European—someone who emigrated from the Old World—marrying an Indian woman.[10] The rest involved Spanish-speaking men from Mexico or Los Angeles wedding Indian companions.[11]

Though marriages with Indians declined, gente de razón men still had many ways to find a companion. Some witnesses claimed that Indian women often felt compelled to offer their bodies for sex. Salvador Vallejo, a resident of northern California, remembered that the Indians had long used their wives and daughters to win the favor of powerful men. Exaggerating a bit, he observed that the Indians of the inland valleys "exercised that horrid and infamous right of *pernaje*," or prostitution. He said, "astrologers," perhaps a reference to people we now know as shamans, could with "impunity . . . take the maidens . . . who suited them best." If "the unhappy creature," that is the girl or woman, "offered any resistance, the astrologers appealed to the mothers, fathers, and brothers who restrained the victim while the deceiving hypocrite violated her."[12]

Other californios suggested how pernaje took new shape in provincial settlements. Poor Indian women, often at their family's urging, sought to make money by selling their charms to soldiers and townsmen. Diego Olivera, a soldier from Santa Barbara, recalled that before secularization Indian women and girls often pursued the troopers assigned to defend the missions. After some time, he noted, the "pobrecitas [the poor dears] gave us their infant children."[13] The historian Antonia Castañeda rightly notes that the situation was usually the reverse: it was the soldier, not the girl or woman, who made advances. The Indian could resist, but the military man would press his case until he got what he wanted.[14]

Olivera's remarks, however, contained some truth.[15] If Indians sought the soldiers' company, some wanted to make money. He called the women and girls pobrecitas, a term that often expressed pity, but also could describe individuals living in poverty. By the 1840s, with the missions closed and many Indians reduced to meager employment, some women and girls offered their bodies to improve their circumstances. The writer Richard Henry Dana remarked that around 1842, "I [knew] . . . an Indian to bring his wife, to whom he was lawfully married in the church, down to the beach, and carry her back again, dividing . . . the money she got from sailors."[16] At the same time, several gente de razón describing themselves as "Los Cuatro Indigenas"—the Four Indians—wrote the Father President of California and lamented the ex-neophyte's ruin. The writers, their identities unknown, but presumably individuals who felt for the Native Californian's plight, complained that since secularization, "the young women [had] prostitut[ed] themselves."[17] As time progressed, Indian women continued to sell their charms. By 1846, if the petitioners in Los Angeles were correct, Indian prostitutes did a brisk business with gente de razón men.[18] That same year, other observers lamented that the angeleños "increased prostitution amongst the Indian classes."[19]

The Indian women and girls had to entertain a diverse crowd. The historian Donald Courtwright explains that in the American West, a region including Mexican California, single young men down on their luck desired any pleasure to forget their cares. Alcohol and a turn at the gaming table helped ease the mind, but sex, usually for a price, brought the best relief.[20] When we turn to Los Angeles and evaluate the 1836 census, the numbers show that the city possessed enough drifters and troublemakers to keep prostitutes in business. The surveyor noted that ninety-two men did not have an occupation and, in the appropriate space set aside in the survey, he wrote "N" for ninguno, meaning "none."

From these men, we eliminate thirty-two; fifteen were married, and to give them the benefit of a doubt, these men possibly felt tempted to visit city fleshpots, but the call of wife and children often kept them at home. The other seventeen were over forty, and if modern crime figures supply hints about male misconduct, once a man advances into middle or old age the urge to commit mischief declines. It is also difficult to imagine an angeleño old-timer sneaking off somewhere with a prostitute. For the rest, we can cut out the five boys between fourteen and ten years of age who earned an "N," but we make an allowance for anyone above fifteen. In a place where adolescents probably took on jobs or apprenticeships early in life, it is reasonable to think that some fifteen-year-olds had acquainted themselves with the women who offered their affections for a price. Of the remaining gente de razón men between the ages of fifteen and forty who were unmarried, fifty received an "N," nearly eight percent of the 608 non-Indian males who lived in Los Angeles.

On the other hand, we may be too quick to say that scoundrels delighted in a prostitute's company. Perhaps other individuals, more respectable, even prominent, had the worst of roving eyes. Once more, the census helps our understanding. According to the 1844 count, unemployed men and boys did not swarm the city. Only twenty men, none of whom appeared in the 1836 census, lacked a livelihood. Of these, a good number in 1844 do not meet our criteria as potential troublemakers. Six were married, with another six too old for ribald or scandalous pursuits. The remaining eight, almost one percent of the 627 gente de razón men in 1844, had to be a formidable bunch to worry municipal leaders.

We must also consider that one needed silver to entertain a prostitute. The gente de razón could rely on the winnings from a card or dice game, and an intrepid few could fatten the wallet through stealing. But for a good number of men, gambling or committing crimes would be uncertain ways to earn money. They needed a more reliable source of income.

As a consequence, it seems that in most instances only successful men had the means to support their dalliances with Indian women. The angeleño farmer or craftsman with loose coins in his pocket could certainly afford some pleasure. A more prosperous citizen, the landowner with ample acres, the successful merchant, and maybe, at times, a priest, also had enough money to secure entertainment.[21] But some, because of their position, did not have to pay a prostitute. They could use their authority to make Indian women consider a proposition.

Hugo Reid, a Scottish immigrant who, incidentally, married a neophyte woman from San Gabriel Mission, suggested how often respectable men searched for Indian companionship. He related the tale of a man standing trial in Los Angeles. The accused had retained two lawyers to defend him, while on the other side, the prosecutor sought a conviction. Reid identified no one, nor did he give the particulars of the case; indeed, he may have concocted the story. But the account, however fanciful, could have drawn on real circumstances. Reid noted that the prosecutor lived with an "Indian girl." One of the defending lawyers had married an Indian woman, a match he wished to keep "secret." The accused, meanwhile, had a habit of making a nightly trip to the ranchería to sleep with his Indian paramour. Reid concluded by recording the comments of a female observer who, unaware of all the entanglements with native women, turned to a friend, and declared, "any man who wants [to] cohabit with an Indian places himself at the level of beasts."[22]

Reid apparently wrote the piece in the 1850s, years after the end of Mexican rule. The principals of his story seem to be Americans, and one could say that a Yankee's passions did not interest the gente de razón. But when Yankee lawyers pursued Indian women, and we may think that other prominent Yankees followed suit, they did nothing new. Angeleño men of influence had sought the Indians' company for years.

The prominent gente de razón, however, did not necessarily parade about with Indian companions. A troublemaker, who had no name to protect, could be immodest when chasing his loves. But others, more substantial in provincial affairs, thought people of their rank should exercise discretion. Antonio María Osio, for instance, a resident of Los Angeles in the late 1830s, recalled how the ardor of Governor Nicolas Gutiérrez violated all sense of decorum. Provincial chief in 1836, Gutiérrez so enjoyed the company of Indian women that word of his intimacies upset the residents of Monterey, then the capital of Alta California. The governor's friends, distressed by the murmuring and gossip, claimed he was a "victim of unrequited love." To keep Gutiérrez and his paramours away from the public, they found ways to help him "obtain what he wanted" without causing a scandal. The friends directed Indian girls to the governor's residence and encouraged him not to advertise his affairs.[23]

The uproar inspired by Gutiérrez reveals how sex presented many complications. Some men, especially those who kept paramours, could have played the moral paragon to hide their appetites. If we are correct, when an angeleño denounced the mixing of Indians and gente de razón, he sometimes confessed his own conduct. But there is another possibility. Once more, we see the expectation that men had to control, but not necessarily ignore, their urges. When some gente de razón men scoured the streets or the ranchería to find a companion, they lacked decorum. In the case of Gutiérrez, his offense was not necessarily chasing Indian women. He only caused concern when his passions had gotten the best of him. Gutiérrez restored his name when he sought pleasure in the privacy of his home. Other prominent gente de razón men, and maybe a few a bit more modest in rank, seemed well aware that they could indulge their passions as long as they practiced discretion.

Antonio Coronel, one of the signatories of the 1846 petition, apparently knew how a successful man could satisfy his desires. Coronel, by the standards of the era, seemed quite proper and dignified. He made a modest profit during the early months of the Gold Rush in 1848, and returned to Los Angeles to earn an appointment as county assessor in 1850. Three years later he won the race for mayor, and he closed out his political career by sitting as state treasurer.[24] Helen Hunt Jackson, the author of *Ramona*, the great California romance, visited Coronel in his later years and, at least in the opinion of a modern historian, she found the old man to "be sympathetic to progress, reform and the advancement of civilization."[25] But in 1848 before he went off to the diggings, Coronel fathered a child by María Soledad, an Indian domestic from the secularized mission of San Juan Capistrano.[26] The parents did not wed, and the baby, a girl, stayed with the mother. According to the 1850 census, Coronel resided in his father's household, but there is no sign of the baby or her mother.[27] There is no way to tell when she yielded to Coronel's advances. But the affair could have continued for a number of years. If so, María had endured Coronel's kisses since 1846, the year that he signed the petition condemning Indian revelry.

The censuses suggest that other men, if they could afford to employ an Indian domestic like the Coronel family, had ample chance to find paramours in the household. According to the surveys, many Indian women, along with girls, worked as *sirvientes*, or servants, one more way of describing a domestic. If they toiled in a home, some probably had to face a man, or one of his sons, who did not always have the most honorable intentions. The censuses, however, sometimes lack specifics. Following Mexican practice, the gente de razón and Indian populace appear in different parts of the survey and it is difficult to tell for whom Indian women or girls worked.

Enough information exists, however, to entertain reasonable guesses. The 1836 survey counts 109 Indian women and girls who worked as servants. But we must caution that the number is unreliable. In some spots, names are illegible, or so whimsical that they seem to be a joke played by the census taker or gente de razón employer. (There is a woman named Cebolla—onion—in the census.[28]) The surveyor confuses matters further when he only provided the ages for sixty-seven women and girls. The others, without ages, could be too old or young to be of any use in the household. But of the Indian females for whom the surveyor gave an age, forty-five are between twelve and forty. Any person below and above this range could have worked as a domestic, but we only concern ourselves with those who could bear children, or possess the looks that could catch a man's attention. The 1844 count, compiled by a surveyor who took greater care entering information, contains 102 women and girls who meet our criteria.

To judge from the censuses, many masters, or any other male in the house, could pursue an Indian domestic. Some men might have enjoyed a loving relationship with their paramours. On the other hand, it could be that the Indian woman encouraged the man's advances. In some instances, the man was the member of a respectable family, and think what flattery it would have been to receive the attention of so illustrious an admirer. But in all circumstances the woman's opinion mattered little. When the man strode forward with arms outstretched could she resist? By running off, she would lose her job and ruin her reputation with potential employers. An Indian domestic, leaving her employers so abruptly, and possibly under questionable circumstances, would not be an attractive candidate. She could have fought back with a swift kick, but the man, probably far stronger and bigger, would have no problem retaliating. The woman, therefore, often had no choice but to surrender if she wanted to keep her income or a roof over her head.

Prominent citizens would not be the only ones who desired Indian women and girls. Some Franciscan priests also succumbed to temptation. In the eighteenth and nineteenth centuries, the task to win souls could make the most faithful priest despair. During a dark night of the soul, the aggrieved cleric would welcome, and maybe seek, a neophyte woman's companionship. On the other hand, a Franciscan could thrill to the responsibility of managing a mission with hundreds of neophytes. With admiring native women and girls before him, the cleric might take liberties. Then again, an opportunist could be loose in California. In his study about a French priest accused of sorcery in the seventeenth century, the English author Aldous Huxley quotes the disgraced cleric's philosophy: "For the young male, continence is impossible. Therefore no vow involving such continence is binding."[29]

If a Franciscan had no intention of remaining celibate, a mission with reverential women and girls provided many candidates for seduction. To be sure, we do not know which attitude, from despair to expediency, impelled priests to stumble, nor do we know how many, like Governor Gutiérrez, fell "victim to unrequited love." All we have are vague references to Franciscan weakness. But the details, even the most meager, accumulate, and we see that some priests claimed an Indian partner. Fray Geronimo Boscana, a priest at several California missions, raised suspicions that he often strayed from his vows. Bancroft notes that many people accused Boscana of having "immoral relations with his *neofitas* [female neophytes]," a charge some scholars have denounced.[30] Other Franciscans also stood accused of eyeing Indian women or girls. Blas Ordaz, a missionary for nearly thirty years in California, supposedly had a difficult time remaining chaste.[31] One observer claimed that Ordaz fathered several children by Indian women. The priest baptized one infant, a boy named Vicente, and perhaps others as well.[32] Another cleric, Antonio Jimeno at San Buenaventura, reportedly used the mission sanctuary to seduce neophyte women and girls. One Indian witness remembered that Jimeno and his Indian companions had "sex right in the mission itself."[33] Another Indian at San Buenaventura claimed that a "certain priest," he supplied no name, would enter the *monjeria*, the dormitory for single women and girls, and have sex with any partner he selected.[34]

In many instances, the man felt reluctant to recognize the children born to his paramours. Any wish to avoid paternity would explain why many Indian and gente de razón unions seemed barren. Of the approximately 1,526 baptisms performed at the Plaza church and the nearby missions, only eighteen children seemingly come from mixed parentage.[35] Records from the Plaza church show that ten children, eight of whom the priest described as "*hijos naturales*," or illegitimate, had a gente de razón and Indian parent.[36] Farther north, at Mission San Fernando, four children, each from a legitimate union—there is no indication otherwise—received the sacrament. Meanwhile, at Mission San Gabriel, another four youngsters, presumably the fruit of a legal marriage, were bathed and anointed in the water and oil of baptism. These numbers, though, seem too low. Given the testimony and inferences of gente de razón men seducing Indian women, more children entered the world than anyone cared to admit.

The death records from the Plaza Church might identify the children fathered by the gente de razón. If Indian women led a miserable life, they would be unable to provide for a baby. The toddler, lacking proper nourishment, would soon die. Many times, when a youngster succumbed, the priest recorded the names of the parents. But, between 1826 and 1838, the period with the most complete records, sixty-eight Indian children breathed their last without the priest identifying either parent. The cleric sometimes wrote "padres no conocidos"—parents unknown—in the death book. At other moments, the priest wrote that gentil or neofito parents watched the funeral.

Either description is sufficiently vague, and provides no hint if the little one had a gente de razón father. But the second entry speaking of gentil or neofito parents could suggest other scenarios.[37] Perhaps the priest pitied an Indian woman when she, and no one else, presented an infant for burial. With the Indian woman often at the mercy of her gente de razón partner, a circumstance well known to many in Los Angeles, a priest conceded the mother a small kindness for the little one's funeral. In death, if not in life, the youngster, with the cleric saying so, had a family present. He could not necessarily say that a gente de razón parent stood at the graveside. Some clerics did, but in most instances, a priest, aware of gente de razón sensibilities, kept quiet. He wrote that the dead child had an Indian mother and father—the gentil or neofito notation entered in the death book—when in fact one of the parents was a member of the gente de razón.

Thus the term "same," did not necessarily bemoan the angeleños' habit of sleeping with Indians. The 1846 petition condemns "polygamy" and "prostitution," but the angeleños could pursue other arrangements when seeking the Indians' company. If anything, the passionate encounter with Indians, especially in later years, only confirmed the angeleños' arrogance. Few required a wedding ceremony, and a trip to the bridal chamber, to experience an amorous moment. They could enjoy intimacy at their leisure.

But in seeking to define the word "same," we do not completely discard all references to crime and illicit sex. The illegal or immoral deed, and all it suggests, expands the term's meaning. Any kiss or embrace the two groups exchanged, while a sign of tenderness in some moments, can also describe force. Intimacy, after all, by referring to bodies pressed together, may describe other activities that require one partner to hold his companion face to face. With this image, the sight of one person entangled with another, but neither individual feeling respect or love, we come to the subject of war and the angeleño meaning of the term, "same."

War and Rebellion

Sex, or its variant, intimacy, while not necessarily a mark of war, nor war's equivalent, nonetheless supplies descriptions that speak of armed conflict.[38] The historian Edward Linenthal says many societies venerate the blood shed by warriors. When the hero falls in battle, the life that spills out of him helps renew the nation.[39] In California, the gente de razón used war and its imagery of reproduction to envision their struggles in the most vivid, intimate ways. Passion, the thought of one body near another, the moment of release at the end of frantic activity, became, for many gente de razón, the means to describe what happened when enemies or lovers faced one another. Each, sex and war, is intense and emotional. One, then the other, describes personal contact. In one instance, the lover offers the hand, the fingers spread to stroke or arouse. But at another moment, during war, the hand becomes a fist and delivers a blow. The offspring from this passionate moment, in short the act of reproduction, may not always represent the siring of heroes or the renewal of the nation. In Los Angeles, and other parts of California, the intertwining of war and sex gave birth to scenarios and creatures the gente de razón wished to avoid.

The question arises if references to war and violence truly reside within the word "same." The petitioners, for instance, did not speak of war or its devastation. But within the term "same," the angeleños, and by extension their contemporaries in Mexico's interior, acknowledged that liberal ideas could culminate in bloodshed. The fear of war, and where it would explode, addressed the role of the Indian. In the years after independence, Mexican thinkers used the idea of racial equality to elevate the Indian's position. The regard for the Indian provided commentators with a way to condemn Spain and Europe. Before suffering conquest, many liberals argued, the Aztecs and Maya of Mexico had created a culture whose sophistication rivaled the glories of the Old World. But all was not lost. Upon independence from Spain, some liberals looked to Pre-Columbian achievements and boasted that there was precedent to show that Mexico would flourish.[40]

In California, the settlers with liberal sympathies shared the enthusiasm to celebrate the indigenous past. The California *diputacion*, the body of citizens elected by municipalities to advise the governor, proposed in

1827 to rename California, "Montezuma," the name of the Aztec ruler who received Cortés. The members also suggested a new coat of arms for California in which an Indian with a plume, bow, and a quiver would stand inside an oval bordered by an olive branch and an oak.[41] Neither idea came to pass, but the Indian legacy continued to encourage all sorts of fancies. Governor José Figueroa told the diputacion in 1830 that in "California you will recognize the country of your ancestors. You will see the original homes of the Aztecs before they moved onto Tenochtitlan [the Aztec capital] and founded the empire of Montezuma."[42]

But the promise of racial equality presented problems. The historian Florencia Mallon explains that liberals, and quite a few conservatives, worried that Indians could not handle the responsibilities of citizenship.[43] When the "same" as any other person in the nation, the natives in Mexico or California supposedly lost all sense of deference. Some liberals feared that the Indians would desire any consideration enjoyed by others in the nation. If they felt wronged, or believed they had been denied an opportunity, the Indians would use violence to secure their advantages. War, or so some liberals insisted, seemed the result of racial equality.[44]

Any californio, like compatriots in the interior of Mexico, might remember one struggle in particular that confirmed their worst fears. When Father Miguel Hidalgo proclaimed Mexico's independence in 1810, he called on Indians and poor mestizos to join the fight. Thousands answered Hidalgo's appeal. The rebel force advanced through the countryside sacking towns and haciendas. At Guanajuato, in the center of Mexico, Hidalgo's army fell upon the city and massacred white inhabitants. During the attack, the rebels stormed the Alhondiga, the royal granary, and refusing calls for mercy, and even the orders of their officers, they butchered much of the white populace taking refuge behind the walls. For decades thereafter, the memory of Hidalgo's excesses convinced liberals that it would not be wise to arouse the masses during political disputes. The historian Toricuato S. Di Tella summarized the national mood, saying, "throughout the first decades of independence, Mexico lived under the fear of the scenes of 1810."[45]

Mexican thinkers, noting that Indians totaled more than two-thirds of Hidalgo's army, explained why the rebel force supposedly went on a rampage. Lorenzo de Zavala, one of the framers of the 1824 Constitution and later one of the leaders of the Texas Revolution, complained that the Mexican Indian was "lazy, [slept] much of the time, [and] whiled away the hours."[46] The conservative thinker Lucás Alaman offered that sloth did nothing to temper the Indians' passions. He explained that the Indians "were guilty of being a cruel and vengeful" people.[47] José Luis Mora, another contributor to the 1824 Constitution, found reasons for the Indians' volatile and violent nature. The Indians' "frontal lobe is not elevated as in the whites," Mora announced. He added, however, that the Indians' brain was nowhere as feeble, "as that of the Negro."[48]

In all truth, no californio document speaks of Hidalgo. But the evidence suggests that the gente de razón had good reason to think that Indians could overwhelm Los Angeles or other californio settlements. In 1830, the year with the best population estimates for all California residents, the Indians, from neophytes who resided in missions to those who lived in provincial settlements or rancherías, totaled almost 98,000 individuals. The settlers, meanwhile, numbered 10,000.[49] Even if the settlers did not know the precise figures for the populace, some had other ways to recognize the dangers they faced. Nearly all gente de razón lived along the coast, their backs to the ocean, while before them stretched mountains and desert. The expanse, at once bleak, limitless, and then breathtaking, would only remind the settlers that they were vulnerable to attack. For in the settlements, toiling in kitchens and tending herd, or deeper in the interior, shooting hard looks, or so the gente de razón suspected, lived many Indians who resented the settlers' presence.

When the angeleños and californios spoke, they repeated, in their own fashion, the Mexican warnings about Indians. During ayuntamiento meetings, municipal leaders and citizens condemned the Indians as "*proletarios*." The word, perhaps more than its equivalent in English, "proletarian," seemed well suited to convey thoughts of Indian attack. Proletario comes from the Latin, *proletarius*, which suggests that a person's only contribution to the state was to produce children.[50] But to create child after child, especially if one lacked the means to feed the youngsters, could lead to danger. A person with many mouths to feed, and with no intention to stop reproducing, might entertain criminal notions. Robbery, theft, perhaps even more brazen pastimes, gave parents the chance to provide for the family.

When observing the Indians, even if they lacked full knowledge of the word's history, the angeleños thought proletario an appropriate term. The Indians, large in number and always multiplying, seemed beyond all constraint or limitation. Early in 1846, citizens complained to the ayuntamiento that the ranchería "is composed of Indian proletarios."[51] In other instances, even when observers did not use the term, the word's meaning continued to surface. The ranchería, reported two ayuntamiento members in 1847, featured many "disorders."[52] Only a proletario, nothing more than an unruly Indian, seemed capable of creating such disturbances. In the American era, the term remained in use. Two members of the city council stated to their colleagues that the "proletarian class is composed of Indians . . . who partake in all excesses."[53]

The Indians, with their appetite for "excesses," could inspire images of Hidalgo's army. Many gente de razón, aware of the Indian multitude before them, feared that if war came they risked annihilation. Few would have disagreed with Juan Bautista Alvarado's description of Indian wars during the 1820s, accounts that could apply to any other period. Alvarado, who resided in northern California, explained that when the Indians reached for weapons, they wanted to destroy the province. During one uprising in 1824, Alvarado remembered that the Indian insurgents wanted to "destroy all the missions, cities, towns, estates and ranchos of Alta California." Another revolt in 1829 posed even greater dangers. Alvarado speculated that had "these barbarians [possessed] greater prudence in going into battle, they would have easily been able to conquer California."[54]

Other gente de razón offered their own vision of what would happen if Indians formed ranks. Carlos Antonio Carrillo, California's delegate to the Mexican Congress in 1831, told his colleagues that the national government should think carefully about secularizing the missions.[55] Like many of his constituents, Carrillo dreamed of a landed estate and welcomed any attempt to distribute church property. As fate would have it, in two years, Carrillo applied for, and received, title to a property that once straddled Missions San Buenaventura and San Fernando.[56] Carrillo, though, at least in 1831, did not let ambition interfere with his thinking. Survival mattered more. Carrillo feared that secularization would release Indians from the stern hand of priests. The Indians, with no one to discipline their passions or direct their energies to more productive pursuits, would supposedly turn violent and threaten California's settlements.

In his presentation to the Mexican Congress, Carrillo argued that the missionaries and their establishments served as a defense from Indian attacks. Before the missions came, he declared, California was an "uncultivated land inhabited by savages."[57] But with the arrival of the priests, the Indians became "useful workers in agriculture and the arts."[58] Carrillo, who had pursued rebellious neophytes into the California interior, remembered the devastation of Indian war. He told his congressional colleagues that the provincials were a "weak population" who had "no other protection than the missionaries."[59] If the government removed the priests and closed down the missions, the act "would mean nothing but the province's political death."[60] Weakened, California would "fall to a foreign nation" or, in a possible reference to Indian war, revert "to its primitive, savage state."[61]

Three years later, California Governor José María Figueroa wrote an appeal protesting the national government's plan to secularize the missions all at once.[62] Figueroa was no friend of priests, however. He only thought that the effort should proceed more gradually. Offering a plan that eventually would become law, Figueroa proposed to secularize the missions over three years, and suggested that only some Indians would receive freedom. The Native Californians who did not meet the requirements Figueroa had set—for example, they could have been too old or too young to be emancipated—would have to remain at the mission. But if all Indians ran free, Figueroa expected devastation. "Legal equality," he insisted, the idea that inspired some Mexicans to propose secularization, "would unhinge society." Figueroa, warning of war, concluded that those who supported unconditional secularization would see their names entered "in the annals of fratricidal strife, in civil disorders, in the farcical notions of the anarchists—that ominous sect abominated in America and Europe."[63]

Most californios, aware that Indian attack would devastate the province, appreciated Figueroa's approach to secularization. Juan Bautista Alvarado claimed that when Figueroa died in 1835, the provincial settlers mourned their dead leader. As Alvarado implied, many of Figueroa's constituents appreciated the attempt to slow the Indians' emancipation. "[The californios] weep for the man who extinguished the torch of discord," noted Alvarado, and "prevented the virgin land from being drenched in the blood of its sons." Intimating that Figueroa rescued California from potential ruin, Alvarado concluded that the governor, "consoled the widow, sheltered the orphan . . . helped the soldier . . . protected merit and encouraged learning—in a word, he labored to regulate our social order."[64]

Carrillo and Figueroa echoed the worries of constituents who feared that attack could come from any quarter. The Indian servant, for instance, seemed well placed to participate in any plot. He would defer to the master and each day handle some burden or obstacle without complaint. But no one would know what designs he contemplated. What he did during his leisure hours would prove equally mysterious. Maybe, as some gente de razón feared, he would retire somewhere with confederates and plan the master's end.

The angeleños no doubt had heard about events in San Diego. Sometime in 1838, Indian servants unlatched doors during the evening to allow easy entry for raiders.[65] The plot, to the californios' relief, failed. But the gente de razón might have shuddered nonetheless. The conspiracy required organization, the stockpiling of weapons, the passing of secrets from one Indian to the next. Perhaps, in the days after the thwarted rebellion in San Diego, the settlers in Los Angeles and elsewhere studied the Indians' faces, hoping to see in a grimace or smile some murderous intent.

The neophytes also commanded the experience, and sometimes the weapons, to present a formidable threat. After the privateer Hippolyte de Bouchard sailed up and down California's coast looking for plunder in 1818, some priests raised an Indian force to defend the missions. In southern California, Father Ripoll at Mission Santa Barbara organized and trained 180 Indians. One hundred served as archers with fifty men wielding "chopping knives." An additional thirty rode as cavalry. At nearby Mission La Purísima, Father Mariano Payeras mustered another detachment of neophyte defenders. Payeras did not relate the size and strength of the Indian troop, but when the neophytes wheeled around the mission in formation, the priest wrote Governor Pablo de Solá, "It would cause me joy if you could see the preparation of these Indians."[66]

When the Chumash rebelled in 1824, an upheaval that involved neophytes at the Santa Barbara and La Purísima Missions, the Indians turned their skills against provincial authorities. Antonio María Osio remembered that at La Purísima the neophytes converted the mission into a fort. Indian marksmen manned the walls and individuals skilled in artillery mounted two cannons on carriages to blast any approaching force.[67] In northern California, José Sánchez, a Mexican sergeant, suggested in 1825 that fugitives from San José Mission taught attacking Cosumnes how to use a cannon.[68]

The Indians also proved to be excellent students in tactics. Osio recalled that when Estanislao, a fugitive neophyte from Mission San José, led an upheaval in 1829, the rebels built a fortress with "primary, secondary, and tertiary stockades."[69] To move easily from one stockade to another, and confound any attacker who approached, the Indians dug "underground passageways" which connected with "trenches" ringing the redoubt.[70] Sergeant Sánchez added that Estanislao and his followers created "an impenetrable fortress along the Stanislaus River."[71]

At times, the neophytes formed ranks with gentiles in the interior. The idea that the two sides would band together caused great concern. When

Indian thieves ran off with cattle or horses some gente de razón suspected that the alliance had finally come to pass. One brigand, maybe two, at times a couple more, would provide enough irritation. But the swift parry and thrust of warriors rustling cattle might announce the beginning of a full assault. To some gente de razón with a frightful cast of mind, somewhere in the California fastness, beyond the handful of raiders, lurked a larger force comprised of neophytes, or ex-neophytes, who had instructed their gentil allies in weapons and tactics.

The fear of devastation inspired the gente de razón to go on the march at a moment's notice. In Los Angeles, between 1833 and 1842, men gathered in the town square three times to prepare for attackers. In 1834, for instance, two hundred Mohave warriors advanced on San Gabriel Mission. Lieutenant José María Ramírez commanded a force that drove off the enemy.[72] Later the same year, settlers mounted up again after receiving word that Colorado River Indians planned to invade "the Los Angeles District." The war party attacked San Bernardino sixty miles to the east and killed thirteen people, but advanced no further.[73] Eight years later, defenders again grabbed weapons after word came that Indians from deserts to the east prepared to attack Los Angeles. The story proved false, but the thought of Indians on the move no doubt rattled angeleño nerves.[74]

During the same period in San Diego, south of Los Angeles, inhabitants sounded the alarm another three times to muster defenders. In 1833, Tajochi, a Quechan chief, wanted to organize gentiles and ex-neophytes who had fled into the desert. The provincial militia captured the chief, however, and the threat died.[75] Four years later, according to the ayuntamiento records of Los Angeles, an Indian force threatened San Diego in May. The municipal body, agreeing to help their beleaguered neighbors, sent defenders south.[76] Afterward, in July or August of 1839—the record is unclear—three hundred Indians occupied the Otay Mesa some ten miles southeast of San Diego. They threatened to recover "lost territory" and drive all gente de razón to the sea. The assault never came, though, and the Indians retreated to the interior.[77]

Nonetheless, what the gente de razón meant by the word "same," or how violence and intimacy intertwined, still awaits explanation. To find an answer, we return to the events of 1810. The historian Torcuato Di Tella says that mestizos, mixed bloods that did not necessarily pursue an Indian way of life or live among Indians, made up a smaller portion of Hidalgo's army.[78] Some mestizos who joined the rebellion had no greater ambition than to find glory or plunder. But other mestizos who fell into formation wanted to claim opportunities that fate, or their social betters, had denied them. When Hidalgo asked for volunteers, they saw a chance to improve their circumstances and rise to a rank that best suited their talents.

In California, with some alteration, the fear persisted that non-Indians would turn against their neighbors when the war cry sounded. Admittedly, the gente de razón did not speak of mestizos joining the Indians. The record suggests that the term "mestizo" had passed out of the californio lexicon by the 1830s. Instead, the gente de razón used other words or images when they worried that their compatriots awaited the chance to march with Indians. It mattered little that few actually fought alongside Indians. But any word of californios riding with the other side encouraged worries that many more bided their time before slipping into the interior to attack provincial settlements.

The people who aroused suspicion present some mystery. For some individuals, all we have is a brief mention in a city report. In 1846, some angeleños worried about the "Indian proletarios and *jornaleros* [day laborers]" spending time together in the ranchería.⁷⁹ Who were these day laborers? They could have been Indians. But if so, observers would not have distinguished day laborers from the Native Californian proletarios. Perhaps they were poor gente de razón who worked the same jobs as the Indians and visited the ranchería when the day was done. The two might drink together or play cards to try their luck and do nothing more. But some angeleños would not forget what kind of people made up Hidalgo's army. They likely feared that a destitute gente de razón would consider the Indian a compatriot. The two would put aside simple diversions and supposedly consider bolder, more violent measures to escape their poverty. Meanwhile, other sorts supposedly cast their lot with Indians. None seemed destitute. Nor did they bear particular grudges that required satisfaction. They only wished to find riches by riding alongside a chief and his warriors.

Thus, any reference to the "same" seems fitting. When some gente de razón acted the "same" as Indians, they betrayed friends and neighbors. The tie between some gente de razón and Native Californians, already strong in so many ways, took on a more frightful appearance during threats of attack. To a degree, the gente de razón could tolerate contradictory, even hypocritical conduct. They could enjoy the Indians' company as long as they retained their authority. But once that sense of privilege came into doubt, as it would during times of war, uncertainty eroded gente de razón confidence. The Native Californians, large in number and supposedly eager to attack, reminded the gente de razón of their vulnerable position.

The sense of productivity and work many gente de razón used to create unity now began to unravel. In good times, the angeleños from different backgrounds could reconcile, but not eliminate, their differences. Any lingering suspicion one group had about the other reemerged upon news of war. Unable to feel secure, the gente de razón turned on one another. They believed that some individuals who lived amongst them supported Indian attackers. When reports came that a few gente de razón had sided with Indians, their fears received confirmation. To see what would transpire if their compatriots and Indians joined forces, the gente de razón needed only remember Hidalgo's march through the Mexican interior. Alarmed, the gente de razón lived in a state of "what if?": What if other gente de razón tired of life in communities like Los Angeles? What if they looked for other forms of fulfillment? What if they did join Indians?

War, more than any other activity, provided answers that frightened the gente de razón. As with intimacy and its relation to reproduction, war can create a bond. Love and passion, though, did not bring individuals together. Violence provided the link. Any connection to family or community, the ties that comprised the gente de razón existence, would stand obliterated. New bonds arose, with gente de razón and Indians becoming one, and multiplying, amid the blood of defeated troops or slaughtered innocents. War, fulfilling what the angeleños meant by the word "same," often granted pleasures that exceeded any comfort offered by Mexico. During war, good sense, discipline, faith in law, and the Almighty, all representing some tie with the Mexican interior, soon vanished. War, with its promise of booty and the thrill of behaving with abandon, offered proof to "what if" the gente de razón acted the "same" as Indians.

The most detailed accounts about Indian–gente de razón cooperation, more elaborate than any reminiscence about revels in the ranchería, concern war. At times, fear consumed good sense and convinced some gente de razón that provincial leaders sided with Indians. According to one tale, Governor José María Echeandía enlisted neophytes in 1832 to fight against his rival, Agustín Zamorano. The Indians, thrilled to leave the missions, went on a rampage; they drank, gambled, and fought with each other. It was only a matter of time, many gente de razón believed, before the Native Californians turned on the settlements.[80] Two years later, José Híjar and Francisco Berduzco, Mexican army officers, reportedly convinced neophytes and gentiles to march against Governor José María Figueroa.[81] Even

Governor Figueroa fell under suspicion of inciting the Indians. On one occasion, the governor supposedly boasted he had Indian blood. Antonio María Osio, believing the remark was a call to attack, later claimed that Figueroa's words emboldened neophytes and gentiles "to steal horses without fear of being punished."[82]

Each story, though, rang false. The first two episodes, suggests Bancroft, fail to stand up to scrutiny. In neither instance, Bancroft explains, is there proof of mischief. Once freed by Echeandía, the Indians did not riot. Híjar and Berduzco, meanwhile, when one studies the charges against them, might not have thought it a good idea to promote war. Any Mexican officer, especially if he remembered Hidalgo's attacks, would not risk plundering the province to promote his interests. There were easier ways to seek opportunity. As for Figueroa's boast, a point Osio does not examine in great detail, common sense suggests that the governor did not wish to issue a battle cry. The governor's dread of immediate secularization would suggest that he would not do anything to provoke restive Indians. Moreover, his military record provides some hints why he dreaded to think of Indians on the attack. Before he came to California, Figueroa had fought Indians in Sonora, a ferocious and violent enterprise that would make the most ardent soldier long for peace.[83] It is doubtful that Figueroa wanted to revisit his experiences in Sonora and encourage the Native Californians to take up arms.

Still, to think that the tales gained currency suggested that the slightest hint of Indians and non-Indians in formation made many settlers think the worst. War, providing the medium that brought the two groups together, supplants sex and intimacy. The moves and gestures that accompany the stark, physical act, now played out amid the frantic, hurried deeds of men at war. As sex leads to procreation, so it was with war, with Indians and gente de razón supposedly generating more of their own, one in league with the other.

We can see how war drew the Indian and non-Indian together. At one turn, the gente de razón, dominant, stands over the Indian. In the next moment, war encourages an intimate exchange, creating doubt about who controlled whom. For example, as an old man, José Francisco Palomares remembered that on a campaign against the Yokuts, an Indian group from northern California, he suffered a wound.[84] An arrow had pierced his left side, its head lodged near the heart. Pedro, an Indian captive, tended Palomares. The Native Californian chewed *yerba de jarazo*, an herb, and practically kissed Palomares's wound. Or as the soldier put it, Pedro "put his mouth to the entrance of [the injury] and expelled juice to the interior from the latter."[85]

Another veteran, José María Amador, recalled how arrows wounded him in battle. "I was left half dead," said Amador. Dazed, he found an Indian helping him. The Native Californian "chewed [a root] . . . called yerba de jarazo." The next moment, Amador stated, the Indian "rubbed [the juice] in my wounds."[86] Amador did not explain how the Indian discharged the juice from the mouth, but we can certainly imagine. The Native Californian bent low, lips inches from the injury, and administered the healing balm.

Antonio Coronel, while not pierced by an arrow, remembered that when he tried to escape the advancing Americans in 1846, he ran into the mountains east of Los Angeles. For reasons we will soon present, he had changed from boots to sandals. Footsore, he found refuge in an Indian ranchería. An old woman approached and washed his tired, bloody feet in an "infusion of herbs." "All pain was gone immediately," Coronel recalled, "and my feet have been tougher ever since."[87]

At times, the touch and contact supplied by war occurred in other ways. In 1829, after Estanislao threatened to lead gentiles and neophytes against provincial settlements, californio leaders organized an expedition to defeat the rebels. On the second day of the campaign the gente de razón troops failed to tend the cattle that would supply food and discovered that some of the animals had wandered off. From fifty-seven cows, the expedition lost nineteen. Concern arose that there would be nothing to eat if the men remained on campaign for a long time. Joaquin Piña, the diarist for the expedition, stated that the Indian auxiliaries allayed worries when they "caught fish for the troops."[88]

The Indians proved even more valuable after the shooting started. When Mexican cannon blasted a hole in Estanislao's defenses, Antonio María Osio claimed that the auxiliaries, numbering between fifty to two hundred men—accounts differ—rushed the gap and "anxious to avenge old grudges [against the villages aligned with Estanislao] threw themselves" upon the rebels.[89] Estanislao escaped, but Indian allies punished any enemy who fell into their hands. One rebel received immediate execution with an arrow into the brain. Others "known to be especially evil" found a noose of wild grapevines slipped around the neck and "were hung . . . to the highest trees."[90]

Indians offered aid in other fights. Nearly a decade later, Estanislao, if he was indeed the same individual, returned to live at Mission San José, which, by the mid-1830s, had been secularized by the provincial government. Presumably pardoned for his offenses, he worked as a carpenter and cowboy for the civil administrators running the mission temporalities. When two ex-neophytes, Paisco and Nilo, left the mission in 1837 and plotted trouble, Estanislao joined troops to catch the fugitives. It is difficult to see the old rebel doing the bidding of his enemies, much less imagine gente de razón officers calling on Estanislao's expertise, but he apparently played a prominent role. José de Jésus Vallejo, a resident of northern California, explained that Estanislao helped kill two rebel followers and badly wounded Nilo.[91]

At the final turn, war extinguished all the differences between Indians and the gente de razón. In battle and its aftermath, when standing side-by-side, or face-to-face, the two soon became one. While Coronel was running from the Americans in 1846—a scene we described earlier—he found refuge in the village of Chief Alejo. The Indian leader, possibly a Yuma—Coronel does not say—agreed to help. He lent Coronel, a "blanket, a palm hat, and a pair of leather sandals."[92] The outfit, probably intended to be some sort of disguise, elicited little comment from Coronel. But it goes without saying that in the mountains, draped in a blanket, with hat and shoes of Indian manufacture, he would look like a member of Alejo's band, namely a Native Californian. If pursuing Americans spied him in indigenous dress, Coronel apparently knew he would raise little suspicion.

Later, in 1848, Juan Bernal, a resident of San José, a settlement well north of Los Angeles, remembered that he and twenty men chased Indian horse thieves into California's interior. When the pursuers found the culprits encamped by a lake, José de Jésus Bernal, the narrator's brother who bore the nickname "El Cacalote," [the Crow], a reference to his appearance or sharp eye, went for a look. José, "a man experienced in following tracks," stripped naked, and "coiling like a snake among the [reeds] . . . he [observed] . . . the Indians without their detecting him."[93] Meanwhile, the Indians relaxed in camp, becoming so careless that they failed to post a guard. Some, feeling secure, stripped off their garments and swam amongst the reeds.

The Indians, reputed to be close to the natural world now, in the scene described by Bernal, fall under the gaze of a man named for a bird and resembling a snake. And some of the naked Indians reflect the guise of José de Jésus, "El Cacalote," also naked. If we take one more look, matters may change a bit. Perhaps the Indians were not at play as Bernal claimed; they too could have swum out to search for the enemy. The Indians and

"El Cacalote," both dripping, each without clothes, prepared to attack. One could thus see his form in the other.

At times, neither side could deny the resemblance. Estanislao, remembered Juan Bojórquez in 1877, "was a man of about six feet in height, of skin more pale than bronze, of slender figure, with a head of heavy hair and a heavy beard on his face."[94] Another description, this one of a gente de razón male, may suggest that some angeleños and californios looked more indigenous than they wished. In 1842, Roberto Pardo, a man who, noted Bancroft, was either a "Mexican or Indian" officer stationed at Santa Barbara, described the angeleño Mariano Silvas for the prefect of southern California.[95] Though Pardo's purpose is unclear, he related Silva's attributes for posterity. Silvas was five feet in height with gray eyes and stooped shoulders. He possessed a Roman nose and a swarthy complexion—"dark" said Pardo—framed his features.[96]

True, the recollections could be tainted or altered to suit the speakers' intentions. Bojórquez, for instance, like many of his gente de razón compatriots, preferred to think that Estanislao was white. The rebel, smart and tough, had to be, to soothe the californios' hurt pride, part European. For the matter of Silvas, it is possible that Pardo erred and embellished his description.

But the opposite could hold true; as with Estanislao and Silvas, men for whom the category of Indian and gente de razón could switch from one to rest on the other, many californios and Mexicans could compare with, or resemble, the Native Californians. A look at the pictorial evidence reveals the indigenous heritage some may have wanted to obscure. Juan Bandini, a prominent merchant from Peru who made his home in Los Angeles and San Diego, dons a neat European cut of clothing in a photograph, but his dark features and severe, sharp expression seem more indigenous than European. Pio Pico, another prominent resident of southern California, looks the statesman in a photograph; upon closer look, however, one can see that his Indian and black forebears lent more gravitas to his pose.[97]

But it is during war or the violent moment that the gente de razón and Indians achieve union. Each, it seems, by sharing a resemblance, stand complete, indeed, the "same," becoming, when at arms, so alike that neither could stand apart from the other. The bonding of the two groups involved various individuals. At times, Spanish speakers and Indians, on occasion joined by Anglo-Americans, came together to raid the ranchos east of Los Angeles. Called *changuanosos* by the californios, the raiders' very origins and the composition of their numbers eluded explanation, and if confusion or uncertainty prevented identification, their fearsome reputation only increased. Most commentators claim the raiders came from New Mexico. In fact, the names changuanoso and New Mexican seemed interchangeable. For the angeleños, and other californios, to speak of one group was to speak of the other.[98]

But here we use caution. Not everyone who traveled the route, even with New Mexicans and Indians riding together, seemed to be a troublemaker. Eugene Duflot de Mofras, the French diplomat who visited California and Oregon in 1841, stated that once a year a caravan from New Mexico arrived in Los Angeles. The pack train consisted of two hundred men escorting mules laden with wool blankets and serapes. Setting out in October, the caravan took nearly two and half months to reach the Cajon Pass, a route through the San Bernardino Mountains that lay seventy miles east of Los Angeles. The traders would then disperse, some going north, others heading south to San Diego.[99]

But more dangerous types, Indian and non-Indian, joined the caravan or followed in its wake. Some of these men could be soldiers of fortune or perhaps what Anglo-Americans would later call gunslingers. Narciso Botello, a resident of Los Angeles in the early nineteenth century, remembered that the men from New Mexico, or changuanosos, to use his term, were "good riflemen" and longed for a fight.[100] José María Estudillo from San Diego added that the "New Mexicans" [his words] were "reputed to be good shots" and even could be "engaged to pursue Indian raiders."[101] If employment proved wanting, some changuanosos found other ways to make ends meet. Most times, they stole horses. In 1840, the prefect of Los Angeles reported that Indians and New Mexicans, who together made up the ranks of the changuanosos, often made off with someone else's mounts.[102]

On several occasions, Anglo-Americans, many of them mountain men, joined the attackers. During one raid, Pegleg Smith and Jim Beckwourth helped Walkara, the Ute chief, harass ranchos near Los Angeles. (It seems that in this instance no New Mexicans were present.) Beckwourth rode ahead to gain the trust of cattlemen and banish any suspicion. He returned to his party, and the raiders, armed with the information gathered by Beckwourth, roared out of their hiding places to make off with five hundred horses. In time, some angeleños grew frustrated with the raids and soon referred to the mountain men as "white Indians."[103]

As with the changuanosos, other interlopers emphasized what would happen when Indians and non-Indians joined forces. In 1842 the gente de razón dreaded the arrival of *cholo* troops, Indian and mestizo conscripts from Mexico. The cholos, commanded by the new governor Manuel Micheltorena, who marched through California to take office in Monterey, spread panic as they advanced through the province. Some cholos supposedly stole produce from trees or helped themselves to a chicken or two; when food was lacking or was hidden by owners, some cholos reportedly went to homes and demanded meals. At other times they downed alcohol when they stopped to rest, and picked fights with each other or any person who blundered into their path.

Juan Bautista Alvarado expressed one more fear. He recalled that the "cholos are like the tigers of India, which if they by chance get a taste of human blood, wild animals will no longer satisfy their appetites. . . . [W]hen they find a man they charge him and devour him."[104] The bloodthirsty cholo seemed a popular image. Antonio María Osio remembered that cholos attacked a French sailor and tore him apart. Rescuers found the man "lying unconscious on the ground, bleeding from different parts of his body and missing a few fingers."[105] Angustias de la Ord, a resident of Monterey, recalled the troubles of another sailor. She said cholos stabbed the man, leaving him "permanently crippled."[106]

Alvarado's description, while an exaggeration, holds more interest. At once Indian and non-Indian, the cholo seemed the product of war, or even made for war. The cholo, remember, was a soldier. When in uniform, and on the march, he, or it, because if fashioned for combat and violence, he assumed a monstrous look, the cholo sought destruction, or desired to make others like him. If pursuing the second choice, to create more like him, he did not depend on sweet persuasion or some sort of tenderness to achieve his ends. He relied on violence.

The cholo trooper, perhaps an Indian, perhaps not, wolfed down the gente de razón. The cholos, of course, ate no one, but at one stroke, the image of eating, suggesting and surpassing a kiss or embrace, emphasized the disappearance of boundaries. The sight of a californio disappearing bite by bite, into the cholo gullet, presented what Alvarado and compatriots dreaded most. The gente de razón became one with the cholo. The cholo, meanwhile, with a settler in the stomach, took on the attributes of his victim. In sum, each turned into the other and became the "same."

The creature that emerged from this union, at least in Alvarado's opinion, took the form of Captain Miguel González, one of the cholo commanders. The officer, claimed Alvarado, earned the "nickname . . .

'*el macaco*,' [the ape], a very appropriate nickname—for if there was ever a man who looked like an ape it was Captain Miguel González."[107] If an ape in appearance, a comment on his ferocious or ugly face, González had the demeanor to match. (Experience shows that any form of the name Miguel González can impose quite a burden.) He was supposedly cruel, vicious, the commander of "tigers" or man-eaters with fierce appetites.[108] González, a man of modest talent, incapable, perhaps, of possessing the evil character his detractors claimed to see, would not have been any more ambitious or conniving than Alvarado, who, between 1837 and 1838, waged a long struggle to sit in the governor's chair.[109]

What matters more is how Alvarado and his compatriots observed González. The captain, a man of Spanish and Indian ancestry, perhaps favoring more the indigenous side, possessed, or so the californios thought, the temperament all would have if the gente de razón sided with Indians. A society, if composed of people like González, would not last. The gente de razón might wear different clothes, take shoes, or put on a hat; but remove the garments, and the body of the settler and Native Californian might seem more alike than different. On the other hand, if the two did not look similar, all, or at least a good number, might have enjoyed the same habits. But however they became one, they suggested frightening possibilities. They compared with Hidalgo's troops destroying all around them. Or, they resembled the cholos and changuanosos, the products, and creators, of war.

Now we can see why the gente de razón loathed the Indian. Some gente de razón, knowing they drew close to the Indian during war, or even at times of peace, admitted how much alike they both seemed. Comparable in appearance, and beholding their image in the Indian, some gente de razón did not like what they had, or could, become. But more alarming, and perhaps the greatest source of worry, the Indian multitude reminded the gente de razón of their weaknesses and meager numbers. Their predicament proved so disturbing that some wondered if they could ever claim any advantage over the Indians.

But there was hope. If war offered a way for Indians and gente de razón to unite, the same means, violence and combat—the tactics of war—provided a way to separate each group. For example, during his account about the hunt for horse thieves, Juan Bernal declared that some gente de razón saw the Indians as family members. But, when referring to blood ties, the gente de razón admitted, yet again, that war, not sex or love, encouraged intimacy. After Bernal and his party stormed an Indian encampment, one californio, Cornelio Hernández, rushed upon a badly wounded warrior to deliver the fatal blow. Summoning his last bit of strength, the Indian leapt to his feet and shot Hernández in the throat with an arrow. The Native Californian, his energy expended, fell backwards dead. Hernández, knocked to his knees, with blood gushing from his mouth, dragged himself to his dead rival, and with a broken knife, gashed the corpse, struggling to reach the heart. "He was repeating," said Bernal, "'I forgive you, brother; I forgive you brother.'"[110]

Family images appeared in other ways. When we last saw José María Amador, an Indian treated his wound with yerba de jarazo. After he recovered, he went on campaign again to chase Indian horse thieves. He and his party enjoyed great success. They captured the culprits and planned to mete out severe discipline.[111] Amador in particular seemed the most inspired to bring down punishment. Helped by some of his comrades, he killed half of the prisoners, and proposed to dispatch the rest a day after. When a Mexican officer protested, Amador replied, "if my own father stood before me I would kill him."[112]

In each instance, Hernández' call for "his brother" and Amador's reference to his father, could be, in the heat of the moment, stray random remarks. But during war, a time to create or destroy any bond, the gente de razón confessed that the Indian was indeed family. With relative pitted against relative, there was none better to deliver the fatal wound. Hernández discovered as much when he wrestled with his Indian foe. During a desperate, violent moment, there is no time for artifice or the careful, deliberate word. With each man locked in a death struggle, the first thought could be the most honest. Did Hernández, during the fight, acknowledge his resemblance to the Indian? His dead brother? Amador, meanwhile, seemed more cautious. Apparently he took his time to execute the prisoners, hardly the passionate moment one would associate with combat. But despite the delay, the intensity and bloodlust one may associate with battle still influenced Amador. Filled with anger, perhaps worried about the loyalty of his companions and the compliance of prisoners, he did not use reason or rational argument to present his views. Amador mentioned the thought closest to his heart and used the term "father" to refer to Indians.

In the final analysis, the term "same" bore great freight. The word did not always refer to gente de razón associating with Indian criminals or paramours. Rather the word suggested that war brought the Indians and gente de razón together. But with each side so close the gente de razón again relied on war, the very cause of their distress, to reestablish differences. War worked well, but was not the only method. The gente de razón needed other ways to distinguish one from the other and reaffirm their connection to Mexico. The mighty, the lowly, the strong, or weak, thus needed more advantages the Indians could not enjoy.

February 19, 1846

To your excellency the Governor [Pio Pico] we come before you the undersigned, and say that since the Indian ranchería was removed to the pueblito—a move calculated to end excesses and thefts—the aborigines . . . taking advantage of their isolation . . . steal from [neighboring orchards]. . . . [O]n Saturdays [they] celebrate and become intoxicated to an unbearable degree, thereby resulting in all manner of venereal disease, which will exterminate this race and . . . be **beneficial** to the city. To preserve the public health and do away with the vice of polygamy . . . [and] the excesses of prostitution [so that] the residents of Los Angeles would not be encouraged to do the same, we ask that the Indians be placed under strict police surveillance or the persons for whom the Indians work give [the Indians] quarter at the employer's rancho.

Signed:
Francisco Figueroa and Luis Vignes

Signatories:

Felipe Lugo	Ricardo Lankem (Laughlin)	—?—Villela
Juan Ramírez	Samuel Carpenter	Tomas Serrano
Januario Avila	Agustin Martin	Mariano Ruiz
José Serrano	Guillermo Wiskies (Wolfskill)	Antonio Salazar
Manuel Sepúlveda	Luis Bouchet	Casciano Carreon
Gil Ybarra	Maria Ballesteros	Maria Anta. Pollorena
Desiderio Ybarra	Francisco López	Vicente Elizalde
Miguel Pryor	Estevan López	Antonio Coronel

CHAPTER FOUR

"Beneficial"

The Rewards of Disciplining Indians

WE NOW CONTEMPLATE why many angeleños found reward in disciplining or abusing Indians. On the battlefield, gente de razón troopers subjected Indians to all sorts of punishment. The home, too, where we find Indian servants, provided one more setting for angeleño attacks. In both places, some gente de razón watched the Indian's suffering with grim satisfaction. Each strike, a stab with the bayonet, the thrusting of an Indian into chains, seemed a blow, and yet one more blow against the Native Californian's vitality. In time, many angeleños hoped, the Indians would vanish and cease their torments. Delighted that they, and no one else, would live in Los Angeles, the signatories declared in the middle of the 1846 petition that the Native Californians' demise "will be beneficial to the city." Admittedly the petitioners said little about violence and only argued that disease and too much drink would doom the Native Californians. But when hearing or reading the petition's description of the Indians' decline, any settler with murderous thoughts might feel triumphant. After all, what would it matter how death carried off the Native Californian? The Indians could die by the hand of the gente de razón or succumb to misfortune.

But the gente de razón's desire to kill Indians reveals a contradiction. It would seem odd that the gente de razón would applaud when war or disease struck down the hired help. Many Native Californians tended the fields of angeleño farmers. A few more helped the cattleman watch the herds. At home, Indians worked as domestics or cooks. If the Native Californians died, angeleño industry and enterprise would suffer. Profits would decrease and the angeleños would lose their chance to purchase clothes or stock the home with a fancy mirror or divan. The Indians caused trouble, but to lose money would present just as many difficulties. In the end, there would be nothing "beneficial" about the demise of laborers.

The dilemma, perhaps a muddle to us, found resolution among the gente de razón. As we will see, when Indians died, or labored for an employer, each fate served the same ends. The Native Californians lay prone and helpless, the object of gente de razón whims. Nearby, dominant, and feeling victorious, stood the soldier, or, in a different setting, the master and mistress. When forcing Indians to submit, the gente de razón revealed why they employed the term "beneficial." The angeleños took one more step to put the Indians behind them. With the Indian removed or defeated, the angeleños felt they could pursue Mexican habits without distraction. A liberal persona awaited them, as would the satisfaction, and maybe the fantasy, that they now had more in common with the residents of the Mexican interior than their Indian antagonists who seemed all around.

Indian Killing

We first look at gente de razón troopers in the field to see how they used the knife and rifle butt to remove all indigenous influence. But the wish to kill could draw on simpler, more fundamental reasons. Some evidence suggests that the gente de razón only wished to punish Indian outrages. When native raiders stole livestock, the proprietors, needing the animals for food or trade, demanded some sort of compensation. At times, the animals' recovery was all the gente de razón wanted. But other gente de razón, especially in northern California, wanted to punish the culprits. José Palomares recalled that sometime in the 1830s Indians raided his *caponera*, a fattening pen for gelded roosters. With three men, he dashed into the Sierra foothills east of San José and found six Native Californians he blamed for the crime. Four Indians escaped, but two fell into Palomares's hands. One met an end we will describe below. The other individual suffered a painful death. Spread on the ground by stakes tied to his hands and feet, the second Indian screamed for mercy when Palomares approached with his knife. Palomares, described by one historian as a man with "psychopathic tendencies," castrated the prisoner and tossed the testicles to circling crows.[1]

Around the same time, José María Amador led an expedition to the Stanislaus River—at least three hundred miles north of Los Angeles—to capture Indian horse thieves. Feigning friendship, Amador invited the raiders to a banquet, and once all sat to "feast on dried meat," Indian auxiliaries and californio militia leapt out of hiding places to capture the stunned guests. Amador divided the captives into two groups of one hundred. Christian converts comprised one group, gentiles the other. He marched the Christians to a road and forced them to kneel in sets of six. Reminding the Indians that they should pray for forgiveness, Amador ordered the auxiliaries and militia to execute the prisoners with arrows. For the remaining one hundred, all gentiles, Amador and another officer baptized the prisoners and shot them in the back.[2]

Other times, the gente de razón wanted to avenge any atrocities perpetrated by the Native Californians in battle. Joaquin Piña, the Mexican soldier who marched against Estanislao in 1829, recorded in his diary that his detachment found "at the foot of an oak tree . . . the charred bones of two soldiers . . . killed [by the] enemy." The Indians apparently had strung up the unlucky pair and burned them.[3] Other gente de razón added to the list of Indian barbarities. Sometimes they exaggerated, but their tales related the terror of fighting a tough and relentless foe. Juan Bojórquez, a member of the militia at San José, recalled that Estanislao tortured captive troopers for the amusement of Indian onlookers. One man, dangled from a tree by his captors, served as a target for Estanislao's archers. After the prisoner died, the Indians "took him down and burned him."[4] José Palomares agreed that gente de razón troopers sometimes met a fiery end. He remembered that Indians "would burn [a captive trooper] alive over a slow fire."[5]

With the thought of dead friends and relatives vivid in the mind, the californios rode off to seek retribution.[6] The californios knew, or at least had a good idea, that they sometimes attacked innocent Indians. But to the avenger astride his steed, pistols cocked, shotgun slung across the saddle, it mattered little who suffered his wrath.[7] Joaquin Piña, joining the hunt for Estanislao in 1829, remembered that when the troops approached an Indian fort they found "three old women" hiding in the bushes. The soldiers, he claimed, shot the "three Indians on the spot."[8] Some moments later, they flushed out another Native Californian—a fugitive neophyte it turned out—and watched Indian auxiliaries fill the poor man with seventy-five arrows. When the neophyte clung to life, his body bristling with shafts, a cavalryman stepped forward and "shot him in the head."[9] Piña and his compatriots, their blood up, hunted for other Indians in the fort. When no more rebels materialized, a trooper turned and shot an Indian prisoner, leaving him dead.[10]

A decade later in San José, José Palomares saddled up to avenge, among other things, the "murder of gente de razón." Palomares, remembering how Indians hung dead troopers from trees, contrived a similar fate for his enemies. Tying the end of one rope to a tree, and fastening the opposite end to a tree some distance away, he strung up Indian prisoners along the line "like beads."[11] In another attack, Palomares surrounded a sweat lodge filled with occupants and set it afire. Indian "men, women, and children were there in confusion," he recalled, and "from one moment to the next, one heard more and more the terror and screams of pain."[12]

But beyond seeking revenge, some californios used violence to cut all ties to Indians. José de Jésus Vallejo, a resident of northern California, explained why some compatriots wanted to torment Indians or let loose with a fusillade. He complained late in life, "I have heard it said that the Indians are of Latino origin. [B]ut neither the faces or eyes [of the Indians] resembled the eyes and faces of the Latinos."[13] By issuing a denial, Vallejo confessed that he and others knew they shared some similarities with Indians.[14] When a trooper studied his reflection in a glass or mirror, he sometimes witnessed, gazing back, a striking, indigenous face. Or at dinner, the herbs or game his wife used to prepare a dish compared with the table set by an Indian family. Enraged, or at least frustrated by the similarities, some troopers showed no quarter in battle and slaughtered the Indian foe.[15]

Sometimes at battle's end, the Indian's face continued to rankle. In the native countenance, rigid in death, or gasping for a final breath, a few gente de razón beheld their image. José de Jésus Vallejo admitted as much when he noted, and then denied, that the Indians and gente de razón resembled one another. The Indian's expression, the shape of his mouth or brow, perhaps the very tilt of the head, emphasized a common heritage. Victory in battle, therefore, was not enough; only obliteration would do. Some gente de razón, weapons at the ready, walked among the Indian dead and wounded. If concerned by what they saw, the troopers or vengeful settlers destroyed the face that could so compare with their own.

We do not necessarily speak of gente de razón mutilating Indians during battle. With bullets and arrows flying, one used any means to kill an enemy. Agustín Albiso, for instance, a trooper who fought against Indians in the late 1820s, once bashed out the brains of a warrior, in effect granting his enemy a new appearance.[16] Nor do we imply that the gente de razón cut up Indians to collect a bounty. In other parts of Mexico's northern territories, settlers received money from provincial administrators when they turned in Indian scalps, ears, and heads.[17] But there is no record of this practice in California. Mutilation apparently brought other rewards.

By focusing on the face, some gente de razón wanted to remove the one feature that reminded them of a legacy they preferred to ignore. Even if the gente de razón destroyed only part of the face, their enthusiasm to cut and slice would leave enough damage to cast doubt on any similarities. We revisit the prisoner left in the hands of José Palomares, who wanted justice for his stolen roosters. One Indian had already suffered castration, but the other faced a different fate. The last thing seen by the captive was the knife's flash. Palomares put out the eyes and confessed that the captive's screams "split the heart."[18] Other times, the gente de razón went after the ears. Juan Ibarra, a Mexican lieutenant stationed at San Diego, pursued Indian raiders in 1826. In one fight, he and his men killed forty-four of the enemy. The victors sliced off the ears and sent them to Governor José Echeandía. (But presenting the gift apparently provided its own joys. There is no record that the troopers received money for collecting the ears.) Sometimes there was competition to cut up Indians' faces. East of San Diego, also in 1826, Native Californians allied with the provincial militia killed three rival chiefs and fifteen of their followers. The auxiliaries followed common practice and collected the ears.[19] The gente de razón troops demanded the trophies, but their Indian allies wanted to brandish them during a victory dance. The outcome of the dispute is unknown.[20] The practice of taking ears persisted over time. During a fight against Indian raiders in 1848, a witness remembered that Demesio Berreyesa, a resident of northern California, cut off Indian ears and kept them as souvenirs.[21]

With the above tales, we can imagine the meaning of other vague, muddled descriptions presented by the gente de razón. The angeleño José del Carmen Lugo remarked that in a battle against Indians, he and his men "made a great slaughter." Afterward, the gente de razón "amused themselves" by killing three natives who refused to surrender.[22] Amusement implies pleasure, and we can only wonder what kind of entertainment Lugo and his companions found on the battlefield. Throughout history soldiers have made sport of mutilating their enemies, and the californio troopers, who were no exceptions to cruelty's attractions, might think that the Indian body was for their fun or amusement. But to see the Indian dead, wounded, or helpless before the knife would give Lugo and his compatriots the chance to heed other compulsions. Some likely took the opportunity to abolish any resemblance they had with Native Californians.

We can also consider what some witnesses do not say. Their silence may hint at the californio urge to disfigure their enemies. F. W. Beechey, a British naval officer who visited California in 1826, hinted at gente de razón designs when he described the triumphal entry of soldiers who had defeated the Cosumnes Indians. The returning troopers marched into San José "with trophies of the field." "Trophies" could refer to many things. Captives, said Beechey, even a cannon operated by Indians, filled the gente de razón's victory train. Other types of booty, among them clothes and trinkets, also passed in review, but a trooper would not necessarily swell with pride if he returned with a shirt or shell necklace. He probably coveted other things. In 1839, after another battle against Indians, troops marched into San José bearing the head of Yozcolo, the chief who dominated the area east of town.[23] Beechey could have documented a similar sight, a bloody memento at the head of a pole. The naval officer, though, provided no confirming details. But given the enthusiasm to collect ears and occasionally send them to a grateful governor, a trooper could have brandished any number of things that brought cheers from onlookers.[24]

Indian Captives

Meanwhile, inside Los Angeles or neighboring settlements, other gente de razón also wanted to strike their reflection from the Indian's face. The punishments imposed on Indians, at least as practiced in the settlements, often followed a pattern first conceived on the battlefield. As the soldier had his way with dead bodies and prisoners, the settler exercised similar liberties when laying hands on an Indian adult or child. We expand the meaning of mutilation and disfigurement, however. The soldier used a blade and bayonet. The settler, though, only needed to purchase or seize an Indian captive. Of course, the Indian who willingly worked for a wage often endured rough treatment in the master's home. But captives, sometimes more than any other Indians, suffered the greatest amount of pain. With the harsh word, or maybe a quick strike with the hand, the master or mistress broke not the body, but the Indian's will. In either instance, on the battlefield, or within the home, the gente de razón exacted a high price. Each blow and every curse beat down the Indian. At the same time, by inflicting punishment, or shouting an oath, the gente de razón sought to purge, a little at a time, the indigenous shape from their person.

War and toiling in someone's employ may seem an odd comparison. Then again, maybe not. At times, service in the home, or any other duty on the family property, presented one more face of war. In Los Angeles many Indian workers seemed to be captives seized after a battle or raid. To test our conclusion, it is best to count the Indians in the employ of masters and mistresses.

The padrón of 1848 helps our investigation, but caveats are in order. The time is two years after the end of our study. Even more uncertain is the inclusion of citizens who may not have lived in Los Angeles during the Mexican period. The newcomers' conduct may not reflect the habits of earlier years. Nonetheless, when examined line by line, the document seems one of the best ways to determine the number of captives in Los Angeles. The padrón, compiled to identify the landowners who used water from the zanja, or irrigation canal, also counted the peones each landowner sent monthly to repair the dikes and channels. The padrón shows that eighty-six angeleños dispatched at least one peón to fix the zanja. Some proprietors, though the reason is not revealed, sent two, perhaps three individuals, to perform the needed repairs. If the tally is correct, 103 *peones* labored for angeleño proprietors.

We linger over the number a bit longer. Who precisely was a peón? The word peón, derived from the Latin *pes*, for foot, merely described a day laborer who possessed no special craft or skill. Some peones could count as captives, but many were not. A few were gentiles; others appeared to be ex-neophytes. An additional number, probably very few, may not have been Indian.[25] But to keep our eye on the Indian peones, many apparently received some sort of inducement to labor for a boss. A few earned good sums for their labor, but most Indians received meager compensation. Some had to make do with the promise of shelter and food.[26] Others received, one witness said, a "lump of beef and a dollar a week."[27] An unlucky few found themselves in debt and they offered their services to creditors to fulfill all obligations. The most unfortunate individuals found themselves sentenced to a work gang. If they were found guilty of drunkenness or disturbing the peace, the prisoners marched off to repair roads and buildings. The Los Angeles ayuntamiento decreed in 1836, for example, that the city constable should "arrest all drunken Indians and compel them to work on [the] zanja."[28]

With all these workers, we might have trouble identifying captives. There is a way, though. First we find the gente de razón who called on workers to handle the chores. Next comes our estimate about how many Indian peones toiled in Los Angeles and environs. Any Indian who does not fit the category of peón, and who labored for a gente de razón employer, may count as a captive. But none of our reasoning will work until we calculate how many angeleños needed workers. In the 1836 census for Los Angeles there were 298 gente de razón households. Families made up most of the households, but a small number featured those who took in a friend or lodger. The 1844 count had 309 households.[29] We state, to be conservative, that a third of the households used an Indian laborer to help tend the property. Why a third? Remember that in the 1848 padrón eighty-six proprietors had peones. We assume that all eighty-six had the money to retain, or purchase, the talents of a peón, who in this instance, for the sake of example, was an Indian man. Perhaps only a man, more than an Indian woman or child, received the command to work on the zanja or any other public project. We may test good sense by using figures from different periods, but in the face of meager evidence there seems no other way to go. Eighty-six of 298 and 309, the tallies from the 1836 census, and then the 1844 count, is roughly one-third of all angeleño households.

Things grow more challenging when we try to count the number of Indian peones, the most critical part of our proof. Once we arrive at a figure, we can then look for captives. The 1836 and 1844 surveys do a poor job listing the age and sex of Indians. At times, especially in 1836, the census taker only entered the name and nothing else. Age and sex rarely made it into the record. As for the 1844 count, the census taker proved even more haphazard. He did not count the Indians at the ex-missions of San Gabriel and San Fernando, nor did he bother to inquire about all the gentiles who lived in the area.[30] But all is not lost. We study first the tabulations for the gente de razón to reach an estimate about the number of Indian men. In the 1836 census, 603 gente de razón men, out of a total of 1,675 people, made up more than one-third (thirty-six percent) of the populace. Meanwhile, the 1844 survey counts 627 gente de razón men, again roughly a third (thirty-three percent) of 1,847 residents.

As with the gente de razón, a third of the Indian populace could have been men. Thus, in 1836, we estimate that there were 184 adult males, out of an Indian population of 550. Eight years later, from 650 Native Californians, we may find 210 men. Of course, drink, disease, the wear and worry of a harsh life would reduce the proportion of Native Californian men, the people we are calling peones for the time being. Still, to pursue the point, the ratio of one-third still holds. If we are right, with 184, and then 210, Indian males in each Mexican census, there would have been at least two peones for each of the eighty-six households who needed workers.

But we may be too conservative. No doubt more gente de razón needed work to be done, implying that half of all households, not a third, desired Indian peones. From a ratio of two Indian workers per family, the number sinks to an average of little more than one, a meager figure for the landowner or merchant who needed many laborers. We can even abandon the idea that some gente de razón always required the services of the male peón. A field hand, as most peones appeared to be, seemed poorly suited for more delicate tasks in and around the house. To meet the demand for more workers or find individuals to handle domestic tasks, the angeleños relied on captives.

The Native Californians seized at gunpoint could include people of any age or background. Indian chiefs and warriors submitted to their gente de razón captors, as would their wives and children. We consider first the men, not boys captured in their youth and later maturing in the employer's service, but men, adults taken by californio troopers. Any Indian man who survived an attack might feel fortunate. As we recall, during a battle, or afterward, when the fighting stopped, the californios often slaughtered their Indian rivals. But in some instances, an Indian man received mercy and served out his days as a captive.[31] In 1836 for example, some angeleños had captured, or purchased, six tulareño men, Indians from the *tulares*, or the marshlands in California's Central Valley.

Behind the men, or at times alone, came children. The angeleños often called their young charges *sirvientes* (servants) or *domesticos* (domestics).[32] Many Indian children also carried the title *huerfano*, or its feminine form, *huerfana*, Spanish for orphan.[33] Admittedly, the term could apply to a nephew or niece adopted by angeleño family, but in an era when the gente de razón often seized Indian children, a huerfano could have been a captive torn from his parents.

The gente de razón used various methods to get their hands on children. An old angeleño remembered that in 1857 a Mexican using the alias "Francisco Castillo" entered the city plaza and sold Indian youngsters to local residents.[34] Castillo, or whoever he was, followed others who had long offered children to buyers. New Mexican traders traveling between Santa Fe and Los Angeles often raided Paiute settlements to carry off youngsters. At other times, the traders did not resort to violence, and they purchased children from destitute parents who needed guns, horses, or, as some witnesses remembered, a "plug of tobacco."[35] If returning to Santa Fe, the New Mexicans took the children home. The traders, concerned that the youngsters' "weak and helpless" appearance lowered their value, provided the little ones with food to fatten their bodies. When the New Mexicans struck out for Los Angeles, the youngsters, presumably plump and healthy, went along. The New Mexicans either sold the youngsters along the trail or they waited until they reached settlements like Los Angeles.[36]

At times, Indians also seized captives, and they scoured the Great Basin looking for victims. Walkara, for instance, chief of the Utes, preferred Paiute children, a popular choice it seems, or went after Piede, Yuma, or Mohave youngsters. He and his men rode to California, where they found a good market for their human wares. Walkara did not want cash, but preferred to exchange the children for weapons and livestock.[37]

Most New Mexican and Indian traders pressed a hard bargain. The historian Leland Creer explains that when either group traveled to Utah they used threats to make Mormons buy a boy or a girl. The Mormons often claimed it was against their religion to purchase captives whereupon the traders countered that they would hurt the child if no buyer approached. Sometimes, instead of making a threat, the flesh peddler would beat the youngster until a Mormon, moved by guilt, offered money or an item—often a gun—to deliver the innocent from his captors.[38] It is not known if the New Mexicans or Indian chiefs tried to intimidate buyers in southern California, but a club or gun aimed at youngster's head probably inspired more than a few takers.

Soldiers grabbed their share of children as well. F. W. Beechey, the British naval officer who described the campaign against the Cosumnes in 1826, explained that after victory the triumphant troops marched, among others, young boys into Mission San José. José Antonio Sánchez, the *álferez*, or ensign, who led the attack, claimed that the priest enrolled all the prisoners in the mission "except for a nice little boy." The youngster, found in the arms of his dead mother, went to Sánchez "as a reward for his services." Sánchez seemed unmoved by the youngster's predicament. The boy wept and wept, but soon, the officer explained, the little fellow "became reconciled to his fate."[39] Sometimes, at least in the opinion of provincial superiors, troopers and settlers turned wild when they snapped up youngsters. Governor José María Figueroa complained in 1835 that the residents of San José, presumably searching for Indian raiders, did not distinguish between "the innocent and the guilty." The gente de razón attacked a village and made off "with seven children" to serve their captors.[40]

The children, though, would not remain young forever. If they lived to be adults, some gente de razón families freed them. Other gente de razón, though, kept the captives as part of the household, and perhaps paid them a modest salary. In return, families sometimes expected the Indians, especially the men, to perform more demanding work. A few, when needed, possibly went to labor on the zanja, while others followed their masters on various adventures. The angeleño Antonio Coronel remembered that during his hunt for gold in 1848, two Indian servants accompanied him. One, explained Coronel, was an "Indian child" captured in New Mexico and "raised by my family."[41]

An Indian woman and adolescent girl often excited the greatest interest among gente de razón buyers. The historian Howard Lamar explains that up through the mid-nineteenth century, many New Mexicans on the march against Indians seized females as war prizes.[42] In California matters would not be different. A soldier might think the female captive a handsome reward for valor in the field. F. W. Beechey, when witnessing the victory march at San José, saw a fair number of Indian women and girls enter with their captors.[43] More than a decade later, in 1839, Captain Santiago Estrada captured seventy-seven Indians, among them many women who lived out their captivity in Monterey.[44] A year later, Ramón Amezquita, one more resident from the Monterey area, reported to the governor that he captured, along with "several men," nine women.[45] Bancroft notes that as late as 1846, the angeleños continued to seize women. After one raid, they distributed captive women among local "ranchos to work and be educated."[46]

Some individuals possibly thought that they could turn a nice profit selling an Indian woman or girl. Along the Santa Fe Trail, New Mexican traders offered girls for sixty to eighty pesos. Women, we would think, especially if young, might cost an equal amount. There is no evidence of Indian females commanding a similar price in California, much less costing anything, but the gente de razón would not be blind to any business opportunities. Joaquin Piña reported that during the expedition to defeat Estanislao, troopers shot "three old women" on the spot. Yet earlier in the day, Piña explained, soldiers captured three other women and spared them the bullet. He did not say if the women were young, but because they escaped death, something, their youth, or fresh faces, saved them from execution.[47] The soldiers could have put the women to work in their household. Or, a trooper, knowing that a girl or young woman commanded a good sum, would keep her alive to make a sale. The old women, on the other hand, perhaps too fragile for work in the home, and having little chance to intrigue buyers, had no value. They met a quick end before californio gunfire.

By squaring the above descriptions with the Mexican censuses, we can count some of the Indian captives who toiled for the angeleños.[48] Of the 553 Indians listed in the 1836 survey, twenty-seven may have been captives. Five girls and five boys appear. Three women make up the smallest category of captives. Men, however, numbering at least fourteen individuals, figure as the largest group. The angeleños had no preference for young or old captives. At least in 1836, any age would do. Among the oldest, we see the six tulareño men, who range in age from twenty-nine to thirty-three. Two Yumas from the eastern deserts, Miguel and José Antonio, both eighteen, occupy the middle range. The youngest, meanwhile, is five-year-old Manuel Montezuma, an Apache. The 1844 census shows that thirty-seven Indians, out of a total of 650, were captives. Of these unfortunates, twelve adults, three women and nine men, make up the smallest group. Ten girls and fifteen boys, for a total of twenty-five children, account for the rest of the captives. José Antonio, a Yuta, an Indian from the Great Basin, ranked as the oldest at fourteen. Meanwhile, at Rancho Puente, several miles to the east of Los Angeles, Mateo, a youngster from Sonora, saw "servant" entered as his occupation. But at the age of three there was probably little he could do.[49]

In one sense, the results may prove frustrating. Pages before, we suggested that the peones who earned a wage or served out their sentence in a labor gang could not perform every chore. Captives, or so we surmised, helped meet the angeleño need for labor. Some trooped to the zanja in 1848, or tended other chores. Our calculations, even if we throw in children like three-year-old Mateo, suggest that captives made up a small part of the labor force. It stands to reason that more captives worked in Los Angeles. Of course, the cost of feeding and clothing a captive could drain the family purse. But, an extra pair of hands helped make life more comfortable for the proprietor and his family. If crops sat in the field waiting to be picked, or the family needed more help in the kitchen, a smart angeleño would not pass up the chance to take a captive. Nonetheless, how to count the additional captives and where to find them poses a problem that requires resolution.

Masters and Indians

By reversing matters and focusing on masters and mistresses, we may see that many more angeleño households used captives. Our approach comes in two parts. At the beginning, we consider how the census takers' tabulations often point to a greater number of captives than previously assumed. Next, our focus, which has largely concentrated on angeleño men, turns to women. A widow or an unmarried woman sometimes relied on Indian captives to perform chores.

Of the two methods, the census numbers best test the imagination. To begin, we turn to the 1850 census, tabulated by the Americans, and assume that the figures present some consistency. What is true in mid-century would have followed patterns inherited from the past. In fact, the 1850 count presents a better sense of who lived in an angeleño household. It identifies all the Indians and non-Indians who lived under the same roof. The Mexican censuses, as we remember, followed a different format. The gente de razón appeared in one section, the Indians in another, making it difficult to tell who lived with whom. There is no such problem with the 1850 count. Of the 194 Spanish-speaking families inside Los Angeles, twenty had at least one Indian who meets our criteria for identifying captives.[50] These twenty, from the total of 194 families, made up ten percent of the households within the city.[51] If, as we said before, the proportion from 1850 had held true for at least a decade, then an equal number of angeleño households put captives to work earlier in the nineteenth century.

The way surveyors chose to record, or overlook, information increases the likelihood that more captives lived in Los Angeles than we suppose. An Indian man, in particular, seemed a difficult person to identify and record. No male captive from the 1836 survey appeared in the count eight years later. Apparently a good many could have come and gone in the eight-year interval between surveys. At other times, the census taker could have stumbled when recording information. In 1836, for example, the census taker did not enter the ages for nearly half of the Indian population. If he failed to list the ages for more than two hundred men, it could be that he overlooked details that would help us identify other individuals who fell prey to angeleño captors.

In some instances, the surveyors could fail to count female captives in gente de razón households. To be fair, they might have found it difficult to identify each person in a family, but enough information exists in the censuses to find Indian women or girls who marched into Los Angeles against their will. The case of Estefena and María Antonia Soto, or as written in 1836 census, Zoto, suggests that some Indian women, if taken captive when young, might have passed as gente de razón. The sisters, both listed as orphans, one fourteen, the other six, lived in the home of Bernardo Higuera.[52] The pair, lacking the Higuera name, and by all appearances separated from their biological parents, seemed to be Indians. One can counter that the two girls were gente de razón whose family could not maintain them and passed the pair on to friends or relatives. There is a Francisco Soto at Rancho Santa Ana, one of the few people named Soto in the census, and quite possibly the girls' father.[53] Maybe with hard times ahead and lacking money, Señor Soto gave up custody of his daughters.

Eight years later, however, their circumstances suggest that they were captives. The age of each, for example, is incorrect. María Antonia is twelve, two years younger than she should be, and Estefena is eighteen, rather than twenty-two. In an era when few people were literate, especially women, a person who would not know how to read and write might lose track of the calendar as the years rolled by. But most other angeleños present in the 1836 count gave their ages accurately eight years later. It may be that the girls, as Indian servants, always had someone else give their age for them. María Antonia, the youngest sister, certainly spent her early years in the service of others. In 1836, she lived in the Higuera household. For the next count, she resided with three widows, all above sixty, María Ygnacia Amador, María Rochín, and Rosalia Valenzuela.[54] Estefena, the oldest, had married José Bermúdez. She might have found contentment, but more than a few husbands could rival a demanding master.[55]

Children especially could test the census taker's ability to sort and categorize. As was customary in the Mexican era, the surveyor had a separate count for the gente de razón and Indians. At times, though, making distinctions could prove difficult. A household would often obtain an Indian child and bestow the family name after baptism. When the surveyor appeared at the door to count the members of a household, he would not know what information to enter when seeing what he thought was an Indian youngster running about. In some instances, he would guess correctly and place the child in the "Indio" section of the census.[56] But on other occasions, especially in 1836, he would scratch his head and wonder about a youngster's status. We can imagine the raised eyebrows that greeted José Miguel, a five-year-old who clung to José García's leg. García, details suggest, had never married. In an age when divorce was rare, it is likely that his wife had died, but the census taker would have marked him as a widower, not as a single man. At thirty-three, the older García might strain belief, as he could have insisted, that he was the five-year-old boy's brother. The census taker no doubt looked equally bemused when he met another José, the three-year-old son of José Alanis.[57] The surveyor possibly wondered if Alanis's wife, age forty-nine, and well past her prime, could have borne children. Of course, the García and Alanis families could have taken on the children of deceased relatives. But, the capture of innocents seemed so common that any youngster who lacked parents would more than likely be an Indian. At the end, the census taker himself could not decide the truth. He identified José Miguel and little José Alanis as huerfanos, the category often applied to Indian children, and attached a question mark.

Gente de razón women make up the final category of angeleños who probably had more captives than we imagine. Though a woman and her captives often escape mention in the Mexican censuses, the bequests made in a will suggest that many mothers or widows could command captives. María Gabriella Pollorena, preparing for the hereafter in 1832, declared that she "has a Yuma Indian, almost a daughter, named Teresa." The girl went to Pollorena's natural daughter, whom the Indian "will serve."[58] At the start of the American era, María Ruperta Martínez agreed to support an Indian girl given to her by a priest. The child, "evidently an Indian," speculated the priest, received baptism and thereafter entered Martínez's service.[59] Around the same time, Juana Ballesteros conferred her orphaned godchild "to her son." Orphan was a familiar reference to an Indian. "The minor," warned Ballesteros, should receive an education until "he grows up."[60]

Other bits of evidence confirm that women obtained captives. Looking once more at the 1848 padrón for water fees, we note that of the eleven women who appear, ten sent a peón. The peón could be anyone, even an impoverished gente de razón looking for work. But again, the laborer might be an Indian captive. Seized as a boy, the Indian, once mature, now trudged on a woman's command to tend the zanja.

The American survey in 1850 suggests that women in Los Angeles continued to rely on a captive's services. One, Carmen Johnson, the widow of an Englishman, had a house swarming with lodgers, young relatives, and her own children, a total of ten people.[61] The crowd could have been a bit demanding, but Carmen had two Indians, María del Carmel, age sixteen, and Tomás, two years younger, to help with the cooking and cleaning. We skip the other three women with Indian youngsters—María Amador, with one Indian child; María Reyes, with two children; and María Ballesteros, also with two—and move to another angeleño household to find Isabel Guirado, age seventy, and quite likely Carmen's mother.[62]

In Señora Guirado's house, eleven people, most of them her grown children and their families, took up residence. Among the clan appeared two Indian girls, María Antonia, age sixteen, and perhaps her younger sister by three years, Celedonia.[63] Maybe the Señoras Johnson and Guirado, like the women we do not describe, had relied on their husbands, now deceased, to procure Indian children. Or, just as probable, each woman bargained with a trader and purchased captives on her own. Granted, it might be hard to see an aged Isabel Guirado haggling over the price of two adolescents, but her daughter Carmen certainly had the spirit to help her mother. James (or Santiago) Johnson, Carmen's husband who died years earlier, had a "variable temperament," said Bancroft. If Carmen could weather her spouse's volatile moods, she could dicker with slavers.[64]

We can then wonder how many peones were indeed captives. When returning to the 1848 padrón, and applying the figure of ten percent, our number drawn from the American census that counts the households compelling Indians to work, we may find that eight or nine angeleños, out of eighty-six proprietors, sent captives to repair the zanja. But the captives of 1848, most of them, if not all, Indian men, would not include women and children toiling in angeleño homes. If we add these others to our total, many captives worked for angeleño proprietors. We cannot give precise numbers, but with so many captives about, a good number of angeleño households possessed Indians, considerably more than the ten percent average calculated earlier. Whatever the number, angeleño masters and mistresses compared with soldiers in the field. They, like the troopers, had enough opportunity to torment Indians.

The Benefits of Taking Captives

At the start of the chapter, we asked what "beneficial" would mean to the petitioners and their neighbors in 1846. As we proposed, the angeleños wished to erase the Indians' influence. The Indian, dead, or defeated on the battlefield, presented no challenges. On the other hand, a captive, sweating for a master or mistress, offered little resistance when complying with all commands. In either instance, the Indian vanquished in war, or sentenced to household duties, freed the angeleño to embrace Mexican ways.

But the question may arise that our answer is too complex. Simpler explanations might seem more fitting. A soldier's reasons for punishing Indians have received mention, but the wishes of a master and mistress need more investigation. Some angeleños used captives to increase the family's profits. They had no other motive or compulsion that needed attention. A few more angeleños welcomed any riches the captive produced, but a sense of prestige would bring greater satisfaction. A nice home—with furnishings—a gaily stepping horse, the good cut of one's clothes, could make neighbors envious, but a captive, maybe two, following behind the master might impress all the more.

Some gente de razón thought that they had saved captive Indians from a benighted life and therefore deserved praise for performing a good deed.[65] When Governor Figueroa died in 1835, a few gente de razón believed that Indians would mourn the man who secularized the missions and emancipated the neophytes. Juan Bautista Alvarado, Figueroa's secretary, imagined how Indians would receive news of the governor's passing. "The child of the wilderness, the unsophisticated Indian," Alvarado claimed, "shows, although in primitive fashion, the sorrow he feels."[66] In later years, José Francisco Palomares described the faithful service of an Indian captured in battle. The prisoner, named Pedro, who, as we recall from the previous chapter, rescued Palomares when he lay on the battlefield with an arrow in his side, "served [me] faithfully for six years, sowing and reaping corn." But, said Palomares, he, not Pedro, deserved gratitude for acts of mercy. Pedro received threats that warriors in the interior wanted to kill him for helping a californio. (How word filtered back to Pedro is not explained.) Because Palomares granted the captive shelter, Pedro, supposedly relieved, "refused money [for his services] . . . stating that he was sufficiently rewarded for having his life saved."[67]

Wealth or prestige, the sense of contentment in doing the Indians a favor, seemingly granted the angeleños enough reason for taking captives. But the word "beneficial" still haunts. The 1846 petition does not dwell on seeking wealth or prosperity. Nor do the petitioners necessarily appear as the Indians' saviors. Punishment, pain, forcing an Indian into the master's house, the extinction of all Native Californians, seem to be the most compelling concerns. Though the wishes stood at odds—remember the petitioners in 1846 wanted the Indians dead, but, at the same time, confined to the master's home—the statements do reconcile. Each fate testifies to the strength of the master or mistress. The gente de razón remain in power, while the Indian languishes, weak and defeated.

Any benefit, then, did not always revolve around the master's wish to increase profit or acquire more prestige. Rather, when taking captives some masters wished to remove or beat down the Indian's presence to make room for other, more salubrious influences from Mexico. But there is something else to the gente de razón's approach. Worry, and at other moments, fear, especially in relation to Indians, often attended their every move. If they did not kill or discipline the Native Californian, the gente de razón believed, they might lose their advantage. Soon enough they would slip, and above them, with the whip hand erect, would tower the Indian.

Sadly, the angeleños, or any other californios, did not reveal all their thoughts on Indians, much less explain why they needed captives. But with one avenue closed, we seek another. It may serve us well to study the angeleños' contemporaries, the Anglo-Americans in the antebellum south. Many commanded captives of a different sort: black slaves. By reviewing the beliefs of white southerners, we may see what kind of thoughts the gente de razón entertained. The historian James Oakes says that the small farmers and planters of the antebellum South believed that owning slaves promoted freedom among white men.[68] As a sign of that freedom, the white master could regard his slave as property, and do all he could to increase the value of his investment. All the more, freedom, at least as defined by the masters, afforded them privileges no black person could claim. The humble farmer, even if destitute or bankrupt, could share a sense of prestige with the mightiest planter. Even if he did not own a slave, the impoverished white, as a sign of his freedom, had the right to buy an African American. Thus, the poor and rich man found unity in their privilege. Whatever rank they occupied, as white men they would never lose their freedom and become slaves.

The master in California possibly followed similar logic. Admittedly, in Los Angeles or anywhere else in California, no one argued that owning Indians advanced freedom, liberty, or any other quality cherished by the Mexican republic. But Oakes' ideas apply nonetheless. Regardless of their rank or occupation, many californios welcomed the thought of taking captives. To many, the captive represented every form of gente de razón supremacy over the Indian. Captive, *cautivo* in Spanish, comes from the Latin verb *capere*, "to take." When the gente de razón stood over the Indian warrior, they had the power to take all they wanted. They took the Indian's life, even taking a harvest of ears or limbs. Or, they could leave the warrior's life, but take him prisoner. The same advantages emerge when the gente de razón dealt with Indian women and children. Once more the gente de razón master could take what he wished. He took their labor, time, and well-being. If the master could, he took their innocence and virtue. In the act of taking, the gente de razón proved they had the authority to give, refuse, and keep all the Indian would deem precious. The merest gesture—a soldier scanning the battlefield for trophies, or the sweep of the master's hand—suggested that the Indians would always be subject to some form of the captive's fate, for they would feel probing, grasping fingers ready to grab and take hold.

There is some mystery as to why the *dueños*, the Spanish word for masters and mistresses, favored Indian captives who came from remote places. Presumably the wish to appear dominant would find fulfillment when any Indian, especially one from a local ranchería, fell into the dueños' power. Nonetheless, Indians from distant lands held particular appeal. Some prisoners, like Paiutes, traveled hundreds of miles with their captors before an exchange of guns, livestock, or even money, landed them in the angeleños' household. Meanwhile, many local Indians, among them the coveted woman and child for domestic service, lived in or around Los Angeles. A Cahuilla or Serrano, for instance, Indians from nearby, could easily have performed any job in the household. Neophytes, too, before and after secularization, seemed well suited to help out in angeleño kitchens and living quarters. A gente de razón dueño who minded his pennies no doubt knew that a local Indian would also be cheaper to employ. Captives from far away lands might command a high price, a problem for any family with a strict budget.

Still, the angeleños continued to acquire captives from distant regions. We dismiss the reason that the gente de razón wanted to ransom innocents from slave traffickers. Some dueños would have purchased a prisoner regardless of how cruel or kind the captor was. One could say that syphilis or smallpox had so ravaged local Indians that the gente de razón would think that no home risked infection when served by a Paiute or Yuma. But, by the 1830s, we can assume that some form of pestilence had already swept through what is now the American Southwest. If Indians dwelled along the Santa Fe Trail, as did some Paiutes and Yumas, it is likely that they met diseased soldiers and traders. Even for indigenous people who lived in the upper reaches of the Great Basin, far from Los Angeles or Santa Fe, visiting Indians from California or New Mexico could have spread infection. Moreover, if disease truly worried the gente de razón we would have to question the sincerity of their fear. Smallpox or syphilis rarely concerned angeleño men who visited Indian companions in the ranchería.

One might make a stronger case that the gente de razón did not want drunken Indians in their service. After secularization, alcohol attracted many Indian drinkers. But when traders brought their wares to distant villages in California or the Great Basin, alcohol, along with guns and other implements, probably attracted a good number of customers. It would be the odd Indian who had never sampled, or even seen, a bottle. On the other hand some dueños might think a child from far away would escape the evils of alcohol. If true, however, the angeleños, thinking that a little one would not drink, would welcome any child, especially one from a nearby village. But the young Paiute captive, or any other child from a distant land, no more innocent than a local youngster, continued to attract the angeleño master and mistress.

At times, the demand for captives made the gente de razón embrace contradictions. Some sympathized with the victims of slavery as long as they did not have to admit they mistreated and abused Indians. As evidence of their dislike for bondage, the gente de razón, like their fellow citizens throughout Mexico, felt compassion for blacks, the people who had suffered slavery for centuries in the New World. Many Mexicans, wishing to stop American slaveholders from moving into national territory, supported emancipation laws. A presidential decree abolished bondage in 1829, but the gesture was largely a formality. Ever since independence in 1821, many Mexican states had outlawed slavery. In communities where bondage continued, residents pooled their money on Mexican Independence Day to buy a black slave's freedom.[69]

In Los Angeles, the gente de razón seemed just as disposed to welcome blacks. According to the 1836 census, two black men, one a seventy-year-old named Joaquin Africano, the other nearly half as young, Juan Wilson, resided in the city.[70] We know little of the men. It is unlikely that they were slaves who owed their freedom to gente de razón generosity, but they apparently found Los Angeles a congenial place. Wilson—of the two, there is a bit more information on his life—arrived on a whaler in 1826, and remained in Los Angeles.[71] He could have jumped ship to escape bad treatment. If he had, Wilson would likely flee Los Angeles once he experienced more hostility. But as of 1836, ten years after arriving, he still lived in the city, suggesting that he liked life with the gente de razón. Joaquin Africano also found Los Angeles to his liking. He had married "Lucia," a local woman (an Indian?) and attended to his life's pursuits before expiring toward the end of 1836.[72]

The gente de razón's need for Indian captives seemingly escapes explanation. Indian prisoners could be an expensive purchase. They possessed no special talent that would surpass the abilities of Indians living nearby. It is equally doubtful that they were healthier or stronger than local gentiles or neophytes. For those gente de razón who welcomed the principles of the Mexican republic, a captive in the household belied claims that they sympathized with any person forced to work for another.

Here we revisit Oakes to solve the puzzle. If we understand his argument correctly, white slaveholders often rejoiced that they were not slaves.

A black suffered constant humiliation, but the white masters, rich or poor, knew that if nothing else, they would never experience a slave's sufferings. But let us rearrange Oakes's argument and imagine the slaveholders' attitude if the blacks threatened to turn the tables and make the white masters play the servant. Fear, doubt, the slaveholder's constant need to assert superiority, more so than existed already, would always be present. As Oakes implies, the master's supreme air, or ease with privilege, would hide uncertainty. One mistake or advantage granted black chattel could have reversed circumstances. Now ruled the slave. The master, disgraced, hopped to the other's commands. Dreading any challenge that endangered his position, the master might scream louder or adopt a more arrogant manner to prove his authority.

We apply the twist in Oakes's logic to the gente de razón in Los Angeles. In some letters and reminiscences, the angeleños spoke with confidence when regarding Indians. On occasion, though, the triumphant tone softens, and in its place appears the fear that Indians could play the master. The evidence suggests that some angeleños had sufficient reason to worry. Of the thirty-six cases magistrates brought against Indians between 1830 and 1850, at least fourteen involved some sort of offense against gente de razón. From this number, twelve concerned the stealing of cattle. An Indian may have only wanted the animals for a meal, but many Indians would know that the angeleños slaughtered cattle for hides and tallow. A Native Californian, angry at a paltry salary or poor treatment, could run off with a cow and, with a knife to skin the beast or scrape off its fat, he could profit as did the master.

At times, Indians resorted to more violent conduct. The prefect for southern California reported in 1842 that "the Indian Maximo and two confederates" often made trouble in Los Angeles. Agustín Janssens and Juan Bandini, officers of the prefecture, "order[ed] the three to leave" the city. Maximo and friends ignored the order. When pressed to comply, they "insulted and threatened Janssens."[73] Another Indian in Los Angeles proved especially defiant. Torcuato, an Indian from San Juan Capistrano, broke into the house of Enrique Sepúlveda in 1842.[74] Two years later, Torcuato, with Julian, another Indian, murdered Ignacio Ortega. When caught, the pair earned the death penalty and met their end before a firing squad.[75] Indian defiance, already a serious matter, took a more deadly turn in 1846. Bancroft reports that "captured" Indians revolted at the San Francisco rancho, a cattle spread east of Los Angeles. The gente de razón shot eighteen Indians before restoring order.[76]

When the gente de razón looked deeper into California's interior, they perceived more threats to their authority. Pio Pico remembered that the "desert tribes" sometimes swept into southern California to kidnap "señoras and señoritas."[77] In 1837, Mohave warriors sprang out of mountain hideaways and attacked ranchos north of San Diego. Among the loot they carried off wiggled one, or perhaps two, gente de razón boys.[78] The same year, the wife of Cosme Peña, secretary to Governor Juan Bautista Alvarado, fell into the hands of Indian captors. Apparently tired of California life, she returned overland to Sonora, but Indians attacked her party and seized Señora Peña.[79] News eventually reached Los Angeles that an Indian chief had taken the Señora as his wife. Several years later, Joaquin, an ex-neophyte from San Gabriel who suffered a branded lip and severed ear as punishment for an unknown crime, swore revenge on Mexicans. He gathered followers around him, some of them ex-neophytes who carried similar grudges, and attacked travelers who rode along the Mojave trail from Los Angeles. In one raid against a caravan, Joaquin killed the men and captured two Mexican women. He could have kept the pair, but more likely he rode into the Great Basin to trade the captives for guns or horses. The angeleños never saw either woman again.[80]

In all the examples above, it was the gente de razón, not the Indians, who absorbed kicks and blows. The men, especially, seemed most concerned about Indian insolence. As for the women who commanded captives, it is not known if they experienced the anxieties that burdened their male counterparts. But with Indians presenting many threats, there is enough cause to think that some angeleño wives and mothers might have insisted that the Native Californians deserved stiff treatment. Men, therefore, probably exhibited behaviors that applied to women. Already worried that somewhere, at some unknown time, an attack would come, the men who heard about the capture of californios seemed disturbed that a gente de razón woman or child now had to call the Indian master. The man, meanwhile, dead or driven off—for how else would a woman and child be in an Indian's service?—had failed to provide protection. Shame might pour down on his head if he survived the attack. Or, if dead, the loss of a woman or child could blacken his legacy.

Such anguish seethes beneath the surface of many californio documents. Many letters and declarations from the Mexican period suggest that the gente de razón men dreaded to think that they looked weak and powerless. For the most part, men were the most literate individuals in provincial California. When they wrote, they wrote to other men. The images they used often involved bravado and exaggeration. But once we study each phrase, there sits one man saying to another that he never wanted to concede any advantage to Indians. Lieutenant Romualdo Pacheco expressed the men's wish to remain strong. In 1826, Pacheco, ordered by the provincial government to open a route to the Colorado River, struck out east from San Diego, and en route commanded that his men camp for the night next to an Indian village. The troopers expected attack and asked Pacheco to consider moving elsewhere. He exploded, and with an eye to the Native Californians standing close by, Pacheco announced, "my honor and that of the nation were very sacred . . . and they would be sacrificed [first] rather than" retreat.[81]

Pacheco did not have to fight, but when conflict came, some gente de razón men feared that Indians tested their manhood. In the first of two expeditions against Estanislao, Sergeant Antonio Soto approached the rebels' camp hidden "in a dense willow wood" to gather information for an assault. Suddenly, Estanislao called out, "Coward, coward come on Soto"—How Estanislao knew the soldier's name is unknown—"Come into the woods if you are a man." In the second campaign against Estanislao, Corporal Pablo Pacheco sent a messenger to demand the Indian leader's surrender.[82] The reply came quickly: "I'll do nothing of the kind. Let your soldiers come in here if they are men."[83] In Los Angeles, meanwhile, bold Indians issued similar challenges. The Indians who "insulted and threatened" Agustín Janssens in 1842 asked in so many words if the angeleños "were men."

Indian insolence often prompted gente de razón writers to fill political pronouncements with images of slavery and tyranny. To a californio man the image of a captive announced submission. The dramatic descriptions could be for effect, but with the thought of Indian outrages ever present, all talk about servitude would not be rhetoric. To read an appeal nailed to a post, or hear it at a public assembly, the man acquired confirmation that toiling for another threatened a dreary fate for him and any person in his circle. Victor Prudon, secretary for the Los Angeles vigilantes of 1836, explained why he and his companions felt compelled to mete out justice: "Unless we strike at the shackles which bind us, wrongdoers will make our decrees null and void."[84] The same year, José Castro of Monterey condemned the arrogant behavior of Nicolas Gutiérrez, the Mexican governor. Castro addressed an appeal to his compatriots, saying "as obedient sons of the mother country, you swore solemnly before God and man to die rather than be slaves."[85] A decade later, when the Americans invaded

Los Angeles, Serbulo Varelas, a Mexican shoemaker, proclaimed, "shall we be capable of permitting ourselves . . . to being subjugated and . . . accept the heavy chains of slavery?"[86]

With the logic turned around to suit our purposes, the import of Oakes's thinking becomes clear. The gente de razón feared that they, not the Indian, risked suffering the captive's shame and humiliation. However, as some men likely thought next, the horror deepened when the father or husband feared that warriors would take his wife and child. We do not know how many gente de razón the Indians seized. Perhaps it was only the few whose fates we described earlier. But in a place where the Indian presence was tenfold to that of the gente de razón and rumors of native forces advancing on Los Angeles made many shudder, the dueños had reason to feel wary.

To prove their superiority, the californios took Indian captives. Sometimes they seized men, but by 1844 the gente de razón apparently fancied women and children the most.[87] (Of the thirty-seven captives we have positively identified in 1844, only nine were men.) In practical terms, it could be safer, and more prudent, to keep a woman and a child for household service. A man, especially if he were a warrior dreaming of retribution, would prove unreliable. But the gente de razón, especially if anxious or worried about their prerogative, needed better assurance that they stood supreme. Ever since antiquity, especially in the Mediterranean or the Near East, a conqueror would take the women and children of defeated enemies.[88] The daughter or wife of a fallen ruler would find a place as a domestic. Or if attractive, the harem awaited. Some boys, meanwhile, especially those of noble birth, might win a spot in the conqueror's retinue. The boys also risked castration and sometimes received the command to satisfy the master's most intimate whims. From the conqueror's perspective, the more boys or young men he collected would show that he was a man among men, or more rightly, a man among boys.

Provincial California was far in time and distance from Macedonia and Babylon, but the impulses that inspired or frightened the ancients could also drive the gente de razón. In Los Angeles, the merchant or farmer, and at times the californio woman, would overcome their feeling of weakness by taking a Paiute or Yuma. Even if a group like the Paiutes rarely attacked ranchos and rode off with captives, the gente de razón did not correct their misperceptions. As Indians from the eastern deserts, the Paiutes earned comparison with the bolder groups who harassed the gente de razón. A local gentil or ex-neophyte toiling in the home did not grant the gente de razón the same sense of triumph. But when taking a captive from elsewhere, especially from places that harbored Indian raiders, some dueños experienced satisfaction. With a prisoner in hand, the gente de razón, like the conquerors in antiquity, would announce, at least symbolically, "burn our property, steal our wealth, but we have your wives and children."

The gente de razón's fear that they had become one with Indians now acquires even more significance. The intimacy that brought one closer to the other now would drive them apart. For the soldier, war, as we argued before, could be an intimate act. The combatants, if unable to kill with a rifle or arrow, would produce a knife, bayonet, or, especially for Indians, a war club to finish the task. When in a death struggle, one gripped the other, and after a knife or club struck home, each man would be locked in mortal embrace, the last gasp, the last splattering of blood falling on the combatants. If the victor was the gente de razón, the final deed was yet to be performed. In a different setting, and with different partners, what would be the lover's caress, now became, with cries and shouts issuing from all around, an act of mutilation. The cradling of the head, the penetration of the flesh—the cutting and slashing of a knife—the treatment of the other's most sensitive organs with personal, heartfelt gestures, showed not love, but anger.

In the gente de razón household, disfigurement took a different shape. The dueño did not mutilate the captives, but the sense of intimacy so dear to the soldier also governed the conduct of the master. For instance, the gente de razón, save for some occasions, never called the captive a slave. To a critic, such reluctance could mask an urge to dissemble. If the Indian were not a slave, but a member of the household, the conscience, and Mexican emancipation decrees, especially after 1829, would be satisfied. But other thinking was often at work. The angeleños, as noted, often called the captives "domestics" or "orphans." Sometimes they preferred to use word "servants." Each term placed the captive on some intimate level with the master. As a domestic or servant, the Indian adult fulfilled his patron's wishes. A young orphan, meanwhile, looked to the dueño as parent and provider.

But intimacy rarely suggested equality. When the trooper drew close, he used the knife to eliminate any similarities. With eyes and ears gone, even at times followed by the head, the Indian, literally cut down to size, bore little resemblance to the gente de razón. In the household, with the captive living among the family, the dueño also found ways to cut and slice. As the knife mutilated an Indian body, the master's command could disfigure the spirit. Even a tender word could wound the Indian. After all, most captives had to comply with a command, even if they preferred not to. Here, then, is what the angeleños found "beneficial." They could treat the Indian as they wished. In the same instance, they confessed that if they relented, roles could switch. The Indians would rule, and the gente de razón had to submit. "Beneficial," when uttered by the angeleños, brought some reassurance. The Indians, and no one else, faced humiliation, and, at times, death. All the same, with the Indian diminished, his influence muted, his image and form supposedly removed, the gente de razón looked to Mexico and created a guise more to their liking.

February 19, 1846

To your excellency the Governor [Pio Pico] we come before you the undersigned, and say that since the Indian ranchería was removed to the pueblito—a move calculated to end excesses and thefts—the aborigines . . . taking advantage of their isolation . . . steal from [neighboring orchards]. . . . [O]n Saturdays [they] celebrate and become intoxicated to an unbearable degree, thereby resulting in all manner of venereal disease, which will **exterminate** this race and . . . be beneficial to the city. To preserve the public health and do away with the vice of polygamy . . . [and] the excesses of prostitution [so that] the residents of Los Angeles would not be encouraged to do the same, we ask that the Indians be placed under strict police surveillance or the persons for whom the Indians work give [the Indians] quarter at the employer's rancho.

Signed:
Francisco Figueroa and Luis Vignes

Signatories:

Felipe Lugo	Ricardo Lankem (Laughlin)	—?—Villela
Juan Ramírez	Samuel Carpenter	Tomas Serrano
Januario Avila	Agustin Martin	Mariano Ruiz
José Serrano	Guillermo Wiskies (Wolfskill)	Antonio Salazar
Manuel Sepúlveda	Luis Bouchet	Casciano Carreon
Gil Ybarra	Maria Ballesteros	Maria Anta. Pollorena
Desiderio Ybarra	Francisco López	Vicente Elizalde
Miguel Pryor	Estevan López	Antonio Coronel

CHAPTER FIVE

"Exterminate"

A Story in Three Parts

IN THE FINAL CHAPTER, we wonder what the angeleños wanted to do after they removed the Indians. As with other ambitions and desires they expressed, the angeleños revealed their intentions in the 1846 petition. In the middle of the document, practically dead center, the signatories looked at the scourges infecting the Indians and proclaimed, "Disease . . . will exterminate this race." The phrase, as with so much else in the petition, offers many meanings. At its most basic, the words repeat the angeleño desire to eliminate the Native Californians. The ravages of disease, at times steady and relentless when attacking the body, reflected the angeleño wish to kill Indians without remorse. At a deeper level though, the petition says other things. The term "exterminate" suggests the removal of someone, or something, so completely that one could think of a landscape stripped of life. If the Indians' removal made the land fallow, so to speak, who, or what, would be planted instead? As one may guess, we will propose that Mexican ways would take root and prosper.

Of course, the petition never mentions Mexico, nor is there an explicit reference to Mexicans. Thus, we must read the petition anew and see each word, not as a separate or distinct item, but together, one combined with the other. For our purposes, a seed and some soil provide the best image. Alone, the seed does nothing. Soil, if left untouched, promises a meager harvest. But put the two together and a grand flowering may result. With the images of seed and soil, what we seek stands revealed; each element, one in concert with the other, suggests how, and by what methods, the angeleños followed Mexican habits.

Into the angeleño soul—our soil—went the liberal seed. The seed contained a copy, or better, an imprint of the ideal person conceived by liberals in the nation's center. Many Mexican liberals spoke of creating the *hombre nuevo* (new man), *hombre positivo* (positive man), or *hombre digno* (dignified man).[1] Each description, though seemingly different, is essentially the same, suggesting, all at once, the title hombre nuevo. Any quality that was positive or dignified, especially in turbulent Mexico, would be welcome or refreshing, hence new.

Any sense of the new, and the shape it took in a man, and at times, the woman, held great appeal. Liberals in Mexico professed, as did some angeleños, that the hombre nuevo broke from the past. Prior to Mexican independence, caste and social rank had great import. The skin's hue, for example, often did much to help or hurt a citizen's reputation. Too dark, and one reclined in low regard; but have fair, rosy cheeks, and the chances for respect would rise. Money could help "whiten" the darkest complexion, but usually an Indian or person of mixed blood had little chance to find an occupation that would bring profit.

After independence the hombre nuevo scarcely worried about tradition. He, not some opinion or habit, would determine his worth. By relying on work and talent, he set his place in the community. Of course, the individual's need to advance could succumb to destructive impulse. Ambition and cupidity, for instance, could corrupt the spirit. As for family and neighbors, they seemed at risk before any person who only cared for success. To liberals, though, the hombre nuevo supposedly went about his affairs in a different way. He practiced respect and moderation, choosing, at all times, to honor the interests of his fellow citizens. When participating in business or politics, explained the historian Charles Hale, the hombre nuevo understood that "the greatest happiness [for all Mexican citizens] is the greatest measure of right and wrong."[2]

As for the seed, especially one that conveyed the imprint of the hombre nuevo, it needed some way to reach California. Books and pamphlets seemed sufficient. But the most exalted term or idea would sit dead on the page if no one appeared to provide explanation. Knowledge of laws or political parties provided one more means to learn. Though, to be sure, such information would remain inert when there was no method of transmission. In need of instruction, the angeleños and their californio neighbors in other settlements often looked to Mexican émigrés to pass on the liberal imprint. The Mexican expatriates, along with some provincial residents, used steady, tender hands to cultivate flourishing sentiments. The ideas surrounding work and productivity bore first fruit, followed in time by other qualities. To see how growth occurred, and who supplied the necessary guidance, we must know how to proceed. Hereafter follows a story in three parts. Angeleño men earn discussion, as do women and children. Though all these individuals contributed to angeleño life, the man set the pattern that others in Los Angeles had to follow.

Men

If Mexican liberals lived in Los Angeles and other communities—all the while transmitting the imprint of the hombre nuevo—we ask how they spread their doctrines to men. A teacher holding forth from a text would be one way. Or a reading group, with citizens gathered around one person holding forth from a book or pamphlet, would be another. And yet one more public display, a surprise we hold for later, seemed the most effective method.

The genesis of the hombre nuevo bears telling. For the most part, the ideal of manly conduct originated during the French Revolution. The tumult in France, much less the triumph and failure of Mexican liberalism, is beyond our scope. But it is enough to say that some French revolutionaries also wanted to create the new man. According to the historian Simon Schama, the new man found his origin in the family. Schools and worthy occupations like farming contributed to his formation, but the new man received his first, and most critical, lessons from the father and mother. Of the two parents, the father displayed the habits that other figures, including the mother, had to honor and uphold. According to some French artists and thinkers in the late eighteenth century, the father resembled a hero from antiquity.[3] He would be austere, strong, and not given to impassioned displays. In his appetites and pastimes, he practiced moderation. The joy of a job well done, or the practice of a simple, abstemious life, granted him rewards as nothing else would. The mother proved to be equally strong. But sentiment, not necessarily austerity or restraint, the father's qualities, seemed her particular gift. She lavished attention on her child and hoped that along with the tough, virile traits instilled by the father, tenderness and compassion, a woman's characteristics, would soon flourish. From watching each parent, the child, the boy especially, learned how to behave. He acquired the father's sense of discipline, but, because of the mother's influence, he would not be so rigid as to lack any feeling or sense of mercy.

In Mexico, liberals admired, and elaborated upon, the French conception of the new man. The new man, or the hombre nuevo, possessed the talents that would help the nation prosper. In the male, given the masculine prerogative of the nineteenth century, Mexico found its leaders, its merchants, the soldiers to fight, and the workers to till the land or practice a trade. At each task, or so liberals hoped, a diligent spirit, not some base appetite, would inspire the hombre nuevo to abandon petty concerns and look to the nation's success.[4]

For the hombre nuevo's nurture and moral development, Mexican liberals wanted parents, especially the father, to reconsider the ways of teaching discipline.[5] As French revolutionaries wished to put aside traditional methods, in the Mexican interior, and elsewhere in the nation, some also wanted to abandon the ways of the past. In the colonial period, men of power, the father, the priest, the king—or his agent, the viceroy—usually relied on fear, and sometimes the threat of punishment, to temper the spirit. The harsh treatment left such frustration that when mature and later a parent himself, the father who endured beatings as a youngster would visit the same terrors on his children. With Mexican liberals, however, the whip and clenched fist declined in importance. Instruction, following the liberal purpose to free the spirit, would prove wanting when delivered by rough treatment. Any lesson seemed best served by the gentle but firm touch. When inculcating parental admonitions, youngsters learned that the conscience, not fear or the promise of a beating, turned eyes and ears away from sinful habits.

There may be doubt that some legacy of the French Revolution moved the angeleños. Common sense alone would say that the distance between Mexico City and Paris was formidable, and that between Paris and Los Angeles, even more.[6] True enough, but the historian Michael Costeloe suggests that French revolutionaries gained admirers from Mexico City to the edges of the republic.[7] Some Mexicans had witnessed the Revolution's outbreaks in 1789. Nearly twenty years later, other Mexicans had attended the Cortes in Cadiz, an assembly whose delegates came from throughout the Spanish empire. A few Mexican participants, along with other colleagues, used the occasion to study the French Revolution and plan reforms. (But it is worth considering how Napoleon's peninsular campaign ruined the French reputation.) In Mexico City during the early years of independence, Voltaire, Rousseau, Montesquieu, and the writings of other French thinkers who had inspired the Revolution, proved a popular item in local bookstores.

Other examples emerge in California. Many angeleño men used the title "citizen," an egalitarian gesture favored by French revolutionaries.[8] In 1836, when the angeleños executed the adulterous lovers, the avengers who gathered for the execution took the title, "Committee of Public Safety"— Comisión de la seguridad pública—a reference to the revolutionaries who claimed to protect France from the plots and counterplots of their enemies.[9] Sometimes, the angeleños closed official documents with the words, "God and liberty," a declaration that rings with another French echo.[10]

French influence took other forms. A look at the angeleño passion for keeping records accorded with the French revolutionary's wish to modernize society.[11] The collection of facts opened up the world, allowing the authorities to identify citizens and instruct them. A name entered in a roll, arranged with other names, the home numbered, filed away, the occupation, and level of expertise, entered in a ledger, impressed citizens that someone, a magistrate or the constable, knew them. If recognized, with no one person invisible, the citizen in California, or France, might feel more obligated to support the law and the state. A review of the ayuntamiento records reveals lists upon lists; lists of men eligible to shoulder weapons, lists of landholders, of men who could read, and those who could not, lists of landholders who used the zanja, lists of citizens and their workers, lists of how much residents paid in fines, lists describing the stores, billiard halls, and grog shops which filled the city.

But the lists and petitions would suggest the worst excesses of the colonial regime where the paper required for government business could drive one to madness. In the same instant, the accumulation of knowledge could be an illusion. Names entered in a file would not mean that the state had control, much less that the citizens would mind their duties. Even so, the lists, with each name appearing clearly and legibly, reflects the French insistence that each person was an individual endowed with certain rights, and, in turn, the bearer of responsibility.

The French left a bigger impression in the way liberals in Mexico and California envisioned the hombre nuevo. Each example above—the vigilante protecting public welfare, the simple title of citizen, the ayuntamiento member's desire to record information—speaks of the man's duty to protect. But a man, if required to abandon poor and shoddy habits, needed an example to follow. To that end, the French revolutionaries often summoned forth the noble Roman or brave Spartan, each a paragon worthy of emulation, and presented one, and sometimes both, in dramatic and vivid form. Art, of all the means to shape mind and spirit, emerged as the most compelling method to instruct men. In verse or prose, in painting, or the robust, elegant lines of sculpture, French writers and artists presented antique themes that pleased the ear, or struck the eye.[12] Art, though, did not exist only for its own sake. When crafting their work, the individuals with the pen or easel tried to seize the imagination.

In Mexico, even with the political upheaval during the first years of independence, orators and artists continued to present the ancients as examples worthy of emulation.[13] Lucas Alamán, a prominent Mexican historian and statesman at the beginning of independence, quoted Cicero to argue that as Rome "[strengthened] the republic to establish its prerogative and remedy the ills of the people," Mexico should do likewise.[14] One can counter that Alamán was a conservative, and imperial Rome would suit his desire for a strong central government. But José Luis Mora, a distinguished liberal, and at times Alamán's foe, agreed, perhaps not word for word, on the need to honor antiquity. Said Mora, "the use of Europe's classical literature would instruct the Mexican people in virtue and morality."[15] The lessons offered by antiquity stretched to other realms. The historian Michael Costeloe explains that by 1835, professors at the University of Mexico agreed to use "ancient and modern classical authors to illustrate Mexico's history."[16] Aspiring artists at the San Carlos Academy in Mexico City produced works that celebrated ancient heroes. If, as happened often, they produced the image of an Aztec warrior, the figure's musculature and noble countenance seemed nothing more than a Mexican guise imposed on the shape of an ancient Roman or Spartan.[17]

In Los Angeles, and other parts of California, the gente de razón could not produce pieces of art, but they found different ways to present the lessons offered by the ancients. The angeleños began with boys in school, who, when hunched over their assignments, learned how the ancients could direct male conduct. As with liberals in Mexico's interior, the angeleños wanted students to appreciate the ancients' dedication to clear thinking. When the boy became a man, he needed a mind uncluttered by distractions and petty thoughts. In one of the primers used by Antonio Coronel, like his father Ygnacio, a teacher in Los Angeles prior to 1846, youngsters learned to write by occasionally copying Latin aphorisms like "Homo sum nihi humanarum ame alienum puto." The saying, by the Roman thinker Terence, then came in Spanish, "Como soy hombre no tengo por extrañas las cosas de los hombres." (Because I am a man, the ways of men are not strange to me.)[18]

In other primers, angeleño youngsters copied the Roman philosopher Seneca in Spanish, not Latin, penning time after time "Wisdom is the gift of heaven." Others struggled with an utterance by the Greek thinker Pythagoras, also in Spanish, "When I am with my friend, I am not alone; however we are not two."[19] A child, to be sure, might have found the ancients mysterious. Indeed, at a later point, we spend more time studying the lessons offered by the primers. Nonetheless, each quotation, its intentions revealed through study, its message, presumably explained by instructors, might prove liberating. After hours of work, hours of hearing an instructor drone on about Pythagoras, Seneca, or Terence, perhaps the moment would come when all would make sense. Discipline, exertion, respect, a responsible manner, all qualities a homage to the ancient hero, and by the nineteenth century, a pledge to the liberal ideal, would sit on the conscience. For some boys, the appeal constituted a tedious reminder, but for others, it became an obligation to honor.

Warnings come, too. Learning, especially at a time when not all attended school, might inflate the head, making the student callous, arrogant, or intolerant. When mature, the student, flush with shallow and intemperate thoughts, provided no benefit to his family or neighbors. To prevent the formation of selfish habits, some primers denounced pride and self-indulgence, perhaps more harshly than they did sloth. In the Coronel primer, classical themes yield to the Bible, and in a paragraph that a youngster read and copied on a tablet, the fate of Nebuchadnezzar provided a chastening example. The lesson introduced the Babylonian king as "one of the greatest princes of the world." Yet when Nebuchadnezzar "made the famous gardens and constructed dikes to contain the Euphrates," he dared think he compared with God. For his affront, concluded the story, the king "went insane and grazed with animals."[20]

If the primers, some laden with classical examples, helped turn boys into stalwarts, perhaps men received the same instruction, though their lessons differed in form and content. But how men learned about the ancients, and the various venues that replaced the classroom, suggests that we must review all ways of transmitting information. Whatever the method, californio speakers and writers mentioned ancient heroes without worrying they would bore or confuse their audience. When Governor Figueroa suspected that the Híjar-Padrés expedition meant to usurp his authority, he mocked the newcomers, writing in a book, one of the first published in California, that they were far removed "from the virtue, from the disinterestedness of the Porfumios, the Cincinnati, the Paprii, and the Fabii."[21] Nearly a decade later, Leonardo Cota, a member of the ayuntamiento, went before his colleagues to complain about dirty streets. The gathering of filth and offal in the city, the remains of butchered animals citizens failed to remove, resembled, he said, a "hecatomb," the slaughter of a hundred cows the ancients offered the gods.[22] When American forces approached Los Angeles in 1846, Pio Pico, then the governor of California, issued a proclamation calling neighbors and constituents to arms by celebrating the Spartans' sacrifice at Thermopylae. Remember, he proclaimed, "the glory won by the death of that brave little band of citizens posted at the pass of Thermopylae under General Leonidas. Hear their motto, 'Stranger, say to Lacedemonia [Sparta] that we have died here obeying her laws.'"[23]

In one sense, the wish to enlighten compatriots may not have been the intention of speakers and writers. It could be that Figueroa and his contemporaries only wanted to boast of their education. For instance, Figueroa's invocation of Roman and Greek heroes, men whose memory the Híjar-Padrés party somehow violated, most resembles a pedantic exercise. His remarks, published in a volume entitled *Manifesto to the Mexican Republic*, ran for nearly two hundred pages. Reprinted letters, memoranda dashed off to Mexico City, and the occasional rant against Híjar and Padrés, comprised the work. But more galling, perhaps, would be the reference to ancient figures. Figueroa, it seems, discussed people only a scholar would recognize. Porfumios, or more likely Porphyrius, a Greek Neoplatonist, receives mention, as do the Paprii and the Fabii, distinguished Roman gentes, or families. The Cincinnati, a reference to Lucius Quintus Cincinnatus, a patriot who left his farm on two occasions to save Rome from attack, might baffle anyone who knew nothing of antiquity. Cota, too, could have confused his audience. Any mention about ancient rituals, in a statement about the need to keep streets clean and well swept, seems a curious choice. Pico, in a pronouncement destined to be copied and distributed, sounded equally daunting. He referred to "Lacedemonia" the ancient name for Sparta, a bit of information even the most erudite person might not have known.

But it would not serve any person to make obscure references when he needed to make convincing arguments. Each man presented his arguments during some sort of emergency. Figueroa wished to arouse public anger about the intentions of the Híjar-Padrés colony. A dirty street, filled with decaying flesh, flies and vermin feasting on the rot, compelled Cota to shout warnings about threats to public health. Pico had less reason to sound confusing when he needed men to take up arms against the invading

Americans. Apparently the angeleños, as did others in the province, had some way to learn about the ancients, so to grasp the speakers' arguments.

If gente de razón men truly could follow the most learned arguments and acquire any lesson liberals hoped to instill, it would be a remarkable feat. Before 1846, only five percent of the populace could read in the Mexican republic, a proportion that more or less held true in California.[24] But our definition of reading may not always apply to Mexican California. According to modern sensibilities, when one reads, one sits alone with a text and scans words on a page. But "to read," when the meaning is expanded, may also suggest another way to understand or learn new ideas. (And, then, when one reads, we can think of the seed and imprint; for words, when published or uttered, conveyed the hombre nuevo.) When an illiterate person stands beside someone reading aloud, what transpires? In one way, the unlettered person is certainly not reading. The printed word means nothing. But if he listens to the words read for all to hear, he may understand the text as well, maybe even better, than his educated neighbor. The illiterate man, though not scanning the words, may in fact be reading. In Los Angeles, then, the idea of reading may have had a different meaning. Reading possibly compared with a public exercise in which citizens revealed an item's contents to ignorant neighbors.

If we are right, it would seem appropriate to count the number of angeleño men who could read. An 1847 padrón of voters, one of the many lists the angeleños enjoyed compiling, identifies members of the electorate who were literate. Of the 239 voters listed, all male, eighty-eight could read.[25] To aid our calculations, we turn to the 1844 census, which counted 627 men in Los Angeles. Of these individuals, to apply the figure of eighty-eight literate men from 1847, nearly one in seven could have perused a book. The level of competence could vary, but it is likely that some learned men, if moved by public feeling, would take the obligation to enlighten ignorant neighbors about liberal habits.

The inspiration to help others read, or at least divulge the contents of books and pamphlets, originated in Mexico. In the years after independence, José María LaFragues, the Minister of Public Instruction, wished to correct illiteracy. He proposed to establish "reading cabinets"—gabinetes de lectura—to educate the adult populace. LaFragues envisioned that literate artisans and tradesmen would journey to towns, and in the plaza or even the family home, they would teach fellow citizens to read. The plan, however, did not appear until 1847.[26]

Still, materials published at least a decade before suggest that some form of the reading cabinets had long existed in Mexico. For instance, political catechisms, popular with the liberal governments in the early nineteenth century, seemed designed for public readings. Usually thirty to sixty pages long, sometimes even longer, the pamphlets discussed the role of government and explained what rights and responsibilities each citizen had. To make the information easier to grasp, the authors followed the style of religious catechisms. When a penitent, usually a youngster, learned Catholic doctrine, he read simple questions followed by straightforward responses. The Ripalda Catechism, a work popular in Mexico and California, asked, "Are you a Christian?" Next, came the answer, "Yes by the grace of God." Another question challenged, "For what end is man created?" The answer declared: "To serve God and please him."[27]

The political catechisms varied in content from their religious counterparts, but the form remained the same. A question posed a problem and the answer, at times pared down for readers ignorant of the period's political controversies, came after. In 1831, José Luis Mora published the *Catecismo politico de la federación mexicana*, one of many catechisms produced in the early years of Mexican independence.[28] The work, divided into sixteen chapters, and spanning almost a hundred pages, seemed especially detailed, but Mora wanted to cover any topic that might occur to the reader. In chapter one, "On Mexican Independence," a question asks: "when do people have the right to rebel?" The reply explains that the people can take up arms when only one class of people, the "clase ilustrada," the upper class, enjoys advantages. "No one," the answer continues, "has the right to obtain happiness at the expense of others."[29]

With catechisms in hand, the educated man in Los Angeles could have perused the contents for his unlettered neighbors. But the catechisms, at least as we have described them, do not reveal how the angeleños learned about the ancients. To date, only one political catechism has surfaced in any Los Angeles archive, and it says nothing about classical history. Another problem arises. The literate man, if moved by good feeling, might read to his neighbors, but another individual blessed with education could feel reluctant to share his knowledge. Moreover, reading cabinets gathering in a home or in the center of Los Angeles could occur on occasion, but to happen constantly, and impart information about Romans and Spartans, might make for a boring exercise. Despite these difficulties, the one bit of evidence we do have suggests that the liberal wish to create the hombre nuevo and speak of ancient history could take another, more active, form.

To see why a single item holds such promise, we leaf through the pages and wonder what other works rested in the angeleños' hands or rose before their eyes. The catechism, written in 1831 by Colonel D. Tomás Yllanes, and entitled, *Cartilla sobre cria de gusanos de seda*, or "Pamphlet On How To Raise Silkworms," emphasizes the Mexican liberals' hope to transform men into the hombre nuevo. In the preface, Yllanes explains that he wishes to teach the reader "the simplicity of caring for silkworms." The business, he says, can bring the "nation millions of pesos."[30] To instruct the audience, Yllanes deviates slightly from the familiar approach of questions and answers. Instead, he presents the dialog of a play in which one character asks another how to raise the creatures.

At the outset, we meet a farmer who laments, "here you have a poor man ruined by so many revolutions, now the escoces, now the yorkinos [Masonic lodges whose rivalry marked the early years of Mexican independence]." A soldier arrives, and to set the farmer at ease, he explains: "I do not come to speak to you about battles and parties, but to give you advice." The thankful farmer produces mulberries, and invites his guest to eat. Eyeing the fruit, the soldier knows they could be the stuff to feed silkworms. He declares: "How backward you are! These [mulberry] trees can be the beginning of your happiness and that of your children."[31]

The play, comparable to a catechism, could expand our definition of reading. A conscientious citizen could read the work to compatriots who might find the story more entertaining, and thus easier to follow. But, in the same instance, performers could take the play and transmit its message to a wider audience. All the more, if a play about silkworms provided instruction on how to find a worthy occupation, other, more dramatic fare describing the ancients, and praising the hombre nuevo, could have delighted an angeleño audience, particularly the men. Some men would only cheer the derring-do and care for nothing else. But, many would admire a Spartan and Roman traipsing across the stage, and wish, even if briefly, that they could emulate the ancient heroes.

Plays of all sorts lifted the curtain on angeleño stages. The historian Nicolás Kanellos says that from the 1840s up through the early twentieth century, theatrical troupes from Mexico toured California.[32] The actors often performed comedies, but at other times, he implies, they presented more serious subjects. He explains that during the French intervention in the 1860s, well into the American period, touring companies raised money for Mexico's defense. Kanellos does not say what performances they staged, but a comedy seemed inappropriate for so serious a cause. A more sober work, perhaps a play with a patriotic theme, maybe even a melodrama, might have worked best.

Kanellos, however, provides no definite explanation of what kind of theater existed in Los Angeles prior to 1846. But the municipal records suggest that many types of productions entertained the angeleños. We know, for instance, that "Pastorelas," Christmas Plays, proved popular.[33] The city treasurer, meanwhile, recorded in 1836 that "maromas," mummers or acrobats, paid a fee to leap and tumble for the populace.[34] The same year, another troupe of maromas plunked down money to put on shows for five days.[35]

Some troupes possibly offered more dramatic material. In 1840, the city treasurer in Los Angeles noted that, "for an entertainment two pesos were paid."[36] There is no mention of mummers or acrobats, and to be fair such an omission could mean nothing. Nevertheless, the "entertainment" could have been a play. If it were, in 1840, with the conservatives coming to power in Mexico, a concerned troupe with liberal sympathies would have found Los Angeles an agreeable place to perform.

If a play about a soldier and farmer seems probable, perhaps so would a performance about the ancients. With so many references to the classics in an appeal or announcement, the authors presumed that the audience, or a good part of it, would follow along. Therefore, a drama about the ancients appeared as one of the best means to inform the public. In the Los Angeles plaza, or somewhere else in the province, the wellborn and miserable sat to watch classical heroes and villains march across the floorboards.

The Mexican critic Antonio Magaña-Esquivel describes the plays an angeleño audience likely enjoyed.[37] He explains that from 1821 up through the 1840s, antiquity, or what he calls "neo-classical notions," influenced Mexican theater.[38] A good many works have disappeared, leaving nothing more than a title and a brief description. Others exist in fragments, with only a very few surviving intact to the present.

But from what is left, the evidence indicates that playwrights with liberal sympathies often found inspiration in the ancients. For instance, Francisco Luis Ortega, a playwright from the 1820s who took a seat in the National Congress, composed a work called *Mexico Libre*, now lost. Audiences saw characters named "La Libertad," "La Discordia," "El Fanaticismo," and "La Ignorancia" appear on stage. Such characters, all drawing on the ancient practice of using allegorical figures to comment on human virtue and weakness, made the thoughtful viewer reflect on Mexico's troubles.[39]

There would be little wonder about what José Joaquín Fernández de Lizardi intended when, around the same time, he staged *El Fuego de Prometeo* (The Fire of Prometheus). Fernández de Lizardi would not produce a light, romantic farce. He called himself "El Pensador Mexicano" (The Mexican Thinker), a name he affixed to newspaper editorials where he often lamented the dominance of the Catholic Church. Fernández de Lizardi thought the liberal 1824 constitution too conservative. The document, to his horror, did nothing to limit the power of the clergy or break up the church's holdings.[40] *El Fuego de Prometeo*, also lost, could have been a celebration of pagan virtues. Prometheus brought fire, the root of human ingenuity. And to guess what symbolism Fernández de Lizardi implied, the ancient appeals to moderation and reason, as might a flame, would light the way to progress. Catholicism, on the other hand, seemed contrary to what Prometheus promised. The Church's use of spectacle and incantation dimmed reason and its bright, shining qualities.

Finally, with the rise of Santa Anna and his conservative allies in the 1840s, playwrights sometimes used ancient history to comment on current controversies. In 1842, Francisco Calderón wrote *La muerte de Virginia por la libertad de Roma* (The Death of Virginia for the Liberty of Rome), one more play whose name alone survives. The drama, drawing on Livy's histories, recounted the tale of the tyrant Appius Claudius demanding the hand of Virginia, the daughter of a distinguished Roman. The father, wishing to preserve the girl's honor, kills her instead. Few in the audience, suggests Magaña-Esquivel, would have missed the play's references to Santa Anna's outrages. By 1842, the year of the play's production, Santa Anna had seized power. Many spectators possibly thought of Santa Anna when the villain Appius Claudius mounted the stage. In the tyrant's lust for a sweet, virginal girl some would see, in parallel, Santa Anna ravaging Mexico.[41]

We do not know which of these plays, and others like them, came north. The angeleño account books say nothing, save for the mention of an "entertainment" in 1840. Witnesses from the period, in a contemporaneous letter or later in a reminiscence, fall equally silent. If any plays did reach California, some could have been romantic tales or comedies. But, as we argue, this was the age of seeds and imprints conveying the message of liberal Mexico. Because many californios had classical references at their fingertips they may have witnessed some sort of production filled with references to the ancients. First came the maromas, with their tumbling and feats of strength. Next, out stepped the players. If there was a political crisis in Mexico or California, as was often the case, the actors used their craft to address the controversy or appeal to the people's sense of justice.

With the audience engaged, the three plays presented above, or any drama that compared, emphasized the hombre nuevo's temperate and diligent nature. When Appius Claudius walked on stage, hisses and whistles probably greeted his entrance; and if he fell before the knife, at least in the play—in real life he remained vigorous into old age—the spectators no doubt cheered. The jeering of villains, however, had little to do with the message actors and playwrights wanted to convey. Self-denial, on the part of the father, and indeed Virginia herself when she lay down on the altar of sacrifice, seemed the point of the whole proceeding. To draw one more lesson from Virginia's death, stoicism in the face of incredible odds, itself the product of discipline and reason, was another way to subdue a tyrant's brutality. Other Mexican plays sounded the same themes. The blessings of liberty, as trumpeted in the work, *Mexico Libre*, or knowledge, as represented in *Prometeo*, only came through work and application.

The classical dramas, with all their references to ancient heroes and villains, provided the connections that bound erudite angeleños with their benighted brethren. The strength of the bond, and the depth to which it descended, rested upon the symbols or turns of phrase employed in the plays. When unfolding on stage, the performances drove home the lessons that most angeleño men would recognize at the slightest mention. They saw, in the flesh, how the hombre nuevo should conduct his affairs and serve those around him. The plays served as a template, a sort of master plan to which most men made reference. An ancient name, or date, a heroic feat, the demonstration of some virtue, or weakness, would not pass unnoticed. The audience, those who could write and read, and those who could not, watched. All grasped the purpose of the players' art, so that any citizen, even the most obtuse, would learn of Lacedemonia or Rome and know its significance.

Enlightened and entertained by the presentations on stage, and maybe, too, by the reading cabinets, it seems quite reasonable to conclude that many angeleño men understood how classical references defined the hombre nuevo. They knew why Figueroa said that sincerity and honest effort found truer expression in ancient Romans then in members of the Híjar-Padrés expedition from Mexico. Cincinnatus, for instance, one of the figures Figueroa discussed, seemed a man deserving of admiration. When the Roman republic called citizens to arms, Cincinnatus left his plow to join the fight. When victory came, Cincinnatus put aside the sword and returned to his farming. In the conduct of Cincinnatus, as Figueroa certainly hoped, the gente de razón glimpsed conduct worth emulating. During war, they marched off; but after the enemy's defeat, they, like Cincinnatus, would spurn the bloodlust of combat and resume their labors. Or when Cota spoke of cleanliness, his audience grasped his references to slaughter. No one would welcome the thought that the muck and grime filling the streets resembled a great bloodletting. Finally, as Pico hoped, any talk of the Spartans' sacrifice at Thermopylae would inspire compatriots to fight off Americans. (Pico's words did little, however. The californios did not stop the invaders.)

To close, there is reason to think that the angeleño effort to create the hombre nuevo did not always go smoothly. The French examples might seem a bit too exotic. A reading cabinet, and the work needed to peruse a text, required great effort, perhaps more than any person was willing to give. The discussion of the ancients presented more difficulties. Some angeleño men probably did not appreciate the references to classical history. The characters alone, and their Greek or Latin names, could prove confusing. In other cases, as some angeleños likely noticed, classical figures offered examples that seemed unsuitable. One has only to read the *Iliad* to see how the ancients relished cutting each other to pieces. But the lessons continued, or, if we speak of plays, the show went on. In word or print, up on stage or celebrated in a pronouncement, the hombre nuevo took shape and presented the qualities all men should emulate.

Women

And what about the women of Los Angeles? They, too, transmitted Mexico's seed, or better, the liberal imprint of the hombre nuevo.[42] The responsibility, though, often brought little comfort. As some angeleño women likely noted, liberal ambitions granted few privileges beyond the duty to serve or support the man. But it is hard to imagine that any person would endure limitations or abuses without complaint. At some level in the individual's mind, he, or she in our case, would yearn for change. If liberation appeared difficult, she at least found some way to turn events to her advantage. Day to day in Los Angeles there existed some space for women to maneuver. Space, however, at least in the way we mean it, acts as an opening within a schedule of chores and routines, or in the laws and customs that upheld the man's prerogative.

In this place, the space we describe, any constraint imposed on a woman (or girl) either lapsed or turned impotent. She seized the opportunity to use her abilities, and, in some cases, defy the men who brought difficulty and trouble. But, when inside the space, or wishing to bring it forth, she sometimes faced a confusing, muddled existence. Though the chance to contest men brought some relief, a woman would not experience peace of mind. The men issued commands or laid down the strictures that confined the woman's movement. By responding to the limitations that men designed, a woman only reacted to her circumstances. She lacked an opportunity to employ her intelligence and failed to develop a philosophy or way of thinking to improve her life. Thus, we also seek something called consciousness, the idea that when inside the space, the area that allowed a measure of freedom, an angeleño woman found some method to discover contentment. Liberal thought, despite its emphasis on men, offered women the best means to define the reach and extent of the space afforded them. To say that liberal thought, or that any idea, did not inspire angeleño women would lead us back to the notion that women only reacted to their circumstances and had failed to develop their intellect. Any idea could appeal to women, but given the climate of the era, it would be hard to overlook liberal notions. Some women, maybe more than we can assume, recognized the meager opening granted them by circumstance—our space—and they employed liberal thought to secure their position. Once they established a space, they acquired consciousness and learned how to resolve the challenges that sat before them.

Unfortunately, the written record says little about a woman's life prior to 1846. Few californio men in any period wrote about women. When they did make a comment, they wrote brief descriptions or, in the matter of magistrates recounting a domestic dispute during the Mexican era, they did not always dwell on details. Some women recorded their thoughts, but many wrote, or dictated, their impressions well after 1850, a time when memories could fade.[43] Nonetheless, other bits of evidence fill the gap. A woman's actions, from the subtle gesture to direct, forceful displays, might reveal as much as the printed word. The deed, or deeds, might seem a wild jumble, but when "read," the events strung together like words, a story emerges. Through their deeds, angeleño women "speak" and show they relied on liberal ideas to create a space. The woman's utterance, if we may call it that, exists in scattered pieces. School lessons help our cause, as do printed items and public displays, each element showing how an angeleño woman reasoned.

We turn to the following scene described by Antonio María Osio, and with a deft, precise touch, arrange the occurrences like print on a page to see how the mothers and daughters of Los Angeles exercised their will. No other person from the nineteenth century, as far as we know, related the events presented by Osio, who waited more than a decade to record what he saw. Bancroft, drawing most of his information from Osio, gives the incident a brief mention in a footnote, but provides no explanation.[44] Still, Osio offered enough details to help us understand the conduct of angeleño women.

In November of 1836, Juan Bautista Alvarado, a prominent resident of Monterey, imprisoned Nicolas Gutiérrez, the incumbent governor, and claimed the post of provincial executive. Among his first acts, Alvarado declared California free and independent until Mexico reinstated the 1824 Constitution. As mentioned in another chapter, the conservatives in Mexico City had assumed power and proposed to write a new constitution. Few californios welcomed a conservative regime, but Alvarado misplayed what advantage he had when he presented his plans to provincial residents. In a decree dated November 7, 1836, the new governor declared that California would draft its own constitution. The effort, an accomplishment of sorts, although the document never became law, represented Alvarado's attempt to resist the conservatives' grab for power. Of the several reforms he envisioned, Alvarado hoped to establish religious freedom. Alvarado, however, proceeding cautiously, did not wish to challenge "the Catholic Apostolic Roman" faith. Catholicism would remain supreme in California. But all other faiths, if practiced in private, would suffer no persecution.

The angeleños erupted. Many did not welcome Alvarado's thoughts on religion, one of many proposals they found repugnant, and refused to pledge their loyalty. The angeleños, if some were indeed liberal, should have welcomed Alvarado's attempts to promote religious tolerance. But a good number claimed that Alvarado behaved no worse than the conservative usurpers in Mexico City. What was more alarming, one angeleño declared, Anglo-American adventurers had gained influence over Alvarado. They convinced Alvarado to "sow discord, plunder the treasury, and attack private fortunes."[45] Fearing rebellion, Alvarado raised a force of 110 men and marched south from Monterey in early 1837 to force compliance.[46] (In an aside, Alvarado gained victory, but he would return south again a year later to put down another rebellion.) When Alvarado approached San Fernando, the ex-mission northeast of Los Angeles, a cry went up to repel the attackers.

For reasons Osio did not make clear, José Sepúlveda, the alcalde of Los Angeles, ordered one of his subordinates, a man described only as "director of operations," to read Alvarado's decree before a group of angeleño women. Osio, for the most part, did not identify these women, nor did he say where they assembled. But in one spot he turned specific and said that María Serrano Sepúlveda, the alcalde's mother, stood among the listeners. When the women heard Alvarado's views on religion, Señora Sepúlveda, explained Osio, "as well as other women, did not understand very well the tolerance of other" faiths.

When they pressed for more information, the director of operations replied "that the Protestant Fathers would have so much power they would personally seek out the brides and take them into their homes for safekeeping, so that the girl's parents would not interfere with marriage."[47] Young women and girls applauded the news. But other women in the crowd, all of them presumably older, became angry and accused the director of operations "of cowardice." At this point, "women of influence appeared," again Osio failed to identify participants, and all present "pledged to ensure that [each woman's] husband, children, and grandchildren, from sixteen to seventy years of age would take up arms for the family name."[48] Osio explained that the women made good on their oath. They helped recruit nearly two hundred, perhaps three hundred, men to fight Alvarado.[49]

When the angeleño army gathered near San Fernando, some women, if we read Osio correctly, went along to serve "as excellent cooks, tortilla makers . . . and workers," who prepared "an abundant supply of choice meats, greens, and vegetables" for the troops. Other women chose to rally the men's spirits. One of the last groups of men to join the gathering forces carried a message from "the distinguished mothers" to José Sepúlveda, the alcalde now turned military commander. The women wanted Sepúlveda, "to gather their sons together, and tell them on their behalf, loudly, clearly, and with no room for misunderstanding, that they would rather cry for them because they had died on the battlefield than experience the sorrow of reprimanding them for a disgraceful escape."

Osio, following the spirit of the times, invoked the ancients to honor the women. When the angeleño women called on fathers, husbands, and brothers to die like men rather than accept "dishonor," Osio said they resembled warrior queens who often led their men into battle. Osio explained that they "had not the slightest knowledge of the zeal of the women described in ancient history."[50] If they had, "they would have imagined themselves as equally heroic as the women of Gaul and elsewhere, whose exceptional feats embarrassed even those soldiers" who pledged to fight until death.[51] Adding a postscript to the whole affair, Osio wished that the Mexican soldiers and generals who battled the Americans in 1846 "had been the sons of these brave women, for then they could have fulfilled the honorable desires that they expressed."[52]

Osio, when presenting his tale, revealed what the "distinguished mothers," among others, wished to accomplish. By urging men to fight, women, and to a certain degree girls, resisted the man's dominance and claimed advantages a husband or father could not touch. But Osio did not address a single moment in time when mothers and daughters decided, just once, to turn defiant. Rather, as Osio suggested, young and old knew that, when conditions were right, they could call on liberal principles to dictate some part of their fate.

Even so, while a good number of women and girls appeared to welcome liberal thought, Osio implied that the different generations often opposed one another. The girls, Osio explained, "reacted favorably" to the news that religious tolerance would allow them to marry a Protestant, or even a "Jew."[53] Some knew, however, or they would know soon enough, that their freedom amounted to an illusion. Unless their beau converted, neither their parents nor a priest would bless the newlyweds. Still, the girls entertained the hope, no matter how desperate or foolish, that they could marry whom they wanted. The mothers, on the other hand, seemed quite traditional. They shuddered to think that an apostate or non-believer would take their daughter's hand at the altar. "The distinguished mothers," along with other mature women, fearing for a girl's welfare, called on men to defend the family and Roman Catholicism from intruders.

The demands of angeleño women and girls, while seemingly contradictory, did converge. Both groups accepted marriage as part of their life. Girls, despite their apparent defiance, desired a husband. The mothers, meanwhile, wanted some say in their daughters' decision. By upholding wedlock, women and girls acknowledged that inside the household, with all its burdens and responsibilities, they found the space to question, or even challenge, men. But outside the household, as many knew, they often lacked the opportunity to do what they wished.

To see why marriage found favor and provided the space for the exercise of liberal measures, we must reconstruct the circumstances that made life with a husband appealing. It may be ironic that marriage, and by implication family, gave women and girls a way to express their voice. Many women and girls had little choice when selecting a spouse. They may have stated whom they wished to wed, but, as scholars note, parents throughout Mexico and its territories often selected their daughter's mate.[54] At times, the parent's desire to evaluate a suitor often reflected the family's standing.[55] The more prosperous or respectable a family, the more likely it would want to find an appropriate match for the daughter. Any parent who wished to preserve the family's reputation would not want a daughter to marry someone from a lower rank.

When we turn to Los Angeles, a young woman from an aspiring family likely knew that wealth, or signs of initiative, could improve the prospects of any suitor. Indians, who often had no property or chance to pursue other opportunities, often lacked the assets that earned notice. They would not impress a family who wanted the daughter to marry a successful spouse. The gente de razón who had no aptitude for work also failed to draw attention. They, as well, did not seem suitable candidates for the daughter's hand. The men who impressed parents, and if handsome, the daughters, profited in their affairs. The most desirable individuals, and the families to which they belonged, often owned, or at least held title, to their enterprise. A prosperous candidate appeared at the door, and the young woman's parents, who believed that they, too, wrung profits from their holdings, had reason to celebrate. They found someone for their daughter who succeeded at his labors, or at least had the means to make others bring him success.

Other considerations confirmed that the bride's opinion or interests rarely mattered. At times, angeleño families wanted their daughters to marry young. As all parties recognized, a bride's youth and supposed innocence made her more attractive to a potential suitor who wanted a virgin for the wedding night. Practical concerns also persuaded parents to accept a suitor's proposal. In an era when disease or war could shorten life, or the elements might wrinkle and dry the fairest face, some families thought it expedient to match their daughter with the first worthy man who came calling.

As a consequence, many couples that stood at the altar in Los Angeles often featured a bride who was nothing more than a girl. Between 1821 and 1846, there were approximately 210 weddings in the Los Angeles area.[56] Of these, twenty-six involved women nineteen or younger. At times, the groom would be young too, at the most one or two years older than his bride. If the bride and groom were both tender in age, perhaps each partner—but not always—came from poor families. A young man who had not established himself, or had come from a family with meager means, would not impress future in-laws, unless they also came from humble circumstances. The parents, if they cared or were still alive, might think that their daughter had little chance of marrying a more respectable man, so they gave their consent.

An arranged marriage would be more evident when the husband was at least a decade older than his bride. The older man had more chances to lend luster to his name, thus making himself a more promising suitor. At times, it made little difference if the more mature candidate did not come from an established family. His success and good fortune would help overcome any deficiencies in his background. Of the twenty-six matches with younger wives, twenty feature men more than ten years the brides' senior. And, from these twenty marriages, eleven include marriages with girls who were between sixteen and fourteen.[57]

A bride younger than sixteen possibly faced some anxious moments. The biologist Adrian Forsyth explains that girls in modern times begin menstruation at twelve or thirteen, a process that commences when they reach a certain body weight. Yet a century ago, says Forsyth, the first menstrual cycle often came two to three years later. A girl, therefore, might have experienced sexual maturity at fifteen or perhaps sixteen.[58] If true, some prospective brides in provincial California would not be in full flower. Breasts or body hair would be absent, with sexual desire, if at all, simmering in contrast to the men's raging desires.

Some girls certainly needed a formidable spirit when they retired to the bridal chamber after the wedding reception.[59] The husband's caress might bring confusion and doubt. But, to avoid controversy, she would accept his advances and endure the husband's caresses. We can only imagine what kind of thoughts came to María Teresa Sepúlveda, age fourteen, when she took the hand of Miguel Pryor, a man eighteen years her senior. As an older man, Pryor likely had experience with women. On the wedding night, he might not feel any reservations about making a young bride satisfy his demands. Arcadia Bandini, also fourteen, probably faced one of the more strenuous tests. Her husband, Abel Stearns, a merchant of considerable wealth, was twenty-six years older than she. The father was no doubt pleased that his child wed a prosperous man, but Arcadia's feelings might be a subject of debate. Stearns carried a long gash on his cheek. An unhappy customer had once slashed at his face with a knife, nearly severing the tongue. The injury, though, did nothing to diminish his nickname, "Cara de Caballo"—Horse Face.[60] The girl never breathed to anyone what she thought when the disfigured face drew close. Arcadia bore Stearns no children.

Without marriage, the woman often lacked the opportunity to experience success or pursue decent work. Nonetheless, the record implies that a few women found ways to develop their talents. The historian Miroslava Chávez explains that Mexican law allowed widows or single women older than twenty-five to manage their property as they saw fit. Women who did not meet these requirements needed to honor the wishes of a father or husband. But as long as they satisfied the law, or exhibited the knowledge to skirt regulations, women apparently used their holdings to great advantage.[61] Chávez says that nearly twenty-five gente de razón women in Los Angeles controlled a rancho at some point during the Mexican period.[62] Some had no trouble handling a rancho's chores. Pancho Rangel, an old angeleño, recalled that some women "could lasso a steer in the fields the same as a man and bring it in."[63] Antonio Coronel, meanwhile, when describing life on a rancho, remarked that some angeleño women "carried out duties that properly belonged to men."[64] Other women tried their hand at farming. There is no precise figure, but an 1848 padrón suggests that out of 103 cultivators living in Los Angeles, eleven women tilled the soil, a proportion that possibly had held true since the Mexican era.[65]

Women also managed other bits of property. In 1836 alone, the city account books note that of the twenty-three proprietors who served alcohol in Los Angeles, five were women: María Lobo del Tapía, Visitación Valenzuela, Luisa Venancia, Asención Castro, and Rita Villa.[66] The municipal compilations, at times incomplete, missed the women who established businesses in other years. Victor Prudon, for instance, in his description of the vigilantes in 1836, explained that Luisa Cota, "a poor widow . . . occupied with the rearing of her large and worthy family," ran a boarding house.[67] A decade later, María Ballesteros and María Pollorena, the two women who signed the 1846 petition, owned title to some sort of property. They, no different than the men who added their names, could have owned a farming plot, or, just as likely, opened up a tavern or boarding house.

But, even when admitting the prospect of an undercount, the women who pursued ranching and farming, or ran a business, formed a small part of the female population. (Some could have been seamstresses or milliners—hat makers—two more occupations traditionally performed by women, but the records say nothing of these, or other comparable pursuits.) After identifying each angeleño woman during the Mexican era who owned a piece of land or operated a business, essentially all the individuals introduced above, we only count forty-four individuals. If we apply the figure of forty-four to the number of women who appeared in the 1836 census, they would account for a small proportion of 424 gente de razón women who lived in Los Angeles, a bit more than ten percent of the total.[68] Eight years later, in the 1844 count, when we again use the number forty-four, the number shrinks to eight percent, a small fraction of the five hundred women in the survey.[69] The American census, tabulated in 1850 and a bit more careful in identifying property owners throughout the city and county of Los Angeles, suggests that a woman's circumstances did not improve as time progressed. Of the 578 gente de razón women over the age of sixteen, fifty-three owned title to their property, a total of less than ten percent.[70] No doubt countless women helped their families tend land-holdings or serve customers. But, given the legal constraints or customs that determined who had final say over the family's business, many women had to defer to their husbands and fathers.

In other instances, an angeleño woman could use the law to her advantage and bring suit against men. Yet as with the chance to manage property, there is some question if the privilege yielded great benefit. At one look, angeleño records suggest that women often convinced magistrates to discipline a vindictive spouse or companion. In 1840, María Valenzuela wished to escape the clutches of her lover Justo Morillo. The pair, who had never married, shared a house, but over time Valenzuela tired of her companion and wished to leave him. Morillo exploded and threatened to kill her. Valenzuela went to the alcalde and asked "that she be allowed to separate from aforesaid Morillo." The alcalde found in Valenzuela's favor and ordered Morillo to keep his distance. To ensure obedience, the alcalde ordered Morillo to put up a bond of five hundred pesos and his property "in the district of Las Bolsas," an area southeast of Los Angeles. If Morillo approached María Valenzuela and violated the command, he would lose his money and land.[71]

Some sources suggest that a few wives prevailed upon the authorities to dissolve a troubled marriage. In 1842, Casilda Aguilar lost patience with her spouse and sued for divorce. A Los Angeles judge agreed that Señora Aguilar had good reason to leave her husband—the records, though, do not explain what the man did—and allowed the couple to cut ties.[72] Around the same time, Casilda Sepúlveda claimed that the priest forced her to marry and she asked for an annulment. The prefect for Los Angeles agreed with her plight and asked the "ecclesiastical court" in Santa Barbara to grant the request.[73] Though the records do not reveal the outcome of the dispute, she apparently succeeded.[74] The historian Marie Northrop notes that in 1845 Sepúlveda wed another man, Ramón Tapía.[75]

But to look again at the record, we see that few angeleño women earned judgments in their favor. Of the nearly 174 criminal cases heard by angeleño alcaldes or prefects during the Mexican period, eleven concern men abusing women.[76] From these eleven, there are nine in which a man stood accused of assault or rape. One more case involves a man abducting a woman, with another featuring a man charged with incest.[77] It is not clear how the magistrates resolved each case. Even if they handed down convictions, the point remains that few men answered for their mistreatment of women. The wife who wanted a divorce had even less chance of receiving her day in court. We do not know how many women wanted to dissolve their marriage—forgetting, for the moment, that a man could just as well ask for a divorce—but the evidence suggests that few succeeded.[78] At times, a wife received a summons to reconcile with her spouse. In 1840, a woman abandoned her husband and went to live with her mother. The prefect, siding with the husband, ordered an angeleño magistrate to "warn the mother-in-law to desist from hiding her daughter and . . . compel her to live with her husband."[79] A year later, another woman wanted a divorce and asked the prefect to hear her case. He refused, saying that she had no grounds for filing a "petition."[80]

In some instances, angeleño women fell outside the boundaries that marked their life. On one side, law and custom often consigned women to the family home until their wedding day. After the nuptials, she resided in her husband's house. At the other end, property rights granted certain women the power to run a business or landholding as they wished. But for others, they fit in neither place. They had no father or husband to provide support. Or, they lacked property that supplied an income. A few may have handled a rope and plow with great skill, but they had slim hope of finding a job on a rancho or farm. If left with no means of support, a circumstance that could become more severe when a child waited at home, some women pursued another calling that provided an income. They put on some rouge, made the dress more revealing, and added a seductive step to their gait. On the street, in a cantina, or maybe when someone banged on the door to make a proposal, they welcomed any advance and became prostitutes.

Previously we reviewed an Indian woman's choice to enter the trade, but beside her, a gente de razón sister competed for customers. How many angeleño women offered their bodies for sale is unknown. The 1836 census identified thirteen gente de razón women as "mala vidas," a term that often described someone who practiced prostitution. But the term could apply to anyone who had no money, not just one who sold her charms. In the next census eight years later, no woman carried the appellation "mala vida," though three had an "N" for "ninguna," as in no occupation, affixed to their names. "N" could identify prostitutes but there is no way to tell for sure. To solve the confusion, we look at the baptismal records for Los Angeles. An angeleño prostitute, like many women in the nineteenth century, had little or no way of controlling conception. If a woman was sexually active, as would be a prostitute, she might give birth to children by different fathers. But a prostitute, no matter how jaded or ruined by her calling, would want her child baptized. She might think she was on the road to perdition, but she would not want her little one to share hell's torments.[81]

At least nine angeleño women from the Mexican period fit our description. Dolores Varelas, for example, had five children, including one set of twins, a different man the cause of each pregnancy. Apolonaria Varelas, presumably a relative, a sister perhaps of Dolores, had four children by different fathers, as did Pilar Almenarez. Concepción Navarro also bore four children, with Encarnación Buelna and Ricarda Valenzuela having three each.[82] Again, different men fathered the babies.

A few women may have enjoyed their work, but many, especially those who turned to prostitution out of necessity, probably did not. Of these reluctant women, many lamented that they could not restore their reputations. Gossip would constantly blacken their names. An occasional male customer could turn abusive, or he could refuse to pay, putting off requests to make good on a debt. Some women no doubt had a pander or pimp to make business go smoothly, but he, too, might turn brutal when times went bad. Punishment often posed a threat. In 1842, the prefect banished Dolores Valenzuela from the city, "so that it may serve as an example to other women of bad character."[83] It is not clear if she was a prostitute, but any mention of "bad character" suggests that she set a price for her companionship.

But if indeed a prostitute, Dolores Valenzuela, and others like her, wanted to recover some of her dignity. She never left a written testimonial, an omission many in her profession shared as well. Nonetheless, the manner in which she treated her child provides a way to observe her thinking. If Valenzuela could not redeem herself, at least she helped ensure that her child would remain chaste and inviolate. Valenzuela, however, lacked the means to grant her daughter a wholesome existence. All she could do was wish. Valenzuela named her child, María de los Nieves—Mary of the Snows—conferring upon the girl the purity, she, the mother, could not enjoy.[84] Here in a name, Valenzuela spoke for her peers and showed what prostitutes wanted; they wanted respect and dignity, everything that "Nieves" implied. To look at the word Nieves in another way, that is to see the name as a point of comparison, would suggest that Valenzuela, and perhaps any other prostitute, knew how sordid or tawdry their lives had become.[85]

For most women, especially those sensitive to their circumstances, they knew that life granted them few choices. If they had no property, or had little interest in offering their bodies to men, home and marriage seemed the only pursuits open to them. Aware that the household seemed their destiny, some, if not many, women could take heart. They knew that the constraints imposed on them provided some benefit.[86]

Husbands and fathers, to be sure, still had dominion within the household, with a few using force to make sure the home looked neat or that little ones minded their place. But for the man to go any further, and sweep, or maybe change the youngster's nappies, would be too much. The man's influence had reached its limits. He could comment on the way women managed their domestic duties, but to supply instruction and perform the duties himself would diminish his authority. Amidst the clatter and clutter of family life, the man's prerogative had extended as far as it could go, and could go no further. A reversal would occur, with those at the top sinking to the bottom, but those at bottom rising to the top.[87]

At the point where the man's privilege and woman's responsibility overlapped, a space appeared. Inside this space, where strength diminished and the powerful yielded to the weak, the woman acquired consciousness. She, and others like her, recognized how the household granted opportunities. Strength, in particular the man's strength, began to decline inside the home; but opposite, the woman, weak and pushed about, sometimes bullied, managed to grow stronger. She still could not handle property without conditions or rush off to war. Voting, sitting in political office, or joining a Masonic lodge were also forbidden. With some significant exceptions, education remained an elusive prize, as were the advantages of reading and writing. But, family life and domestic duties offered advantages as nothing else would.

The women's wish to turn matters in her favor could betray liberal influence. For it was in liberal thinking that some women found the confidence to challenge the authority of men. The historian Jean Franco notes that after 1821 many liberals in Mexico wanted to expand the woman's duties.[88] They focused on women who came from the middling and upper tiers of society, but wished to include women from the lower ranks. The liberals reasoned that many women, regardless of their social position, had to labor in the kitchen or nursery. The domestic responsibilities, they knew, while a burden, could grant women the chance to show resolve. By playing mother to the nation, in effect giving birth to the ideas and behaviors that created the hombre nuevo, women would find that liberal thought gave them some leverage over men.

To some Mexican liberals, the hombre nuevo received his first instruction in the home. Aside from the father, who exerted great influence, the mother provided other valuable lessons.[89] Children, the boys chief among them, spent their earliest years primarily with the mother. She taught the little ones responsibility. Each Sunday, she took the youngsters (and husband) to church, and at night, she folded their hands and taught them to pray. The love and respect each citizen should express for another would first be learned at the mother's knee. José Luis Mora, the prominent Mexican liberal, elaborated on the mother's contributions to the child's development. He explained that after independence, the mother would spread "virtue, decorum, and prudence." He hoped as well that the gentle graces of "music, drawing, literature, and friendship," qualities apparently in short supply during the colonial period, would now, in the 1820s, be "advanced by women."[90] Mora said nothing about religion, but talk of virtue and prudence, the appeal to decorum or refined habits, suggest the proprieties any cleric would welcome.

As for the man, whether a husband or other adult relative, the woman steadied his hand. She encouraged his efforts, and if circumstances warranted, she might utter more bracing comments. But, all the while, the mother or daughter tempered the man's conduct. She gave him refinement, says the historian Franco, and without inflaming his brutal, violent capabilities, she invited the man to express himself in more constructive fashion.[91]

The evidence suggests that angeleño women acquired a liberal sensibility in various ways. When young, a fortunate few gained their first exposure at school. In the Sepúlveda/Mott collection at the Los Angeles County Museum for Natural History we find an old, undated grammar lesson by Francisca Sepúlveda, daughter of José, the alcalde who confronted Alvarado in 1837, and granddaughter of María Serrano, one of the women who challenged their men to fight. The exercise, of which only half survives, is on ruled paper. Francisca, born in 1826, probably completed the assignment in the latter part of the 1830s.[92] She wrote: "la pereza ha sido siempre . . ." or in English, "the lazy girl (or woman) has always been the . . ."[93] The line, undoubtedly part of a moral exercise, emphasized that liberals wanted women to adopt a diligent personality.[94]

When sitting in school with boys, as she probably did, Francisca also slaved over Terence and Pythagoras. Apparently, Francisca was not the only woman who learned about the classics in school. Osio invites the thought that some angeleño women seemed quite familiar with figures from antiquity. He said that the "distinguished mothers" of Los Angeles behaved like the women of "ancient history" when they told their men to return home victorious or die bravely in battle. From reading his words, it is Osio, and not the women, who employed classical imagery. But it could be that Osio only repeated what the women expressed. They, rather than Osio, invoked the ancients to bolster the spirits of angeleño men. If so, some "distinguished mothers" of Los Angeles had heeded a teacher's words and learned about Romans, Spartans, and Gauls.

Many women, though, would be too old for lessons. María Serrano, for example, Francisca's grandmother, would not labor over a grammar book or sit before an instructor.[95] But Serrano, when challenging her son José Sepúlveda to fight Alvarado, seemed quite capable of citing the ancients. If she did not sit in a schoolhouse, she found her inspiration elsewhere.

Serrano and her compatriots would not have to look far. Reading materials could deliver the instruction that awakened the consciousness of angeleño women. In the Coronel family papers we find two issues of the woman's journal, *Panoramas de las señoritas*.[96] The periodicals, one from October 20, 1842, the other, a month later, dated November 10, came from Mexico City.[97] Conservatives could have produced the magazines, but, as we will see, the references to self-improvement, the ancients, and the wish to create the hombre nuevo, reflect liberal aspirations.

The November issue gives lessons in confidence. Stories of famous women fill the first half; one, a biography on Delilah, implies that a man's brute strength does not always prevail. A quick mind, the reader learned, worked best. But the periodical, though it praises mothers and wives, cannot say that women are smarter than their male counterparts. In nineteenth-century Mexico, the publishers often took care not to offend a man's sensibilities. A woman, the magazine says, has a greater talent for guile, perhaps a more delicate way of describing intelligence. "Delilah," we learn, used "trickery," to pull out the "secret of [Samson's] strength."[98]

Other articles follow, each one saying that the woman had to tend to her own needs. Longevity, announced one essay, depended on "good teeth, regular circulation, a slower pulse, [and frequent] exercise." At all times, declared the essay, a woman needed to possess "latent rather than obvious emotions." One more article took up the topic of hygiene. When a mother tended to her charges, she should know how warm weather heated the body and caused discomfort. Perspiration would run in torrents, and once the body turned hot, good humor waned, with reason evaporating next. A good mother, lectured the piece, needed to understand what clothes cooled the heated brow. "It is wrong [to say]," the reader learned, that "cotton is less healthy than hemp and linen."[99]

The October issue of *Panoramas* reveals why women needed good health and a quick mind, or what the magazine calls "cleverness." As one article declared, women needed to toughen their sons. A contemporary author, however, did not compose the appeal. The editors looked to antiquity and translated "To the Mothers of Families," a letter Theana, the "wife of [the Greek thinker] Pythagoras," addressed to her friend Eulabia.[100] When Theana counseled her friend, she provided wisdom a mother in Mexico City, or Los Angeles for that matter, would find interesting. "I know you want to raise your sons carefully," Theana explained. But in a stern tone that might please liberals she added, "a pleasant education [for boys] will produce nothing more than slaves." A mother may be at a loss about what to do next. Theana, anticipating liberal sentiment, showed the way. "If you want to make men out of your sons," she announced, "remove them from excessive care; let their education be austere." Theana, like those who desired the hombre nuevo, wanted sons with a taste for hardship. The boys needed sinew and muscle, not the fleshy folds of a dandy, to find success. "Let them get used to heat and cold . . . and hunger and thirst," Theana lectured. Such suffering taught sons "to be agreeable to their peers, and respectful to their superiors."[101]

The next article, in a sequence that possibly was no accident, added that the severe, stern habits men learned from mothers required an educated woman. Josefina Ballecchery, the author, apparently did not care if she offended men. She declared, "you can judge the civilization of a people by seeing how much liberty is granted women." Open a school for women, she argued, "so that [their] intelligence will not be subjugated."[102]

The dates of the *Panoramas* issues, while hinting at a problem with the evidence, only demonstrate that a steady stream of periodicals reached California. Each issue comes from 1842, six years after Alvarado's attack. But the possibility exists that some women's magazines had circulated in California for years. The historian Jane Herrick explains that the first woman's magazine, *El Aguila Mexicana*, appeared in 1823.[103] No copy of *El Aguila* has surfaced in Los Angeles, but Mexican newspapers and periodicals often came north in ships or a horseman's saddlebag. Bancroft suggests that in the 1820s, *La Gaceta de México*, a newspaper from the national capital, gained quite a following in provincial settlements.[104] Perhaps alongside *La Gaceta* appeared *El Aguila* or other publications that suited a woman's taste.

When the printed word failed, as would be the case because few women could read, the liberal message found other outlets. Women, like men, could organize a reading cabinet, in which one, out loud, would hold forth from a published work for the benefit of friends and neighbors. If women felt so disposed, they could attend the dramas staged by visiting companies and see the players address political topics. Later, when the reading cabinet was done for the day or the performers had left town, the women could use different venues to exchange ideas. At market, after church, perhaps when doing laundry along the Los Angeles River, wives and mothers had occasion to discuss what they learned.

Admittedly, a penchant for coming together to talk may not confirm that angeleño women always discussed political matters. A child's first steps, or a spouse's troublesome conduct, would often command attention. In other moments, some women likely recognized that their backgrounds frustrated communication. Osio's "distinguished mothers," individuals who presumably came from established families, might not always associate with more impoverished women. As for the "tortilla makers" or "excellent cooks," the humbler women who prepared food for angeleño troops in 1836, some possibly disliked their more elegant counterparts.

Nonetheless, at some point most women recognized that they had to abide by the limitations imposed by men. The "distinguished mothers" seemed quite familiar with the pains of deference. Some were child brides, who, as they grew older, possibly resented how their families had pushed them into an arranged marriage. María Serrano, the woman who challenged her son, José Sepúlveda, and other angeleño men to do battle, was fifteen, by only three weeks, when she stood at the altar.[105] The "tortilla makers" and "excellent cooks," meanwhile, faced other difficulties. Unable to obtain any help for their domestic duties, they cooked, cleaned, lugged water from the Los Angeles River, and when done, they prepared for the same round of chores the following day.

Eager to ease their burdens, some, if not many, had sufficient opportunity to know that liberal thought brought them benefit. In their meetings together, no matter how formal or casual the encounters, they found confirmation, or discovered for the first time that by nurturing the hombre nuevo they acquired authority, even if it was but a wisp in relation to the powers commanded by men. The space between privilege and limitation offered a meager opening, but in the area that emerged they found the consciousness to address their circumstances.

When the opportunity arose to claim some advantage, as it did when Governor Alvarado advanced on Los Angeles, women seized the moment. They called on men to act like men. Any suggestion that girls could marry whom they wished gave mothers a chance to berate husbands and sons for failing to protect the family's integrity. The man who wondered how he would fare before cannon or rifles received a kiss and reassuring words that he would survive. For the man who ignored the call to arms, wives and mothers questioned his courage, or worse, doubted his manhood. As Osio recalled, the women insisted that they would rather watch the man "die on the battlefield" than see him survive by resorting to "disgraceful escape."[106] When the man fell, they treated his wounds, or if death carried him off, they buried him. The boy who watched and heard the mother's exhortations acquired lessons in discipline that only a mother could provide. The daughters, meanwhile, rejoiced that they had a chance to wed the man of their choice. As events would confirm, they often had little say in selecting their spouse, but the girls knew that marriage might present them with abilities they otherwise would not possess.

The liberal climate of Los Angeles, if as extensive as we think, allowed women to act. But, when defying the husband or any other male, the woman knew that boldness had its limits. A woman who went too far might risk a black eye. The wife or daughter who silently endured insult and attack did not go far enough. Somewhere, in between the rebellious act and compliance, flourished the space in which some women found refuge. In this world, where the roles of man and woman sometimes inverted, wife and grandmother, a daughter or sweetheart possibly understood that if they nourished the seed and imprint, the austere, sober qualities a liberal wished to pass on to the nation, they could improve their prospects.

Children

Children, meanwhile, the tabula rasa, or blank slate on which teachers inscribed the design for the hombre nuevo, bore the liberals' hopes for the nation. The youngsters seemed the best candidates to receive the seed, or liberal imprint. As we will discuss, the youngsters went to school, sat in class, read edifying material, and took tests to prepare for positions of responsibility. Of course, a conservative might have pondered how to educate children. But, more than anyone, liberals grasped that Mexico's progress and deliverance from a colonial past would only occur if children received good schooling. An adult's formation remained critical, but he, or she, often had habits that defied improvement. A child, though, held more promise. Even if not the innocent creature many imagined—going to school, minding elders, and heeding commands sometimes failed to invite cooperation—the child exhibited sins teachers and parents could easily correct. Recognizing that a classroom's lessons would help transform Mexico, José Luis Mora expressed the hopes of liberal compatriots when he declared that education was "a work of regeneration."[107]

Lest fancy carry us away, we do not say that the Mexican child, in the nation's interior, or elsewhere, always received the finest education. Throughout Mexico, especially on the republic's fringes where sat California, communities often lacked the resources to instruct youth. Children from wealthy families, or, those who received some sort of bequest, often went abroad to acquire learning. Most young people, though, had no such opportunities.

Despite disappointment, the liberals continued hoping, wishing really, to teach children lessons in appropriate conduct. The historian Anne Staples notes that a curriculum in the newly independent Mexico tried to emphasize a "spirit of investigation."[108] The child learned that elected government, with its encouragement of debate and compromise, surpassed the orthodoxy once promoted by the Spanish crown. Catholicism remained important, but the spectacle of a religious procession or a priest chanting prayers yielded to simpler, more introspective devotions. Prayer, the sacraments, and instruction in the catechism seemed surer ways to nurture the soul. Just as important, a child learned how to apply initiative. But excessive care for one's advancement, a worry that liberals confronted when discussing the man's nature, could splinter the nation. So to temper and control the hunt for profit, teachers reminded young people that respect for neighbors, not necessarily ambition, should drive one's spirit.[109]

The angeleños shared the liberal resolve to overcome all obstacles and instruct children. We make our case by examining one event. In July of 1844, students gave orations at the end of the school year, an annual event to which the ayuntamiento invited the entire populace. One student, Cayetano Arenas, aged nineteen, received polite applause, perhaps even a cheer or two, when he rose to recite his presentation from memory, or read the words he composed on paper.[110] Young Arenas spoke in a cadence and rhythm that accorded with the liberals' wish to create the hombre nuevo. The boy emphasized that he and his fellow students used education to sharpen their minds: "As useless it is for me to find the right words . . . [when] the illustrious body assigned a teacher to us on January 15 [seven months prior] we knew not even the sounds of letters and as a consequence we were ignorant of all the characters which comprise our language."

Discipline helped the students learn. "We would not find ourselves on the road to knowledge," he announced, unless "we [controlled] our disorderly passions." But the quest to resist the pleasures of the flesh, Arenas added, sometimes required help from the Almighty. "Religion," Arenas explained, "obligated" the students to exercise restraint. A sense of denial provided a feeling of accomplishment, but he notes that sacrifice offered other rewards. By acquiring discipline, the students entered the "temple of [knowledge] whose doors would be opened . . . wide." The students, though, did not forget that their elders helped them succeed. Arenas explained that "words of gratitude offer poor tribute" to the parents. But he hoped that when he and his classmates started families they would "receive in our maturity the benefits" that they now lavished on their elders. As for the "respectable body," the ayuntamiento, Arenas, again emphasizing that he expressed the will of his peers, "asks the Supreme Creator to fill you . . . the [municipal leaders] with the gifts you bestowed on us."[111]

The oration's phrasing and elegant imagery, even more impressive in the original Spanish, suggests careful instruction. Young Arenas had the presence of mind to pay the proper tributes. He honored God and worked in a good word for the discipline favored by liberals. Then he turned to his family and expressed his thanks. Finally, perhaps with a bow or some other flourish—young Arenas seemed quite capable of making some grand gesture—he hailed the ayuntamiento. A parent would help dispense lessons, but a teacher provided more guidance. The instructor lectured, used flattery when need be, and perhaps brandished a ruler to teach young Arenas how to deliver an oration.[112] The writing, too—Arenas had to pen his words first—shows that a teacher offered lessons in composition. When Arenas wrote, over his shoulder, watching, ready to scratch out an offending phrase or word, the teacher, or an aide to the teacher, stood by, saying that this word is too prosaic, that one too abstract; avoid this construction; emphasize this point but not that one.

The instructors who helped Arenas, or any other angeleño child, possessed many talents. At times, soldiers fulfilled their duty by serving in the classroom. In 1844, for instance, the teacher who directed young Arenas was Guadalupe Medina, a lieutenant in the Mexican army.[113] Some primers children used in class could be, at times, the creations of Agustín Zamorano, an army captain who served in Monterey and San Diego. Zamorano brought the first printing press to California and, no doubt aware that shipping schoolbooks from Mexico could exact a dear price, he designed and produced the materials teachers assigned.[114] The primers numbered several pages and on the last page, right below the final line of type, the signature "Agustín V. Zamorano y Corral" appeared. The captain had a sense of play. In one exercise in which children read and copied the alphabet with each letter beginning a different word, he began the sequence with "Agustín" and concluded with "Zamorano."[115]

Priests also spent time in the classroom. In 1836, when the teaching post fell vacant, the ayuntamiento invited Father Alejo Bachelot to instruct angeleño children. The cleric made quite an impression. When he received notice of his new assignment in Hawaii, the ayuntamiento asked Bachelot's superiors in Santa Barbara to rescind the order. The request failed, and many in the populace mourned Bachelot's departure.[116] The enthusiasm for clerics persisted through time. Four years later, the municipal body asked the priest in Los Angeles—his name is not recorded—to help share the teaching load with the lone instructor. Though no answer appears in the ayuntamiento minutes, the priest probably agreed to lend his services.[117]

Most times, though, a person who was neither a priest nor an army officer accepted the offer to teach.[118] Salaries might come sporadically, but when the ayuntamiento made good on payday, the reward probably attracted a talented instructor rather than a misfit with nothing else to do. In 1833, the ayuntamiento paid Francisco Pantoja 105 pesos for teaching angeleño youth.[119] The sum is impressive, at least in relation to the money available to spend. A year later, in 1834, the treasurer reported that the city had collected more than 919 pesos in taxes and fees.[120] If the ayuntamiento collected the same amount of money in 1833—for which year we have no tabulation of Los Angeles' revenue—it appears that nearly an eighth of the city's income could go to the teacher's salary.

The pot turned sweeter in later years. In 1844, the alcalde Manuel Requena asked the governor to help finance the angeleño school.[121] Public education, explained Requena, required at least ninety pesos a month from January through July.[122] The total approached 630 pesos, but Requena pared down his request to an even six hundred. The money, which the governor agreed to provide, though he cut the amount another one hundred pesos, would still provide a handsome salary. Even if the rent—to pay for the building—or other expenses consumed two-thirds of the money granted by the governor, and in all honesty we do not know how the ayuntamiento spent the funds, the instructor would still earn at least 150 pesos teaching.

Most persons who chose to work in a Los Angeles classroom, especially after 1830, possessed, with some exceptions, liberal temperaments. The military claimed its share of reactionaries, but, as we saw before, in many parts of California, Los Angeles included, men with more radical views often donned a uniform.[123] Private citizens with liberal dispositions also took up teaching. The Híjar-Padrés colony, some of whose members embraced liberal beliefs, disbanded soon after arriving in California. Several individuals, rather than return to Mexico, found work in a Los Angeles classroom. Victor Prudon, for instance, prior to the time he joined the vigilantes in 1836, tried teaching. One can only wonder if his lessons smoked with the fervor he applied to his quest as city avenger. José Zenon Fernández, a member of the expedition like the others, helped out in the classroom for part of 1838.[124] The same year, Ygnacio Coronel, another colonist, worked as a teacher, and once more the year after. Antonio Coronel, Ygnacio's son, helped his father and during the American period continued the family avocation by helping establish the first public school in Los Angeles.[125]

The performance of Cayetano Arenas, judging by his choice of words and demeanor, no doubt convinced parents that their youngsters would receive a decent education. By 1840, so many children crammed the schoolhouse that the ayuntamiento wondered if the parish priest would help teach another "forty to forty five boys" in the rectory.[126] The lay instructor possibly taught an equal or greater number, suggesting that two teachers had between them eighty to ninety charges. Four years later, the alcalde Manuel Requena reported to the provincial governor that the school "is absolutely full with 102 youth."[127] He was so confident of the school's success that Requena believed that Los Angeles needed a new schoolhouse "with the capacity of holding two hundred or more students."[128]

An increasing number of students in 1844 gave flight to all sorts of ambitions. Requena, for instance, wished to see more girls attend school. There is no way to tell how many girls received lessons, but save for a fortunate few, not enough sat in class. Requena even named three teachers, all women, one each for the first, second, and third grades, to instruct the angeleños' sisters and daughters. Requena apparently expected that the new schoolhouse would have one room for girls, another for boys. But the alcalde provided little elaboration. His plan for a girl's education disappeared, and neither Requena nor his colleagues mentioned the topic again.[129] The same year, popular enthusiasm for education convinced three priests that the angeleños could support a college "for both sexes."

They proposed that citizens could donate money to finance construction and hire faculty. This idea, however, also disappeared from the record.[130]

Nevertheless, if he was so inclined, Requena could boast of other accomplishments. The pupils, out of the 575 gente de razón youngsters tabulated by the 1844 census, account for nearly one in six children in Los Angeles. (Few Indians, if any, attended lessons.) If all could read, as we think they did, they would join the eighty-eight literate men mentioned before in the 1847 padrón. The men who could peruse a text three years into the future probably knew how to do so in 1844. Together, children and adult males, we cannot be sure of the mature women who could read, would total 190 people. They accounted for more than ten percent of the angeleño inhabitants in 1844, the last year we have a full record of the city's population in the Mexican period. (The city had 1,847 gente de razón.) If our proportion is correct, the number of literate people in Los Angeles doubled the national average of five percent.

Even with one, perhaps two teachers providing instruction at any given time, it is a wonder that scores of children learned anything. But if young Arenas acquired his learning and poise in a Los Angeles classroom, then teachers proved quite talented in handling many youngsters. The curriculum alone seemed demanding. Ygnacio Coronel, the secretary of the ayuntamiento in 1844, explained that Lieutenant Medina taught students "writing, arithmetic, analytical thinking, the pronunciation of language, the rules of writing, whole numbers and fractions."[131]

Medina may have had the intelligence to master all the subjects, but how he passed this information to students seems more interesting. He had to teach more than one hundred pupils. Teaching would be difficult enough with a small class, but with many more students, and all of different ages, the challenge increased. At nineteen, Cayetano Arenas was the oldest; the youngest could very well have been four. Medina, too, if he dreamed like others of creating the hombre nuevo, would need time to teach his pupils the required ideals and principles. Perhaps in the scheme of things, it was not the instructor who mattered, though a gifted teacher remained a prized talent. Apparently, the ayuntamiento and parents considered the form of instruction more valuable.

The angeleño teaching method followed practices first tried in Mexico. Many liberals in the home republic, and at times conservatives, recognized at independence that few qualified teachers existed to instruct great numbers of students. More important, at least to liberals, the curriculum needed to teach students the habits and critical thinking any nation needed to progress. In 1822, prominent residents in Mexico City agreed that the philosophy of Joseph Lancaster, an English Quaker, offered the most promise and they established a philanthropic society, La compania lancasteriana, to teach the city's poor.[132]

Lancaster relied on one teacher to preside over a class of one to three hundred students. As is evident, one person could not instruct a packed classroom. But, in a technique called mutual learning, the instructor taught the best pupils, who, in turn, would teach the next brightest students, and so on. In Mexico City, Lancaster's ideas underwent some revision. But the idea of having one student instruct another remained. The Mexican teacher held class in a large hall where students sat ten to a table. At the front table appeared the slowest students—ability, as well as age, determined ranking—and behind those came a group with more talent. The progression continued until the highest rank sat in the back. A monitor, an older student trained by the teacher, sat at each table and helped instruct the pupils. The instructor, sitting on a raised platform, wrote the subject or lesson on a blackboard hanging behind him.

As an example, we imagine the students' day. With a monitor at the table, and having an hour to give the lesson, the pupils probably began the morning by copying Bible verses. Most times, students wrote on tablets to complete the exercise. If the school was poor and no tablets appeared, or there were not enough to go around, students used a box of sand to scratch out letters and phrases. At the conclusion of an hour the teacher rang a bell, and wrote on the blackboard that arithmetic would be the next subject. All switched, students poor in numbers sat at the first table, with the next brightest groups extending to the back. The monitor who was gifted at writing, but not so at arithmetic, moved to the table more suited to his talents. The shuffling continued throughout the day, with lessons commencing at eight and ending at five. The only break came at noon, when all had time to eat lunch.[133]

When the Lancaster system came to Los Angeles is not known. In 1844, an ayuntamiento inventory counted one table, six benches, and thirty-odd books, for "una escuela lancasteriana"—a Lancaster school.[134] The same year, the ayuntamiento secretary noted that the instructor, "Lieutenant Medina, taught by means of 'enseñaza mutua,'" or mutual learning.[135] But it could be that teachers in Los Angeles had used Lancaster's approach for nearly a decade. Most of the teachers attached to the Híjar-Padrés expedition came from Mexico City, or parts nearby, the area of mutual learning's first application in 1822. It is likely they had learned the technique before they left and found Los Angeles a good place to use their skills.[136]

With children before them, the instructors relied on displays of authority to educate children about the liberal purpose.[137] Authority, though, did not mean that teachers always relied on punishing the body. It came in subtler form, gaining manifestation in the word or opinion of onlookers. A teacher judged students. The students, in turn, evaluated each other. At the end of the school year, as we saw with Cayetano Arenas, some students stood before city residents and faced the severest test of all when they presented their orations. The classroom, and its arrangement, with desks open to the instructor's scrutiny, reminded the student that he, or she, would never escape judgment. Some lessons, especially those involving grammar and writing, emphasized even more that when seemingly alone or absorbed in some assignment, the eye of Providence, and the eye of the law, indeed, often the same thing, still watched and judged each act. With authority observing every move, as the school lessons implied, the child internalized the responsibilities of the hombre nuevo. A priest, a parent, or the magistrate could not always be present to pass judgment. But within the conscience, the gaze of authority acquired greater power, reminding students that when temptation beckoned they should keep the mind and hands absorbed in some worthy task.[138]

At the same time, children learned that initiative and application determined merit. In the colonial period, blood or family ties often distinguished one person from another. Matters had supposedly changed in the liberal period. A citizen rose or fell on his talents. If one worked hard prosperity, followed by the recognition of peers, would come. But when one refused to labor, or wanted to rely on the reputation of family or friends to advance, rewards would become meager. Failure awaited, with poverty and starvation punishing anyone who refused to make an effort.

A Lancaster classroom, at least in theory, imparted the required lessons for the liberal age. Diligence won favor from students and teachers; lack of effort or the occasional wisecrack earned the culprit ridicule, and on occasion, a quick whack. We admit that the following example comes from Mexico, but what prevailed in the home republic would have occurred in Los Angeles as well. Once a week, sometimes more, the schoolmaster held recitations. He called on individual students to stand up and answer questions on the material. If the youngster answered correctly, he won sweets or advanced to the next rank. Mistakes could prove costly, however. An unlucky respondent sometimes wore a sign around his neck denouncing his "lazy" or "foolish" habits. In some cases an egregious or flippant answer risked a rap on the knuckles or the ordeal of kneeling in front of the instructor with outstretched arms. For those who answered sincerely but failed to supply the right response, they suffered a demotion and would sink one, perhaps two ranks.[139]

In Los Angeles, with limited supplies for instruction, the pains of performance possibly took other forms. Each student could not huddle over an exercise book, but had to share. For a reading exercise, they had to scan the text out loud, their pronunciation subject to quick correction by a teacher or monitor. A classmate's giggle or the jealous glance from a rival would remind everyone that peers sat in judgment as well.

Exercises in penmanship delivered even more substantial lessons. Several surviving texts allow us to envision their use. Many primers contained a half page of text, with room beneath so novices could copy a printed example. Some had an entire page filled with print while the opposite leaf remained blank for practice. Most primers invited students to copy the alphabet and the numbers zero through nine. Writing these characters and figures for the first time could overwhelm young hands and grids appeared to guide unsteady pens across a page. With few primers available, many students likely shared the same volume and demonstrated their talents in full view of others. A student with peers standing beside him probably took his place at the blackboard to practice writing letters and numbers. Or the student sat at his table, cradling a slate on his knee. If primers were few, slates could be equally rare. And as one youngster demonstrated his writing ability, classmates stood behind and watched, awaiting their chance to take up the chalk.

The content of the exercises offered instruction as well. The 1844 inventory, for instance, which listed the objects in a classroom, added that the children used primers, readers, and religious catechisms.[140] Of these items, religious catechisms probably seemed one of the best means to indoctrinate children. In the Coronel papers, we find a religious tract, combined with grammar lessons and multiplication tables.[141] An individual, even in private, can never rest, the text implies, for the soul is constantly put to the test. To a question about temptation—do not forget that queries and responses comprised most catechisms—we read the answer, "The enemies of the soul are three: the world, demons, and the flesh." How can one fight the lure of forbidden conduct? The answer suggests that in private, as in public, one must exercise discipline. "The cardinal virtues are four," we learn, "prudence, justice, fortitude, and moderation."

Other lessons fill the Coronel tract. The next twenty pages speak of the proper posture for writing. But again we wonder for what purpose a student should sit straight and tall. By the standards of nineteenth century medicine in Mexico, a straight back and rigid countenance promoted good heath.[142] At another look, however, a body at straight lines revealed one's serious intent. "What is the first thing that must be learned to write well?" a query asks. "Place the arm," one is told, "and take the pen with comfort and skill." The limbs and posture properly arranged, the mind, too, alert, because to remain in a stiff position concentration would seem necessary, the student awaited more instruction. The last twenty pages emphasize that one must always possess fine character. Be brave, the pamphlet declares, like San Justine and San Pastor, "one . . . nine, the other seven." Each went to fight the Moors, "but was beheaded." Presumably they died bravely. If either boy slackened in defending the faith, the Almighty would not look kindly on their souls.[143]

What one wrote on a slate for neighbors was not an empty exercise, but a preparation for other behaviors to be etched across the spirit. "The good you do," announces the Coronel piece, "will be engraved on your heart."[144] Surely, what pleased God also delighted magistrates and ayuntamiento members. "Fear God the avenger," the student learned, "and all that may offend him."[145] The thought of an angry God would make quite an impact. Perhaps, when alone, a student might think twice about catching a quick nap or indulging some other whim for fear of being caught. Later, when the student matured and entered adult life, any thought about the divine gaze, or its companion, public opinion, could quell temptation.[146]

In another primer, the principalities of heaven and earth find their needs interwoven. The pamphlet, comprising six paragraphs, each in a different cursive, apparently to make a young hand appreciate various styles of writing, presents morals that would please angeleño parents and municipal leaders. In the first paragraph, which the student copied in the required style, a respect for divinity prepared the mind for further lessons. "The fear of God is the beginning of wisdom," the student copied. "He who knows the most understands best his own ignorance."[147]

Moderate habits, the youngster learned in the second paragraph, satisfied the demands of heaven and earth. "Wealth and riches complement all the aspirations and fears of a fool," says the exercise, but "the wise man lives independent of fortune and in all his occupations, his guide is his honor, his nourishment virtue, and the greatness of his soul does not interest or diminish with possessions."[148] Seek knowledge, the final paragraph announces. Faith, the lesson implies, comes through study; apparently, the law, too, its intent divined through study, brought rewards more satisfying than riches. With the senses awakened, the mind and soul sensitive to God's will, the student appreciated his obligations. Work would absorb his talents, but the knowledge that Providence was indeed present would shadow every thought.

As for the person who had no chance to learn, or worse, sat in the classroom and ignored every lesson, life would turn dull. His sensibilities lost, or blunted, he resembled an individual who had lost his sight. "A blind man for whom sunlight is unknown," the exercise tells the student, "cannot see the variety of color, nor the beauty of women." The danger, we learn, is that with the light struck from the eyes and selfishness consuming the spirit, the unlucky person "will be like beasts that grow fat from grazing, or become thin from work." For such a person, "virtue, vice, honor, [and] infamy are eternally equal." His mind and soul clouded, even blackened by sin, experience nothing. Only money, or the promise of earning money, excited the spirit. But profit appealed to the worst instincts. Selfishness, ambition, the grab for glory, would provide satisfaction only at the outset. Over time, an individual would lose vitality when succumbing to greed. Or, as the lesson insists, the world turns colorless when wealth "is everything."[149]

The lessons designed for children could have invited various reactions. An impressionable youngster possibly took the maxims to heart. Another could be stricken with anxiety. And another could have ignored the messages altogether. With such varied responses, one might think an angeleño school modestly successful in educating youngsters. But the point is not whether the angeleños managed to impart a liberal ethos to the little ones. Of greater interest is that they tried at all. In making the attempt they lived up to the idea of passing the nation's imprint to children. Into the youngster went the idea for the hombre nuevo, where it flourished or died away. Perhaps, for every failure or misstep, the liberal seed did take root in some students. In 1852, an unknown angeleño wrote to a newspaper and declared, "In all the civilized world, school is considered one of the primary necessities of man, and in republics, the major hope [is] to create good citizens."[150] The words, the imagery, the allusion to liberal notions— think of the word "republics"—presents the thought that the writer attended an angeleño school. Perhaps, from these words, we can surmise that more than a few students paid attention in class, with some taking to heart the idea of the hombre nuevo, the new man.

We have come a long way to explain the term "exterminate." The liberal lessons of Mexico, what we call the seed or the nation's imprint, appeared in books and pamphlets. Mexican immigrants, and any angeleño who followed the liberal purpose, brought the printed word to life by offering instruction. Men learned they had particular responsibilities, as did the women. Children received even greater attention. They, because of their youth, seemed best suited to learn the responsibility and diligence liberals hoped to inculcate in the nation.

But "exterminate" brings up other subjects. Perhaps more than any other term or phrase we have plucked from the 1846 petition, "exterminate," with its implicit hope to destroy the Indian, offers what we seek. Once the Indian died or kneeled in submission, the angeleños could seek some tie to Mexico. Sometimes distant, even infuriating, but valued by many, Mexico remained a beacon. Mexico, often in the form of liberal appeals, lifted the angeleños out of their isolation and connected them to experiences that life in California would never provide. If they remained alone, or in thrall of another power, the angeleños dreaded to contemplate the consequences. As Antonio María Osio argued, without Mexico all the gente de razón, not just those in Los Angeles, would lose "their nationality and all they hoped to create."[151]

The angeleño regard for Mexico adds more perspective to the difficulties modern Californians face in the new millennium. California features many individuals of Mexican ancestry, a population that will only increase in the coming years. With more awareness about Mexican contributions to California's growth, modern residents may take heart that those from the south of their border and their descendants are not strangers, but merely a people who have long made their way north.

The angeleño example may also make those in the present reconsider the way they imagine California's past. History, as we know, often encourages nostalgia in which some admire the qualities and attitudes of a distant age. In the case of California, scholars and residents often see the Mexican era as a time of innocence. One textbook on California history calls the period "Arcadia," and focuses on the ranchos to describe a land rich with bounty.[152] The thought of an abundant, plentiful past illustrates, by way of contrast, the imperfections that now blight the present. For some time now, modern Californians have lamented the price of modernity. Freeways carve up the landscape. Housing tracts stretch into lands once covered in orange groves or strawberry fields. Cities, meanwhile, once reputed to be safe havens, now teem with immigrants, many of them from Mexico, the land, ironically enough, that helped create the myth of a California Arcadia.

The California romance can suit any number of approaches. For those who say that the Mexican occupation of California accomplished nothing, or at most encouraged ceaseless squabbling, the American victory in 1847 seems appropriate. The californios failed to use their initiative and thus ceded the province to a people who could better use the land's resources. It would not work to say that the angeleños and their californio contemporaries often valued industry more than leisure.

On the other hand, the insistence on California's lost glory comforts individuals who dread the problems of modern times. Needing the reassurance that at one time life seemed much simpler, some Californians look back to an inviolate, pristine past where the problems of modern times were absent. Many favor political measures that promise to restore California to its idyllic state, or they hail leaders who somehow will reestablish the Golden Age.

But as the angeleños demonstrated, California was never an innocent place. The angeleños aspired to achieve much, although they did not have much time to experience success. They often succumbed to fear, with many believing that Indians presented a threat. The angeleños, to their discredit, found reassurance by punishing the Indians and claiming that only they, and they alone, could enjoy the liberal promise. Few grasped the irony that they violated, rather than fulfilled, the liberal ideal when they abused the Native Californians.

Perhaps, here, among the desires and thwarted ambitions of the angeleños, we find the most worthy lesson for the current age. By mistreating Indians, the angeleños showed modern Californians that when all do not succeed no one does. On one side will be those who insist that they only seek to preserve California's resources for future generations. On the other will stand individuals who feel deprived. The conflict presents some unhappy prospects. The angeleños resolved their difficulties by punishing the Indians. In the modern era, harsh measures may only provoke the unfortunate and impoverished segment of the populace. The prosperous and comfortable residents may think that discipline would bring peace, but as the angeleño example suggests, there will lurk the suspicion that the individual who bears punishment only bides his time to retaliate. Thus, it would be wise to learn what the angeleños never did, and see that the quest to establish tranquility requires other measures. What these methods will involve we leave to abler minds.

To finish, we recall that, at the start, we stopped and wondered what the angeleños wanted. Having examined angeleño aspirations, we can now move on. But before leaving, we mention an angeleño's hope that "another friend ... with a ... pen might continue the story."[153] We pass on that pen, just as others have passed it to us, and wait for our successors to uncover and tell, or perhaps retell, what more the angeleños wanted to say.

Notes

Abbreviations

AP   Archives of the Prefecture
LAA   Los Angeles Archives (Bancroft Library)
LACA Los Angeles City Archives
SCWH Seaver Center for Western History, Los Angeles County Museum of Natural History

Introduction

1. Douglas Monroy, "The Creation and Re-creation of Californio Society," in *Contested Eden, California Before the Gold Rush*, ed. Ramón A. Gutiérrez and Richard Orsi, 173–95 (Berkeley: University of California Press, 1998). David Weber adds that California, along with the territories of New Mexico and Texas, had "weak links to the nation's core" and became "insular." See *The Mexican Frontier, 1821–1846, The American Southwest Under Mexico* (Albuquerque: University of New Mexico Press, 1981), 280. For more about the de facto independence of Mexican California, and by extension, Los Angeles, see Monroy's *Thrown Among Strangers, The Making of Mexican Culture in Frontier California* (Berkeley: University of California Press, 199); Lisbeth Haas, *Conquests and Historical Identities in California, 1769–1936* (Berkeley: University of California Press, 1995); Richard Griswold del Castillo, *The Los Angeles Barrio: A Social History* (Berkeley: University of California Press, 1979), esp. 4–13; and Leonard Pitt, *Decline of the Californios, A Social History of the Spanish-speaking Californians, 1846–1890* (Berkeley: University of California Press, 1966). For an alternate view about life in Mexican California, see Antonio Rios-Bustamante, "Los Angeles, Pueblo and Region, 1781–1850: Continuity and Adaptation on the North Mexican Periphery" (Ph.D. diss., University of California Los Angeles, 1985). Rios-Bustamante turned his dissertation into a book, *Mexican Los Angeles: A Narrative and Pictorial History* (Encino, California: Floricanto Press, 1992). Both works are examples of good scholarship. It is a pity that Dr. Rios-Bustamante is not cited more in the literature. Also consult Howard Nelson, "The Two Pueblos of Los Angeles: Agricultural Village and Embryo Town," *Southern California Quarterly* 59, no. 1 (1977): 1–11.

2. Hubert Howe Bancroft, *The History of California,* 7 vols., (San Francisco: The History Company, 1883–1887), 1:310–52.
3. Mexico did not officially assume control of California until September 26, 1822. On that day Agustin Fernandez de San Vicente, canon of the Durango cathedral, arrived in Monterey and formally declared the authority of the constitutional government. Bancroft, *The History,* 2:445–47.
4. See Kevin Starr, *Americans and the California Dream, 1850–1915* (New York: Oxford University Press, 1973), 24–25; and Pitt, *Decline of the Californios,* 12–13. Also consult Monroy, *Thrown Among Strangers,* 136.
5. It is difficult to untangle the disputes between northern and southern California, but Bancroft makes an attempt. I speak about events that happened in 1835 and 1845. See *The History,* 3:291–92; and 4:519–20.
6. Griswold del Castillo, *The Los Angeles Barrio,* 10–11.
7. Ibid., 11.
8. Bancroft, *The History,* 3: 9n. 418. Montesquieu was very popular in Mexico in the late eighteenth and early nineteenth century. See D. A. Brading, *The First America, The Spanish monarchy, Creole patriots, and the Liberal state* (Cambridge, England: Cambridge University Press, 1991), 566–73 and 652–55. The original document that cites Montesquieu is from the Los Angeles City Archives (hereafter cited as LACA), vol. 2, April 7, 1836, 188–90, Sp. There are at least three different versions of the ayuntamiento records. In the late nineteenth century, Hubert Howe Bancroft commissioned his scribes to copy the original ayuntamiento records. These copies now sit in the Bancroft Library at the University of California, Berkeley. They bear the designation, Los Angeles Archives, or LAA. The originals, all in Spanish, sit in the city clerk's office in Los Angeles. They take the designation Los Angeles City Archives. An English translation accompanies the Spanish originals. As circumstances dictate, we use all three versions. The English version, though, is the least used. Only when the original Spanish is confusing do the English translations come into play.
9. Graph in the *Los Angeles Times,* October 20, 1999, A3.
10. The writer is responding to an article in the *Los Angeles Times* that discussed Mexico's reluctance to extradite criminals, *Los Angeles Times,* B14, Thursday, May 30, 2002. Other observers think the invasion is complete. When watching Enrique Zedillo, then Mexico's President, come to Los Angeles in 1999, a witness declared, "this visit . . . is a victory parade through a conquered California." Mary Beth Sheridan and Dave Lesher, "Zedillo Courts L.A.'s Latino Community," *Los Angeles Times,* A3, May 20, 1999.
11. At least to one person, angeleño seemed to be the preferred name. "Memoria de Don José Francisco Palomares," Thomas Temple Collection, Box 2, File #28, 25, in Spanish, Seaver Center for Western History, Natural History Museum for Los Angeles County (hereafter SCWH). A copy of the dictation made in 1877 to Thomas Savage. The original dictation sits in the Bancroft Library. Palomares describes the Americans preparing to fight the Spanish-speaking residents of Los Angeles: "[The Americans] would increase to 14 and the object of their meeting was to combat the angeleños." Bancroft, though, prefers the word, "Angelinos." See, for example, 3:588.
12. For the story on Calafia, a character from *Las Sergas de Esplandían* (The Exploits of Esplandian), see James Hart, ed., *Companion to California* (Berkeley: University of California Press, 1987), 466. As for the Latin origins of California's name see Bancroft, *The History,* 1:64–65n. 4.

13. For more on the missions and their importance to the formation of the California's identity in the late nineteenth and early twentieth century, see Kevin Starr, *Inventing the Dream, California Through the Progressive Era* (New York: Oxford University Press, 1985), esp. 31–98.

14. The missions, and their rise and fall, fill volumes. Here follow some significant works: Zephyrin Engelhardt O.F.M., *The Missions and Missionaries of California*, 4 vols. (San Francisco: James Barry and Company, 1913); Gerald Geary A.M., *The Secularization of the California Missions* (Washington D.C.: The Catholic University of America, 1934); Manuel Servín, "The Secularization of the California Missions," *Southern California Quarterly* 47, no. 4 (1965): 133–49; Edwin Beilharz, *Felipe de Neve: First Governor of California* (San Francisco, 1971); Sherburne Cook, "The Indian Versus the Spanish Mission," in *The Conflict Between the California Indian and White Civilization*, 1–194 (Berkeley: University of California Press, 1976); Daniel Garr, "Church-State Boundary Disputes," in *Spanish City Planning in North America*, ed. Dora Crouch, Daniel Garr, and Axel Mundingo, 237–58 (Cambridge, MA: MIT Press, 1987); Daniel Fogel, *Junípero Serra, the Vatican, and Enslavement Theology* (San Francisco: ism Press, 1988); Robert Jackson and Edward Castillo, *Indians, Franciscans, and Spanish Colonization: The Impact of the Mission System on California Indians* (Albuquerque: University of New Mexico Press, 1995).

15. For more discussion, see David Weber, *The Mexican Frontier*, 66–68. Also consult Bancroft, *The History*, 4:48–54; and Antonio Coronel, *Tales of Mexican California*, trans. Doris de Avalle-Arce and ed. Doyce B. Nunis, Jr. (Santa Barbara: Bellerophon Books, 1994), 21–22.

16. *Exposition Addressed to the Chamber of Deputies of the Congress of the Union by Señor Don Carlos Antonio Carrillo, Deputy for Alta California Concerning the Regulation and Administration of the Pious Fund, Mexico, 1831*, trans. and ed. Herbert Ingram Priestley (San Francisco: John Henry Nash, 1938), 6.

17. Ibid., 7.

18. Angustias de la Ord, "Occurrences in Hispanic California," trans. and ed. Francis Price and William H. Ellison (Washington D.C.: Academy of American Franciscan History, 1956), 34. De la Ord is speaking about Padre Magín Catalá.

19. Ibid., 36. De la Ord is describing Padre Narciso Durán.

20. Ygnacio Sepúlveda, "Historical Memorandum to Hubert Howe Bancroft," 1874, trans. Earl Hewitt (Bancroft Library, University of California, Berkeley), 6.

21. Our conclusion comes from the literature. At times record keeping, especially in the early years of settlement, left much to be desired. Nonetheless, the evidence suggests that most settlers came from Mexico. See William Mason, "Alta California's Colonial and Early Mexican Era Population, 1769–1846," in *Regions of La Raza: Changing Interpretations of Mexican American Regional History and Culture*, ed. Antonio Ríos-Bustamante, 169–87 (Encino, California: Floricanto Press, 1993). Also consult Michael Mathes, "Sources in Mexico for the History of Spanish California" *California History* 61, no. 3 (1982): 223–26. Bancroft has a more detailed explanation about the people who settled California. See Bancroft, *The History*, 1:126–39, 1:311–14, 1:341–50. At times, Bancroft admits that he has trouble with the evidence. For example, he says that no manifest for San José, established in 1777, appears until 1781.

22. For more on the plans to populate California, see Salomé Hernández, "No Settlement Without Women: Three Spanish Settlement Schemes, 1790–1800," *Southern California Quarterly* 72 (Fall 1990): 203–33; and Daniel J. Garr, "A Rare and Desolate Place: Population and Race in Hispanic California," *Western Historical Quarterly* 6 (April

1975): 133–48. The other inducements included the cost of transportation, rations, and a stipend. The settlers, in turn, had to promise to stay for a period up to six years.

23. Richard Griswold del Castillo, *The Los Angeles Barrio,* 4–5.

24. For more on Branciforte (later Santa Cruz) and the recruitment of settlers from Mexico, see Bancroft, *The History,* 1:564–73. Branciforte was not a success.

25. For more on the Híjar-Padrés expedition, see C. Alan Hutchinson, *Frontier Settlement in Mexican California* (New Haven: Yale University Press, 1969). Hutchinson says that 239 people came north.

26. *Diaries and Accounts of the Romero Expedition in Arizona and California,* ed. Lowell John Bean and William Mason (Los Angeles: Ward Richie Press, 1962), 86–89. In 1836 alone, one hundred settlers from the Mexican state of Sonora migrated to Los Angeles.

27. Bancroft Research Notes, "Commerce 1841–1848," Heading 1841, Department State Papers, Angeles VI, 77–78. The citation describes the various expeditions that set out from Santa Fe, Mexico. Some expeditions brought settlers, others brought traders, and as we will see in chapter four, some brought trouble. The Research Notes contain the footnotes that Hubert Howe Bancroft used to compile his *History of California.* The Hubert Howe Bancroft Reference Notes, are in the Bancroft Library. The Notes comprise nearly seventy volumes devoted to different aspects of California history. Each volume of the Notes is identified by year and topic. Hence there are individual volumes identified as "Military, 1769–1781," or "Indians, 1848–1850," and so on. Unfortunately, the volumes are not indexed or cataloged. There are no page numbers either, but each item in the volumes is accompanied by a heading listing the year and the source from which Bancroft collected his information. In some instances, the references come from books or documents that are lost or now bear a different name. For more on Mexican migration to California, see Sister Mary Colette Standart "The Sonoran Migration to California, A Study in Prejudice," *Southern California Quarterly* 57 (Fall 1976): 333–57. In the years after Mexico surrendered California to the United States in January 1847, migrants continued to make the trip. By the 1850s, some angeleños had enough of American rule and they returned to Mexico. For more on the angeleño return to Mexico, consult Griswold del Castillo, *The Los Angeles Barrio,* 119–24. To understand how Mexican immigrants continue to keep a flame burning for their native land, see George J. Sánchez, *Becoming Mexican American, Ethnicity, Culture, and Identity in Chicano Los Angeles, 1900–1945* (New York: Oxford University Press, 1993), esp. 17–37. Also see David Gutiérrez, "Migration, Emergent Ethnicity, and the 'Third Space': The Shifting Politics of Nationalism in Greater Mexico," *The Journal of American History,* 86 (September 1999): 451–517. Other works provide more detailed perspectives. Read Albert Camarillo, *Chicanos in a Changing Society: From Mexican Pueblos to American Barrios in Santa Barbara and Southern California, 1848–1930* (Cambridge, MA: Harvard University Press, 1979); and Ricardo Romo, *East Los Angeles: History of a Barrio* (Austin: University of Texas Press, 1982).

28. Enrique Krauze, *Mexico, Biography of Power, A History of Modern Mexico, 1810–1996,* trans. Hank Heifetz (New York: HarperCollins Publishers, 1997), 335. Krauze refers to the inhabitants of Chihuahua, a state in northern Mexico. But the statement could very well apply to the angeleños and their californio compatriots. Octavio Paz, the Mexican man of letters, elaborates on the pull of the Mexican "center." He explains that the center, most of whose influence he attributes to Mexico City, had long exacted a hold over the nation. This influence, Paz says, exceeded all "rational formulation" and became "the order of things." Octavio Paz, *Posdata* (Mexico: Siglo Veintiuno Editores, 1970), 124–25, 132–33.

29. Coronel, *Tales of Mexican California*, 13.
30. As we see in later chapters, the word, "Indian," or in Spanish, "indio," and any variation combined with "indio," such as the term "indios barbaros," contained all the spite and anger the gente de razón wished to convey. The term "gandul," however, seems the only significant exception. The word, from an Arabic term suggesting a youth from modest circumstances who affects an elegant manner, came to describe "savage Indians." Sherburne Cook, *Expeditions to the Interior of California, Central Valley, 1820–1840*, (Berkeley: University of California Press, 1961), 181. For a more complete definition of gandul, see Martín Alonso, *Enciclopedia del idioma, Tomo I*, (Madrid: Aguilar, 1958), 2104.
31. Francisco Santamaria, *Diccionario de mejicanismos* (Mexico, D.F: Editorial Porrua, 1959), 711. The first definition for Mecos is "el indio chichimeca, de este origen o afín de éste." The third definition then adds, "Patán, grosero, indecente, o deshonesto y obsceno, soez; individuo de condición canallesca."
32. For another example on how Indians can shape the self-image of settlers, see James Axtell, "Colonial America Without the Indians," in *After Columbus, Essays in the Ethnohistory of Colonial North America*, ed. James Axtell, 222–43 (New York: Oxford University Press, 1988); Richard Slotkin, *Regeneration Through Violence: The Mythology of the Frontier, 1600–1860* (Middletown, CT: Wesleyan Press, 1977); *The Fatal Environment: The Myth of the Frontier in the Age of Industrialization, 1800–1890* (New York: Athenaeum, 1985); and Michael Rogin, *Fathers and Children: Andrew Jackson and the Subjugation of the American Indian* (New York: Vintage Books, 1979).
33. To confuse matters, any Mexican, who is an individual from a state in Mexico, could also take the name of his point of origin. Someone from Sonora, a state many angeleños could claim as their birthplace, was a *sonorense*. A person originating in Chihuahua, one more state a few angeleños formerly called home, could answer to *chihuahuense*. Or, the points on the compass helped determine identity, with northerner, or *norteño*, providing one of the most common designations.
34. As one example, see the *Pronunciamiento de 24 de Set. 1846*, which Serbulo Varelas wrote in 1846 to resist the invading Americans. Varelas, a Mexican cobbler, penned a document that addressed the angeleños as "Mexicans." See Bancroft, *The History*, 5:310n. 22.
35. See the *Pronunciamiento de San Diego contra el Gefe Politico y Comandante General de California Don Manuel Victoria en 29 de Noviembre y 1 de Diciembre de 1831*. Bancroft, *The History*, 3:202n. 39; 5:310n. 22. He reprints an appeal that addresses the angeleños as Mexican citizens.
36. Antonio María Osio, *The History of Alta California, A Memoir of Mexican California*, ed. and trans. Rose Marie Beebe and Robert M. Senkewicz, (Madison: University of Wisconsin Press, 1996), 343. Beebe and Senkewicz present a good, brief explanation about the various names available to the californios.
37. See Pablo Vejar, "Recuerdo de un viejo," as told to Thomas Savage, 1877. Spanish copy of the original in the Bancroft Library, University of California, Berkeley. The Thomas Temple Collection, Box 2, File #30, 2, SCWH.
38. Osio, *The History of Alta California*, 236. For more on Osio's life, see 6–7. Osio sat on the Los Angeles ayuntamiento, the municipal council, in 1836, and a year later sat on the *diputacion*, a body of notables who assembled in Monterey to advise the governor.
39. Ibid., 232, 236.

40. Juan Avila's description is in his account about the political coup against Governor Manuel Victoria in 1831. Pacheco, who supported Victoria, died during the conflict. Extract from Avila's dictation to Thomas Savage, Thomas Temple II Collection, Box #2, File 8, 2, in Spanish, SCWH.

41. Ibid.

42. Bancroft Reference Notes, "Commerce 1839–1870," Heading 1840, José Arnaz, "Recuerdos," 3. Arnaz lists some of the prices of his goods. The rebozos went for $150. As a sense of scale, in the early to mid-nineteenth century the Mexican peso and the American dollar were of equal value.

43. Pancho Rangel, "La vida de un ranchero" as told to Thomas Temple II, Box 2, File 27, p. 29, in English. SCWH.

44. Don José Joaquin Maitorena to Padre [Tomás] Sánchez, Santa Barbara President to the Mission, 25 September 1828. Thomas Temple II Collection, Box 2, File 25, type-script Spanish and English. SCWH.

45. LACA, Ledger for the period between July 1 and September 30, 1836, vol. 3, 46, Sp. The totals are incomplete, but the ayuntamiento apparently collected 780 pesos during 1836.

46. See the discussion about angeleño men in Chapter Five.

47. For more on the construction of cities in Mexico, see Pamela Voekel, "Peeing on the Palace: Bodily Resistance to Bourbon Reforms in Mexico City" *Journal of Historical Sociology* 5, no. 2 (June 1992): 183–208. Also consult, Francisco de la Meza, "El urbanismo clasico de Ignacio de Castera" *Anales del Instituto de Investigaciones Esteticas* 22 (1954): 93–101.

48. Bancroft, *The History*, 4:629n. 10 For more on the literary societies, see Robert Shafer, *The Economic Societies of the Spanish World, 1763–1821* (Syracuse, New York: Syracuse University Press, 1958). One of the groups that Shafer describes is named "Los Amigos del Pais." The name suggests that the members used their time together to exchange ideas.

49. The ayuntamiento often held public meetings to which all citizens were invited. In one instance, a citizen disagreed with the way the municipal council organized the upcoming election and "read from the fifth book issued by Spain and recognized by the young republic, citing the law of May 19, 1813." See LACA, vol. 3, December 26, 1830, 354, Sp.

50. List of Mexicans in office:

Name	Years	Birthplace
Alcaldes		
Guillermo Cota	1827 and 1829	Baja California
Manuel Requena	1836 and 1844	Yucatan
Luis Arenas	1838	Hermosillo, Sonora
Juan Gallardo	1846	Sonora
José Vicente Guerrero	1848	Alamos, Sonora
Sindico		
Narciso Botello	1835	Los Alamos, Sonora
Manuel Arzaga	1834	Mexico
Antonio Avila	1836	Del Fuerte, Sonora
Antonio María Osio	1836	Baja California

Name	Years	Birthplace
Regidores		
Rafael Guirado	1835 and 1838	Alamos, Sonora
José María Herrera	1836 and 1837	Tepic, Sonora
Rafael Gallardo	1847	Sonora
Luis Jordan	1845 and 1846	Sonora
Francisco Pantoja	1837	Mexico
José María Aguilar	1825 and 1826	Culiacan, Sonora (?)
Juan de Dios Bravo	1835 and 1836	Mexico (?)

An alcalde was usually mayor and chief magistrate; a sindico served as treasurer and city prosecutor; a regidor was an alderman who represented a district. Admittedly the sources convey some doubt about the national origin of José María Aguilar and Juan de Dios Bravo. But the evidence suggests they came from Mexico.

51. LACA, vol. 2, November 13, 1836, 276–78, Sp.
52. Bancroft, *The History*, 3:483n. 4. The ayuntamiento delivered its decree between November 29 and December 6, 1836.
53. Bancroft, *The History*, 3:486–87n. 10. The writer is Luis Castillo Negrete. He wrote his letter on December 5 or 6, 1836.
54. Juan Bautista Alvarado, the man who seized the governor's chair, marched south to impose his authority, and remained in office. See chapter five for more information about Alvarado's attempt to remain in office.
55. Osio, *The History of Alta California*, 256n. 48.
56. Bancroft, *The History*, 5:310n. 22.
57. José Francisco Palomares to Thomas Savage, 1877, Thomas Temple II collection, Box 2, File 28, 25, in Spanish. SCWH.
58. *El Clamor Público*, August 2, 1856. Chicano Studies Library, University of California, Berkeley. For the best account about what happened to the angeleños under American rule, see Leonard Pitt, *The Decline of the Californios, A Social History of the Spanish-speaking Californians, 1846–1890* (Berkeley: University of California Press, 1965).
59. Many scholars have discussed the californio dislike for Mexico. For one of the most recent interpretations, see Monroy, "The Creation and Re-creation of Californio Society," 173–93.
60. The literature on Mexico's condition in the first years of independence is vast, but we list a few significant works: Timothy Anna, *Forging Mexico, 1821–1835* (Lincoln: University of Nebraska Press, 1998); D. A. Brading, *The First America: The Spanish Monarchy, Creole Patriots, and the Liberal State, 1492–1867* (Cambridge, England: Cambridge University Press, 1991); Michael Costeloe, *The Central Republic in Mexico, 1835–1846, Hombres de Bien in the Age of Santa Anna* (Cambridge, England: Cambridge University Press, 1993); Stanley Green, *The Mexican Republic: The First Decade, 1823–1832* (Pittsburgh: University of Pittsburgh Press, 1987); Charles Hale, *Mexican Liberalism in the Age of Mora, 1821–1853* (New Haven: Yale University Press, 1968); Jaime E. Rodríguez, *Down from Colonialism, Mexico's Nineteenth Century Crisis* (Los Angeles, Chicano Studies Research Center Publications no. 3: University of California Press, 1983).
61. Costeloe, *The Central Republic in Mexico, 1835–1846*, 2–3.
62. Timothy Anna, *Forging Mexico*, 1–33. Anna goes into great detail explaining why, at least to some residents, Mexico would not exist as a nation.

63. For a discussion on the angeleños creating a unique way of life in California, see Griswold del Castillo, *The Los Angeles Barrio,* 10–13; and Monroy, "Creation and Re-creation," 180–81. Also consult Lisbeth Haas, *Conquests and Historical Identities in California,* 34, 35–36; Kevin Starr, *Americans and the California Dream, 1850–1915,* 25; Monroy, *Thrown Among Strangers,* 136; C. Alan Hutchinson, *Frontier Settlement in Mexican California: The Híjar-Padrés Colony and Its Origins, 1769–1835* (New Haven: Yale University Press, 1969), esp. 325–26.

64. For more on Mexico's failure to secure California, see Pitt, *Decline of the Californios,* 1–5.

65. Bancroft, *The History,* 3:432–35.

66. Bancroft, *The History,* 3:442. Literally Chico's remark is: "I leave small but I will return big." I have chosen to give his words a more colloquial rendering.

67. Pitt, *Decline of the Californios,* 23–24. Pitt also explains that France also received californio overtures.

68. Douglas Monroy, "The Creation and Re-creation of Californio Society," 180–81.

69. Sepúlveda, "Historical Memorandum," 3.

70. For more discussion on Bancroft's recuerdos, see Douglas Monroy, "The Creation and Re-creation of Californio Society," 173–75. Also review Rosaura Sánchez, *Telling Identities: The Californio Testimonios* (Minneapolis: University of Minnesota Press, 1995); and Genaro Padilla, *My History, Not Yours: The Formation of Mexican-American Autobiography* (Madison: University of Wisconsin Press, 1993). There is some dispute about the number of recuerdos. Sánchez says that "sixty-two old Californios" worked with Bancroft to create the personal memoirs. See *Telling Identities,* 1. Bancroft, though, says that he produced 160 memoirs, half of them coming from "natives (Bancroft's term for the gente de razón) or [those] of Spanish blood." See *The History,* 1:55.

71. For example, in *The History,* 5:14, Bancroft says that during a political dispute between rival californio factions, one of the individuals involved wrote an appeal that was a "an absurd exhibition of petty suspicion and weakness." The description seems a bit harsh considering that the factions debated how best to prepare California's defenses in case the Americans invaded.

72. I present a short bibliography on Vico: For a good, short, and lucid discussion of fantasia see, Isaiah Berlin, *The Crooked Timber of Humanity* (New York: Knopf, 1991), esp. 60–61. Other works, though complex, offer more thorough perspectives. *The New Science of Giambattista Vico, The Third Edition (1744),* trans. and ed. Thomas Goddard Bergin and Max Harold Fisch, (New York: Doubleday and Co., 1961), xxxvi–xxxvii, 62; *Vico, Selected Writings,* trans. and ed. Leon Pompa, (Cambridge, England: Cambridge University Press, 1982), 57–60; Michael Mooney, *Vico and the Tradition of Rhetoric* (Princeton: Princeton University Press, 1985), 101–3; Domenico Pietropaolo, "Grassi, Vico and the Defense of the Humanist Tradition" in *New Vico Studies,* v. 10, ed. Giorgio Tagliacozzo and Donald Phillip Verone (Atlantic Highlands, New Jersey: Humanities Press International, Inc., 1992), 8–9; James Robert Goetsch, *Vico's Axioms, The Geometry of the Human World* (New Haven: Yale University Press, 1995), 90–91. To see how the debate between science and the humanities continues to the present and supposedly corrupts the learning experience for students in an American university, see Alston Chase, *Harvard and the Unabomber, the Education of an American Terrorist* (New York: W.W. Norton and Company, 2003), esp. 40–41 and 199–205.

73. Rangel, "La vida de un ranchero," 29.

74. Berlin, *The Crooked Timber of Humanity,* 58–59.

75. LACA, vol.1, February 19, 1846, 527–31, Sp. Three months later, on May 2, 1846, the police commission, a group of respectable citizens appointed by the ayuntamiento to investigate the complaint, says that there is no harm "in permitting [the Indians] to enjoy themselves in their own style." But the police commission, perhaps wary of angering fellow citizens by not proposing any countermeasures, recommends that the ayuntamiento break up "the Indian ranchería [into] into certain quarters . . . that shall be under the jurisdiction of the municipality." The ayuntamiento, reacting quickly, rejects the proposal, as well as the suggestions made in the petition. It recommends that the "ranchería shall be placed at Avila's spring(?) . . . and be [placed] under the supervision of an honest warden." LACA, vol. 1, May 2, 1846, 527–31, Sp. Apparently, the ayuntamiento succeeded in moving the ranchería. On June 16, 1846, Juan Domingo paid "two hundred pesos [for] the vacant land where the Indian ranchería stood." LACA, vol. 1, June 16, 1846, 316, Sp.

Hereafter comes the petitioners' vital statistics. Most of the information comes from the Mexican censuses of 1836 and 1844. For the 1836 census, see the reproduction in the *Historical Society of Southern California Quarterly* 18, no. 3 (1936): 667–730. We use the pagination of the original. For the 1844 census, see *The Historical Society of Southern California Quarterly* 42, no. 4 (1960): 360–422. We depend mostly on the 1844 census because it is only two years before 1846. Note, however, that our pagination follows the pagination style used in the census, not the page numbers provided by the *Southern California Quarterly*:

1. Francisco Figueroa, 745, born in Mexico, *comerciante* (merchant).
2. Luis Vignes, 782, born in France, *labrador proprietario* (farmer) and *campista* (an individual who owned his own livestock but not the land on which to graze his herd).
3. Felipe Lugo, 781, born in California, labrador proprietario.
4. Juan Ramírez, 747, born in California, labrador proprietario.
5. Januario Avila, 747, born in California, labrador proprietario.
6. José Serrano, 782, presumably born in California, no occupation.
7. Manuel Sepúlveda, 738, born in California, labrador proprietario.
8. Gil Ybarra, born in California, labrador proprietario. Curiously, he is not in the 1844 census. He does appear in the 1836 census, 28.
9. Desiderio Ybarra, 735, born in California, 1844 census, labrador proprietario.
10. Miguel Pryor, 746, born in the United States, labrador (farmer)
11. Ricardo Lankem (Laughlin). He is not in the 1844 census, but appears in the 1836 survey, 11, born in the United States, carpenter.
12. Samuel Carpenter, 1844 census, 746, born in the United States, labrador proprietario.
13. Agustín Martin, no information in 1844 census or the 1836 census. Bancroft makes no mention of Martin as well.
14. Guillermo Wiskies (Wolfskill), 746, born in the United States, labrador.
15. Luis Bouchet, 760, born in France, labrador.
16. María Ballesteros, 782 (?), born in California, no occupation. In the census her name appears as Andrea. But according to Marie Northrop, *Spanish-Mexican Families of Early California: 1769–1850* (New Orleans: Polyanthos, 1976), 55, 186–87, her full name is María Andrea del Carmen Ballesteros. In 1841, she married Vicente Lugo, brother of Felipe Lugo, one of the petition's signatories.

17. Francisco López, 764, born in California, labrador proprietario.
18. Estévan López, 764, born in California, labrador proprietario.
19. (Felipe) Villela, 764, born in Mexico (Baja California), labrador.
20. Tomás Serrano, 762, born in Mexico (San Luis Potosí), no occupation.
21. Mariano Ruíz, 762, born in California, labrador.
22. Antonio Salazar, 764, born in New Mexico, labrador.
23. Casciano Carreón, 765, born in Mexico, labrador.
24. María Antonia Pollorena, 737, born in California. She is married to Hilario Machado, a labrador proprietario. It is likely María Antonia Pollorena helped her husband.
25. Vicente Elizalde, 738, born in California, *zapatero* (shoemaker).
26. Antonio Coronel, 758, born in Mexico, labrador.

76. The Indians, and their gente de razón companions, also went to local watering holes to find a good time.
77. See for example, the petition asking angeleños, in this instance men, to donate money for the celebration of a Mass to honor the Virgin Mary. LACA, September 10, 1838, 3:390, Sp. Luis Arenas, Pedro López, Raimundo Alaniz, Isidro Alvarado, Juan Ramírez, and Ramón Ybarra add their names.
78. In an "extraordinary secret session," the ayuntamiento agrees to send "money, men, and arms to fight hostile gentile Indians marching on San Diego." Each member of the body signs the decision. LACA, May 31, 1837, 2:422–23, Sp.
79. For a good summary of the dispute in which emigrants from Sonora demanded Figueroa's resignation, see Bancroft, *The History*, 3:282–87.
80. For a list of the forty men who demanded that María del Rosario Villa and Gervasio Alipas receive quick justice for murdering Domingo Feliz, see LACA, vol. 2, April 7, 1836, 188–90, Sp. The list suggests that no current, or former, member of the ayuntamiento participated in the execution.
81. Felipe Lugo was regidor in 1832.
82. A *juez de campo* helped resolve disputes over cattle brands and sometimes heard complaints about the boundaries dividing one property from another.
83. Januario Avila was regidor in 1834 and 1835. Gil Ybarra was sindico in 1831 and alcalde in 1832. Desiderio Ybarra was regidor in 1826, 1827, and 1828.
84. Bear in mind that a padrón could be a tabulation of any sort, from a survey to a list of landholders living in the community. In our case, the 1835 and 1838 padrones suggest that four manzanas, or blocks, comprised the settlement. For manzana two see LACA, 3:662, 1835, Sp. Manzana four appears in LACA, 3:650, 1835, Sp. For manzana one, see LACA, 3:669, 1838, Sp. (Some of the people in manzana one appear in manzana two for 1835. We have not attempted to sort out the confusion.) Manzana three appears in LACA, 3:526–27, 1838, Sp.
85. The four who do not have an occupation listed are: María Ballesteros, María Antonia Pollorena, Agustín Martin, and Tomás Serrano.
86. Victor Prudon, "The Vigilantes of Los Angeles" trans. Earl Hewitt, 1–12.
87. Ibid.
88. For a quick count of productive angeleños, see the table in Howard Nelson's "The Two Pueblos of Los Angeles: Agricultural Village and Embryo Town," 10.
89. In the 1840s, the ayuntamiento asked men of "wealth and power" to patrol Los Angeles at night. But the individuals who agreed to police the streets seemed to be merchants and farmers. None of them were cattlemen, individuals who supposedly had the most

wealth. See the Los Angeles Ayuntamiento Archives, Prefect Santiago Arguello to the Juez de Paz, vol. 2, January 25, 1841, 18–19 and vol. 5, April 25, 1844, 165–66, Bancroft Library, University of California, Berkeley.

90. Our idea of productivity comes from US labor history. I have yet to find a comparable discussion in Mexican, Borderlands, or Latin American history. See Christopher Lasch, *The Revolt of the Elite and the Betrayal of American Democracy* (New York: W.W. Norton and Co., 1995), esp. 50–114.

91. The 1836 census has 603 men. The 1844 census counts 627 men.

92. For more on how people see themselves, see Arran Gare, *Postmodernism and the Environmental Crisis* (New York: Routledge Press, 1995), 139–47. I am indebted to my colleague Mark Woods for directing me to this book.

Chapter One

1. See *The Historical Society of Southern California Quarterly* 18, no. 3 (1936): 720 and 730 for the population figures. Curiously, on p. 730, there is an adding error. When the surveyor counted the Indians he reached the figure 553. However the numbers, when tabulated again, come out to 555.

2. The Indian population figures come from the original 1844 census in the Los Angeles City Archives (hereafter LACA). Also see the published and edited version, "The Los Angeles Padrón of 1844," *The Historical Society of Southern California Quarterly* 42 (December 1960): 360–414.

3. For more on Indians in Los Angeles and other parts of provincial California, see George Harwood Phillips *Chiefs and Challengers: Indian Resistance and Cooperation in Southern California* (Berkeley: University of California Press, 1975); and *Indians and Intruders in Central California, 1796–1849* (Norman: University of Oklahoma Press, 1983). Also consult Albert Hurtado, *Indian Survival on the California Frontier* (New Haven: Yale University Press, 1988).

4. A ranchería or rancho refers to two different things. The first, ranchería, always describes an Indian settlement. Meanwhile, a rancho almost always refers to a cattle spread.

5. At times, the census would use gentil, or non-Christian as an Indian name. See, for example, the 1836 census, p. 723, column two, for Indians designated as gentila or gentil, a female and male non-Christian.

6. A. L. Kroeber, "Elements of Culture in Native California," in *The California Indians, A Source Book,* ed. R. F. Heizer and M. A. Whipple, 3–65 (Berkeley: University of California Press, 1971). We also use the linguistic map—compiled by Kroeber—that sits in the front of the *Source Book.* One scholar says that the Indians of Los Angeles spoke up to 135 languages (!). See Kevin Starr, *Inventing the Dream, California Through the Progressive Era* (New York: Oxford University Press, 1985), 8.

7. The Cahuilla Indians sometimes took the name Luiseño, a title inspired by Mission San Luis Rey. See Kevin Starr, *Inventing the Dream,* 9.

8. In modern times, there is an Indian band in the southeast area of California that bears the name "Agua Caliente."

9. Hugo Reid, a Scotsman who had moved to California early in the Mexican period, observed in 1852 that after secularization the neophytes often moved to settlements north of their former missions. See Robert Heizer ed., *The Indians of Los Angeles County, Hugo Reid's Letters of 1852* (Los Angeles: The Southwest Museum), 98.

10. There are other accounts of how Indian drinking often caused concern. See Maynard Geiger, O.F.M., ed. and trans., *As the Padres Saw Them, California Indian Life and Customs as Reported by the Franciscan Missionaries, 1813–1815* (Santa Barbara: Santa Barbara Mission Archive Library, 1976), 89, 105. Consult the "Interrogatorio," Santa Barbara, June 1824," in *Expeditions to the Interior of California, Central Valley, 1820–1840*, ed. and trans. Sherburne Cook, 153–55 (Berkeley: University of California Press, 1962). For a broader view of Indian drinking, see William B. Taylor, *Drinking, Homicide and Rebellion in Colonial Mexican Villages* (Stanford: Stanford University Press, 1979), esp. 28–72.

11. LACA, vol. 1., May, 2, 1846, 527–31. It seems that the person speaking the line about the "bacchanalia" is a member of the *comisión de policia,* or police commission, a group appointed by the ayuntamiento to investigate citizen complaints. The other complaints about Indians are: LACA, vol. 2, November 11, 1844, 939–40, Sp; LACA, vol. 1, May 2, 1846, 1082–84, Sp; LACA, vol. 4, November 3, 6, 8, 20, 1847, 620–38, Sp; and LACA, vol. 4, August 11–14, 1849, 722–24, Sp.

12. LACA, vol. 3, October 17, 1850, 364, Sp. See Manuel Clemente Rojo, *La Estrella,* January 25, 1855. The article is in the Benjamin Hayes Scrapbooks, vol. 43, chap. 10, 172, The Bancroft Library, University of California, Berkeley.

13. LACA, vol. 1, July 5, 1844 (?), 398, trans. [The year is unclear.]

14. LACA, vol. 1, May 2, 1846, 527–31, Sp.

15. LACA, vol. 2, January 22, 1833, trans.

16. LACA, vol. 2, November 11, 1844, 939–40, Sp.

17. Two petitions put before the ayuntamiento come into play here: LACA, vol. 1, February 19, 1846, 527–31, Sp.; and LACA, vol. 4, February 24, 1847, 354, 361, Sp.

18. LACA, vol. 4, October 30, 1847, 616, Sp.

19. LACA, vol. 3, October 17, 1850, 364, Sp.

20. LACA, vol. 4, October 23, 1847, 616, 626, Sp. The ayuntamiento goes on to agree that a guard should be posted at the ranchería's entrance so that no gente de razón could enter.

21. The ranchería had been relocated several times during the Mexican period. See LACA, vol. 1, May 2, 1846, 527–31, Sp., for more information about the fate of the Indian settlement. The ayuntamiento ordered the ranchería to be destroyed, but apparently it rose again. For more on how many Indians lived inside Los Angeles, see Steven W. Hackel, "Land, Labor, and Production, The Colonial Economy of Spanish and Mexican California," in *Contested Eden,* 111–46. For a different view, see George Harwood Phillips, "Indians in Los Angeles, 1781–1875: Economic Integration, Social Disintegration," *Pacific Historical Review* 49 (August 1980): 435–37. To add more spice to the debate about the size of the Indian population, we turn to Bancroft. He says that as of 1845 there were roughly "1,100" Indians "in community or scattered" throughout the district. Bancroft then implies that only "ex-neophytes" made the count, while "gentiles" for the most part did not. See Bancroft, *The History,* 4:628n. 9. The number of Indians could have been larger. We, though, stick with the 1844 census, and stay with the number of 377.

22. See chap. 3 to learn more about the angeleño male's appetites.

23. Our reasoning is as follows: forty-three Indians make up one-third; eighty-six angeleños make up two-thirds.

24. For a good overview of California Indians, see the Robert F. Heizer, et. al., *Handbook of North American Indians,* 17 vols. *The Indians of California,* vol. 7, (Washington: Smithsonian Institution, 1978). Also consult, even if a bit dated—the essay first appeared in 1922—Kroeber, "The Elements of Culture in Native California," 3–65. Also

see Pedro Fages, *A Historical, Political, and Natural Description of California*, ed. and trans. Herbert Ingram Priestley (Berkeley: University of California Press, 1937). Fages, who composed his piece in 1770, was the commander of the presidio at Monterey when the viceroy, Don Antonio María Bucareli y Ursúa, requested a report on California's resources and people. For another view, composed more than a century later in 1877, see Salvador Vallejo, "The Origin of the Californian Aborigines," ed. and trans. Earl Hewitt, Bancroft Library, University of California, Berkeley. Vallejo, when read in conjunction with Fages, suggests that some prejudices about the Indians had not changed.

25. For more on Indian artistry, see Norman Neuererg, *The Decoration of the California Missions* (Santa Barbara: Bellerophon Books, 1996).

26. I relate the story of Pablo Tac and Agapito Amamix. See "Indian Life and Customs at Mission San Luis Rey, A Record of California Mission Life Written by Pablo Tac, an Indian Neophyte" (Rome, 1835), ed. and trans. Minna and Gordon Hewes, in *Native American Perspectives on the Hispanic Colonization of Alta California*, vol. 26, ed. Edward D. Castillo (New York: Garland Publishing, Inc. 1991), 35–59. Also consult Angustias de la Ord, *Occurrences in Hispanic California*, trans. and ed. Francis Price and William H. Ellison (Washington D.C.: Academy of American Franciscan History, 1956), 33, 82–83.

27. Howard Swan, *Music in the Southwest* (San Marino: The Huntington Library, 1952), 86–90. Father Narciso Durán, who, among many roles, served as President of California's missions in the early nineteenth century, composed some of the music that Indians throughout the province learned to perform. Durán, for example, "probably" composed the *Misa de Cataluña* and the *Misa Vizcaína* pieces sometimes performed by Indian musicians.

28. Craig Russell, "Mexican Baroque, Musical Treasures from New Spain" libretto, in *Chanticleer, Mexican Baroque* (Germany, 1994), 10.

29. "Te Deum" is short for *Te Deum Laudamus*, "To, thee, God we praise."

30. Los Angeles City Archives, vol. 2, June 11, 1837, 425–26, Sp.

31. There are a score of books describing how Indians excited forbidden thoughts. With significant exceptions, the best works concentrate on the Anglo-American experience, but they serve nonetheless. One is the most provocative is Michael Rogin, *Fathers and Children, Andrew Jackson and the Subjugation of the American Indian* (New York: Vintage Books, 1979); and Richard Slotkin, *Regeneration Through Violence: The Mythology of the Frontier* (Middletown, CT: Wesleyan Press, 1977). Perhaps one of the more vivid descriptions of non-Indians projecting their violent desires onto Indians appears in Evan S. Connell, *Son of the Morning Star, Custer and the Little Bighorn* (New York: Harper and Row, 1984), esp., 304–5. For the Spanish Borderlands, see Ramón Gutiérrez, *When Jesus Came, the Corn Mothers Went Away*, (Stanford: Stanford University Press, 1991).

32. Gerald Smith and Clifford Walker, *The Indian Slave Trade Along the Mojave Trail* (San Bernardino County Museum, 1965), 9.

33. The historian Hubert Howe Bancroft is unsure if Miguel Blanco—Michael White—is English or Irish. See Bancroft, *The History*, 7 vols., (San Francisco: The History Company, 1883–1886), 5:773. As for the description of angeleño cruelty, see Miguel Blanco's dictation to Thomas Savage, *California All the Way Back to 1828* (Los Angeles: Dawson's Book Shop, 1956), 46.

34. José María Amador, "Memorias sobre la historia de California," in *Expeditions to the Interior of California, Central Valley, 1820–1840*, ed. Sherburne Cook, 197–98 (Berkeley: University of California Press, 1962).

35. For more comment on gente de razón cruelty, see chaps. 3 and 4.

36. Douglas Monroy, "The Creation and Re-creation of Californio Society," in *Contested Eden*, ed. Richard Orsi and Ramón Gutiérrez, 123–95 (Berkeley: University of California Press, 1998). Monroy does an excellent job examining the contradictions inherent in liberal thought.

37. Antonio María Osio, *The History of Alta California, A Memoir of Mexican California*, ed. and trans. Rose Marie Beebe and Robert M. Senkewicz (Madison: University of Wisconsin Press, 1996), 256n. 48. The entire quotation, as translated by Beebe and Senkewicz, is as follows: "However this time it seemed worse, as they [the residents of Mexican California who battled the Anglo-Americans in 1846] began to think about the loss of their nationality and everything they hoped to create." Osio lived in Los Angeles in the 1830s.

38. Osio, *The History of Alta California*, 55–68. Osio seems well aware about the challenges of fighting Indians. See his description about the Chumash rebellion in 1824.

39. Coronel, *Tales of Mexican California*, 81.

40. In Mexico, the word "liberal" could suggest generosity. Or, it could describe the nature of an educated or enlightened person, a definition that could apply to many people, including conservatives. As a political term, liberal presented even more variety. For more on liberalism in Mexico and California, see Charles Hale, *Mexican Liberalism in the Age of Mora, 1821–1856* (New Haven: Yale University Press, 1969). Also see Enrique Florescano, *Memory, Myth, and Time in Mexico: From the Aztecs to Independence*, trans. Albert Bork and Kathryn Bork (Austin: University of Texas Press, 1994); and D. A. Brading, *The First America, the Spanish Monarchy, Creole Patriots, and the Liberal State* (Cambridge, England: Cambridge University Press, 1991). Also consult Michael Costeloe, *The Central Republic in Mexico, 1835–1846, Hombres de Bien in the Age of Santa Anna* (Cambridge, England: Cambridge University Press, 1993); and Stanley Green, *The Mexican Republic: The First Decade, 1823–1832* (Pittsburgh: University of Pittsburgh Press, 1987). Mexican thinkers from the nineteenth century may provide a better perspective of events, see José Luis Mora, "Una vision de la sociedad mexicana" (1836), 71–140; and Lorenzo de Zavala, "La sociedad mexicana antes y despues de la independencia" (1836) 31–68, in *Espejos de discordias, la sociedad mexicana vista por Lorenzo Zavala, José Luis Mora y Lucás Alámán*, Andrés Lira, ed., (Mexico, D.F.: SEP Cultura, 1984). For more discussion on liberalism in California, consult Jesse Davis Francis, "An Economic and Social History of Mexican California," 2 vols. (Ph.D. diss., University of California, Berkeley 1939). Reprinted by Arno Press (New York, 1976). For one more view, see Woodrow Hansen, *The Search for Authority in California* (Oakland, CA: Biopress, 1961).

41. Jean Franco, "En Espera de una burguesía: la formación de la intelligentsia mexicana en la época de la Independencia," in *Actas del VIII Congreso de la Asociacion Internacional de Hispanistas*, 21–35 (Madrid: Comisión Editorial del VIII Congreso de la AIH, 1986).

42. Ibid.

43. See D. A. Brading, *The First America*, 561–82.

44. Franco, "En Espera de una burguesía," 27.

45. Quotation from C. Alan Hutchinson, *Frontier Settlement in Mexican California* (New Haven: Yale University Press, 1969), 166. The speaker is Bernardo González Angulo. He seeks to introduce a bill that will distribute mission lands to Indians and settlers.

46. José Fernández to Francisco Elorriaga, October 13, 1833, Valentín Gómez-Farías Collection, Document 4721. Nettie Lee Benson Library, University of Texas at Austin. It should be said that that Valentín Gómez Farías was acting president. The elected president, the mercurial Antonio López de Santa Anna, did not want to bother with the responsibilities of government and retired to his hacienda in the Yucatan peninsula.

47. Keld J. Reynolds. "The Reglamento for the Hijar y Padrés Colony of 1834" *Historical Society of Southern California Quarterly* 28 no.4 (March 1946): 143–175.

48. *Diaries and Accounts of the Romero Expedition in Arizona and California*, ed. Lowell John Bean and William Mason, (Los Angeles: Ward Richie Press, 1962), 86–87, 89.

49. Stanley Green, *The Mexican Republic*, 89–91. Green presents all the particulars about Mexico's Masonic lodges.

50. Bancroft, *The History*, 3:34–37, 3:47–49.

51. See the entry in *Diccionario Porrua de historia, biografia, y geografia de Mexico* (Mexico, D.F.: Editorial Porrua, S.A., 1964), 186.

52. Bancroft, *The History*, 3:263n. 42; 4:741; and 2:793.

53. Rosaura Sánchez, *Telling Identities: The Californio Testimonios* (Minneapolis: University of Minnesota Press, 1995), 110.

54. Angustias de la Guerra Ord, *Occurrences in Hispanic California*, trans. and ed. Francis Price and William Ellison (Washington D.C.: Academy of American Franciscan History, 1956), 23.

55. Ibid., 25.

56. José María Figueroa, *Manifesto to the Mexican Republic which Brigadier General José Figueroa, Commandant and Political Chief of Upper California presents on his conduct and on that of José María de Hijar and José María Padrés as Directors of Colonization in 1834 and 1835*, trans. and ed. C. Alan Hutchinson, (Berkeley: University of California Press, 1978). For reference to Bentham, see 54.

57. Ibid. For references to ancient philosophers, see 94. The reference to Voltaire, though a bit obscure, is on 89n. 159.

58. For more on the life of Juan Luis (Jean Louis) Vignes, see Bancroft, *The History of California*, 5:762.

59. The information concerning Bordeaux's revolutionary sympathies comes from Simon Schama, *Citizens* (New York: Vintage Books, 1989), 582–84.

60. Tabulations come from the 1836 and 1844 censuses.

61. *Canción sobre el amor del trabajo,* Anonymous, Valentín Gómez-Farias Papers, Nettie Lee Benson Library, University of Texas at Austin.

62. *Cartilla sobre cria de gusanos de seda,* D. Tomás Yllanes (Mexico, 1831), n.p., in the Antonio Coronel Collection, #678, SCWH.

63. José María Váldez' petition for a farming plot, LACA, January 17, 1838, vol. 1, 86, Sp.

64. LACA, vol. 1, August 8–August 27, 1840, 491–94, Sp. In fairness, four angeleños wish to claim the property of Tomás Lucero. They say that Lucero had failed to develop his property. But Felipe Lugo, appointed by the ayuntamiento to investigate the claim, reported that Lucero had indeed developed his property.

65. LACA, vol. 3, 1833–1834, 130–36.

66. Ibid. Enrique Daniel Stone (?) refused to repay Juan Bautista Leandry for a loan.

67. Ibid.

68. Francisco Ramírez, *El Clamor Público*, February 21, 1857, microfilm, Chicano Studies Library, University of California, Berkeley.

69. José del Carmen Lugo, "Life of a Rancher," trans. and ed. Helen Pruitt Beattie, *Historical Society of Southern California Quarterly* 32, no. 3 (1950): 185–236.

70. Horace Bell, *On the Old West Coast,* ed. Lamar Bartlett (New York: William Morrow and Company, 1938), 4.

71. Bancroft Research Notes, "Commerce, 1841–1848" Heading, 1843, Los Angeles Archives, 2:358–61.

72. Bancroft Research Notes, "Agriculture 1841–1854," Heading 1845, from Juan Bandini, "Historia de Alta California," (?), 260–71, 290.

73. Ibid.

74. Bancroft Research Notes, "Commerce, 1839–1870," Heading 1840, from Henry Delano Fitch, "Documentos para la historia de California," 118.

75. LACA, vol. 2, November 11, 1844, 939–40, Sp.

76. The sindico condemns the Indians' conduct. LACA, vol. 2, May 2, 1846, 1082–84, Sp.

Chapter Two

1. Antonio Coronel, *Cosas de California* or *Tales of Mexican California,* ed. Doyce Nunis, trans. Dianee Avalle-Arce (Santa Barbara: Bellerophon Books, 1994), 81.

2. Ibid., 79. Coronel suggests that physical punishment seemed to be a regular occurrence. For more views on parenting in Mexican California, see Leonard Pitt, *Decline of the Californios* (Berkeley: University of California Press, 1971), 11–12.

3. Salvador Vallejo, "The Origin of the Californian Aborigines," 2, trans., 1870 (?), Bancroft Library, University of California, Berkeley.

4. José Francisco Palomares, "Memoria," in Sherburne Friend Cook, *Expedition to the Interior of California, 1820–1840* (Berkeley: University of California Press, 1962), 203.

5. For more on Indians and the way they treated their dead enemies, see Kenneth Stewart, "Mohave Warfare," in *The California Indians, A Sourcebook,* ed. R. F. Heizer and M. A. Whipple, 431–44 (Berkeley: University of California Press, 1971). It is worth remembering that what happened in one group, in this case, the Mohave, would not prevail in another.

6. See chap. 1.

7. See chap. 3 for more commentary on angeleño and Indian family ties.

8. See, for instance, "El Fondo Municipal," The Municipal Fund for Los Angeles. In 1834, to take just one year, the city treasurer collected $337—a peso equaled one dollar in the nineteenth century—from people who sold alcohol. Los Angeles City Archives, "El Fondo Municipal, 1834," 3:18, Sp. I wish to thank Helen Lara-Cea, a colleague at Berkeley, for giving me this insight. She found that the gente de razón in San José often made a nice pile of money selling alcohol to Indians.

9. Coronel, *Tales of Mexican California,* 79.

10. There is an abundant literature on what qualities constitute "whiteness." We draw on works examining the eastern seaboard of the United States and the American Southwest. For a good introduction, see David Roediger, *The Wages of Whiteness: Race and the Making of the American Working Class* (London and New York: Verso Press, 1991); Alexander Saxton, *The Rise and Fall of the White Republic* (New York: Verso Press, 1992); and Neil Foley, *The White Scourge* (Berkeley: University of California Press, 1997). For a good review of matters in California, see Gloria Miranda, "Racial and Cultural Dimensions in *Gente de Razón* Status in Spanish and Mexican California," *Southern California Quarterly* 70, no. 3 (1988): 265–78; and "*Gente de Razón* Marriage Patterns in Spanish and Mexican California: A Case Study of Santa Barbara and Los Angeles," *Southern California Quarterly* 63, no. 1 (1981): 1–21.

11. Jaime E. Rodríguez, *Down From Colonialism* (Los Angeles: Chicano Studies Research Center, UCLA, 1983), 8–9.

12. The idea about color in Mexico can lead to some inspiring discussion. See Patricia Seed, *To Love, Honor, and Obey in Colonial Mexico: Conflicts Over Marriage Choice 1574–1821* (Stanford: Stanford University Press, 1988); and Stanley Green, *The Mexican Republic: The First Decade: 1823–1832* (Pittsburgh: University of Pittsburgh Press, 1987). For a different view of race and color in Mexico, especially in the years leading up to independence, see Rodríguez, *Down From Colonialism,* 8–9. Rodríguez draws the distinction that it was better to be "rich than white." He presents a more thorough discussion in the book he co-authored with Colin MacLachlan, *The Forging of the Cosmic Race: A Reinterpretation of Colonial Mexico* (Berkeley: University of California Press, 1980).

13. The 1818 (?) Padrón, de la Guerra Documentos, Tomo I, p. 125, Bancroft Library, University of California, Berkeley. There is some controversy about the exact date. The padrón could be from 1822, but national law and practice forbade the use of racial categories by that time. Of course, the angeleños could persist in identifying individuals by race and color, a practice from the colonial era.

14. The 1818 survey writes Desiderio's surname as "Ibarra."

15. Briones was so obscure he does not even earn mention in Bancroft's "Pioneer Index," the biographies of settlers he added at the end of his *History of California.*

16. For more on the dilemmas brought forth by the bid for racial equality, see D. A. Brading, *The First America: The Spanish Monarchy, Creole Patriots, and the Liberal State, 1492–1867* (Cambridge, England: Cambridge University Press, 1991). Also consult Stanley Green, *The Mexican Republic.*

17. Juan Bandini, *Noticia estadistitica de la alta California, 1831,* Documentos oficiales para la historia de Mexico, vol. 4, documento no. 21, folios 198–212, Archivo General de la Nación, Mexico, D.F., typescript 9. I thank my colleague Iris Engstrand for showing me this document.

18. Ibid., 4.

19. Ibid., 22.

20. As brother to Desiderio, described earlier as a prieto, Gil could be the same shade. If he was indeed dark, it is curious that he referred to himself as white.

21. LACA, vol. 2, May 31, 1837, 422–23, Sp.

22. LACA, vol. 7, October 17, 1850, 364–65, Sp.

23. Antonio Coronel Collection, #663-A 5, 1850 (?). SCWH. The assignments seem to be from the 1850s, maybe earlier.

24. Salvador Vallejo, "The Origin of the Californian Aborigines," 1, trans., n.d. Bancroft Library, University of California, Berkeley.

25. Ibid.

26. Ygnacio Sepúlveda, "Historical Memoranda," 6, trans., 1874 Bancroft Library, University of California, Berkeley.

27. José de Jesús Vallejo, "Reminicencias historicas de California," 7, Sp., Bancroft Library, University of California, Berkeley.

28. Leonard Pitt, *Decline of the Californios,* 12–17, 26–68. For more on how Anglo-Americans looked at Mexicans in what is now the American Southwest, see Raymund Paredes, "The Origins of Anti-Mexican Sentiment in the United States" *New Scholar* 6 (1977): 139–66. For comparison, see Arnoldo de León, *They Called Them Greasers: Anglo Attitudes toward Mexicans in Texas, 1821–1900* (Austin: University of Texas Press, 1983). Other scholars examine American racism in greater depth. Consult Stephen Jay Gould, *The Mismeasure of Man* (New York: W.W. Norton, 1980); and George Frederickson, *The Black Image in the White Mind* (New York: Harper Torchbooks, 1971), esp. 43–70.

29. J. W. Guinn, "Muy Ilustre Ayuntamiento," *Historical Society of Southern California Quarterly* 4, no. 3, (1899): 206–12.

30. Sherburne Cook, "The Indian versus the Spanish Mission," in *The Conflict Between the California Indian and White Civilization* 1–194 (Berkeley: University of California Press, 1976). The book reprints Cook's extended essays on the California Indian's demise.

31. Ibid., 27.

32. Cook, "The Physical and Demographic Reaction of the Non-Mission Indians in Colonial and Provincial California," in *The Conflict*, 197–233.

33. Ibid., 213–14.

34. The speaker is alcalde Vicente Sánchez. Los Angeles Ayuntamiento Archives, November 17, 1845, vol. 5, 271, Bancroft Library, University of California, Berkeley.

35. LACA, vol. 1, June 15, 1838, trans.

36. Sherburne Cook, "Small Pox in Mexican California," *Bulletin of the History of Medicine* 7, no. 2 (1939): 153–91; also see Los Angeles Ayuntamiento Archives, vol. 3, n.d. 1844–1850, 7–11, Sp., Bancroft Library, University of California, Berkeley.

37. Los Angeles Ayuntamiento Archives, vol. 3, n.d. 1844–1850, 7–11, Sp., Bancroft Library.

38. LACA, vol. 2, December 18,1832, 10–11, trans.

39. LACA, vol. 1, December 19 and December 21, 1837, 441–42, trans.

40. LACA, vol. 1, December 17, 1838, 520, trans.

41. LACA, vol. 3, December13, 1837, 183, trans.

42. Bancroft, *The History*, 2:550n. 19.

43. José del Carmen Lugo, "Vida de un ranchero," or "The Life of a Rancher," trans. Helen Pruitt Beattie, *Historical Society of Southern California Quarterly* 32, no. 32(1950): 190–91.

44. Ibid.

45. Bancroft, *The History*, 2:417–18n. 8–9.

46. Cook, "Indians versus the California Mission," in *The Conflict*, 54.

47. Bancroft, *The History*, 4:190–91n. 1.

48. Bancroft, *The History*, 2:417–18n. 8–9.

49. Bancroft Research Notes, "Agriculture," 1844, n.p., William Baldridge, "Days of '46," 7–8, Bancroft Library, University of California, Berkeley.

50. Bancroft, *The History*, 3:637–38n. 9.

51. Bancroft *The History*, 2:417–18n. 8–9.

52. Ibid.

53. Bancroft, *The History*, 2:550n. 19.

54. LACA, vol. 1, January 19, 1836, 595, Sp.

55. Bancroft, *The History*, 3:637–38n. 5.

56. W. W. Robinson, *Land in California* (Berkeley: University of California Press, 1948), 39.

57. The other maps that exist usually depict pieces of property involved in disputes or property a citizen wished to inhabit. As an example, see the map in LACA, vol. 4, September 4, 1847, 286, Sp. Benito Pedraza, "native of Sonora, married, and with an occupation as farmer, and now resident of this city," requests a plot of land. Pedraza maps out the parcel he covets, denoting in which direction sat north and south, and how close the property sat to the Los Angeles River. The Spaniards, late in the eighteenth century, executed maps of Los Angeles, but no other rendering appeared until Ord's work in 1847.

58. Bancroft, *The History*, 3:588–89.

59. Quoted in Robert Glass Cleland, *Cattle on a Thousand Hills* (San Marino, CA: The Huntington Library, 1951), 75.

60. Ibid., 23–31. Coronel adds that the hosts often hid their daughters from the guests. Coronel, *Tales of Mexican California*, 78.

61. Benjamin Hayes, "Notes on California Affairs," file no. 2, n.p. Bancroft Library.

62. Bancroft Research Notes, "Commerce, 1841–1848" Heading 1842, from Eugene Duflot de Mofras, *Exploration of the Oregon Territory and California*, 1:487–88.

63. Ibid., "Commerce, 1841–1848," Heading 1846, John Marsh to Lewis Cass, *Contra Costa Gazette*, December 21, 1867.

64. Later on in this chapter, we list the rancheros who held title to ranchos in the Los Angeles area. We use the 1836 and 1844 censuses to compile our list. As of yet, at least to this point in time, there is no indication that the wills of any of these people have survived to the present.

65. Los Angeles Archives of the Prefecture, in Los Angeles Public Records, Book A, May 11, 1832, 954, trans. SCWH. There are at least three transcriptions of the Prefect records. The originals sit in the Huntington Library in San Marino, California. The City Clerk's Office in Los Angeles and the SCWH have English translations of the Prefect records.

66. Ibid., Book A, 1855, (?), 86, trans. SCWH.

67. Ibid., City Clerk's Office, October 25, 1847, 396, Book A, trans.

68. Douglas Monroy, "Creation and Re-Creation of Californio Society," in *Contested Eden: California Before the Gold Rush*, ed. Richard Orsi and Ramón Gutiérrez, 173–95 (Berkeley: University of California Press, 1998). Also see Douglas Monroy, *Thrown Among Strangers: The Making of Mexican Culture in Frontier California* (Berkeley: University of California Press, 1990), 99–103. For one more view, see Steven W. Hackel, "Land, Labor, and Production, The Colonial Economy of Spanish and Mexican California," in *Contested Eden*, 111–46. For a definition of seigneurial and seigneur, see *The Oxford Universal Dictionary on Historical Principles*, 3rd ed., (Oxford: Oxford University Press, 1964), 1832.

69. Kevin Starr, *Inventing the Dream, California Through the Progressive Era* (New York: Oxford University Press, 1985), 12–13. Starr, a deliberate and careful historian, shines best when he discusses the Anglo-American impact on California.

70. Dora Crouch, Daniel Garr, and Axel Mundingo, *Spanish City Planning in North America* (Cambridge, MA: MIT Press, 1982), 170–71.

71. Ibid., 156–73. The size of a community's population seemed one more way of reaching the rank of city.

72. Ibid.

73. As one example among many, see the document entitled "The Illustrious Ayuntamiento of this city named for its commissions, justices of the field, and police commissioners, the following gentlemen" LACA, vol. 3, February 3, 1838, 501, Sp.

74. Susanna Bryant Dakin, *An Old Scotch Paisano in Los Angeles* (Berkeley: University of California Press, 1939), 7.

75. Victor Prudon, "The Los Angeles Vigilantes," 1, trans. Earl Hewitt, Bancroft Library.

76. Fernández was a member of the Híjar-Pádres expedition, many of whose members probably came from Mexico City. See C. Alan Hutchinson, "An Official List of the Members of the Híjar-Pádres Colony for Mexican California, 1834," *Pacific Historical Review* 42, no. 3 (1973): 462–79.

77. The diligencias come from the Thomas Temple Collection, Box #9, Files M-2 and M-3—the pagination is sometimes erratic and is unreliable—SCWH. For Francisco Bazo, see the diligencia for August 29, 1831. José Acosta appears in the diligencia dated March 31, 1833. As for Juan Patricio Contreras, see the diligencia for October 23, 1834.

78. Rodríguez, *Down From Colonialism,* 7. For Mexico City and its reputation as the city of palaces, see Guillermo Tovar de Teresa, *The City of Palaces: Chronicle of a Lost Heritage,* 2 vols. (Mexico City: Vuelta, 1990).

79. Crouch, Garr, and Mundingo, *Spanish City Planning in North America,* 153–72. Also see Carroll William Westfall, *In This Most Perfect Paradise: Alberti, Nicholas V, and the Invention of Conscious Urban Planning in Rome, 1447–1455* (University Park: Pennsylvania State University Press, 1974), 25–28 and 60–61; and Donald Hedrick, "The Ideal of Ornament: Alberti and the Erotics of Renaissance Design," in *Word and Image* 3, no. 1 (1987): 111–37. For more on Mexican urban design, consult George Kubler, *Mexican Architecture in the Sixteenth Century,* 2 vols. (New Haven: Yale University Press, 1948), 1:69–71.

80. Daniel Garr, "Los Angeles and the Challenge of Growth," *Historical Society of Southern California Quarterly* 61 (Summer 1979): 147–58.

81. Los Angeles Ayuntamiento Archives, vol. 5, July 22, 1847, 437, Sp., Bancroft Library.

82. Crouch, Garr, and Mundingo, *Spanish City Planning in North America,* 170–71.

83. Los Angeles Ayuntamiento Archives, vol. 4, November 19, 1832, 64–66, Sp., Bancroft Library.

84. After having read nearly all the ayuntamiento proceedings, I can safely say that Leonardo Cota did not make many speeches that entered the record.

85. See the *Diccionario de la lengua española* (Madrid: Real Academia Española, 1956); for a comparison see the meanings for rancho in the *Oxford English Dictionary,* 2nd ed., (1983).

86. Francisco Santamaria, *Diccionario de mejicanismos* (Mexico City: Editorial Porrua S.A., 1959), 915.

87. Ibid.

88. When growing up in Los Angeles, I often heard family members use the terms *a rancho* or *a ranchera* to condemn inappropriate behavior.

89. José María Figueroa, *Manifesto to the Mexican Republic which Brigadier José Figueroa Commandant and Political Chief of Upper California Presents on His Conduct and on that of José María de Híjar and José María Padrés as Directors of Colonization in 1834 and 1835,* ed. and trans. C. Alan Hutchinson (Berkeley: University of California Press, 1979), 76.

90. Los Angeles Ayuntamiento Archives, vol. 5, n.d., 1844, 7–11, Sp., Bancroft Library, University of California, Berkeley.

91. J. W. Guinn, "Muy Ilustre Ayuntamiento," *Historical Society of Southern California Quarterly* 4, no. 3 (1899): 206–12.

92. Bancroft, *The History,* 2:783.

93. Coronel, *Tales of Mexican California,* 78, 81.

94. José del Carmen Lugo, "Life of a Rancher," 214–17.

95. Here follow the fifteen. First we present the ten men who claimed to be rancheros and campistas, but apparently did not hold title to their properties: José Manuel Cota was regidor in 1832. In the 1836 census (p. 672) his residence appears as labrador proprietario (?), but his occupation is ranchero. Leonardo Cota, regidor in 1845 and 1846, follows his brother: In 1836 (p. 672), his residence is labrador proprietario, but his occupation is ranchero. In 1844 (p. 757), however, he lives in Los Angeles, but now lists his occupation as labrador proprietario. Guillermo Cota was alcalde in 1827 and 1828. He, too, like his sons, José Manuel and Leonardo, lists his residence as a labrador proprietario (1836 census, p. 672), but he identifies his occupation as ranchero. Manuel Domínguez, alcalde in 1832 and 1839, lists his occupation as "grazier" in the 1850 American census,

Census of the County and City of Los Angeles California for the Year 1850, ed,.Maurice Newmark and Marco Newmark, (Los Angeles: The Times Mirror Press, 1929), 77. In the two Mexican censuses, (1836, p. 672, and 1844, p. 758), Domínguez lives in Los Angeles and lists his occupation as labrador proprietario. Antonio Machado, regidor in 1833 and 1838, sindico and alcalde in 1839 (?), lists his occupation as "grazier" in the 1850 census. He as well, has a curious history. In the 1836 survey (p. 697) he lives in Los Angeles and is a labrador proprietario. Eight years later, in 1844, (p. 779) he lives in Rancho San Pedro, but remains a labrador proprietario. Ignacio Palomares, regidor in 1835 and 1838, alcalde in 1848, does not appear in the 1836 count. But in the 1844 survey (p. 738) he lives in Los Angeles and lists his occupation as labrador proprietario. In the 1850 census (p. 98) he says he is a grazier. Bancroft says, however, (*The History*, 4:766) that sometime between 1837 and 1840 Palomares received title to Rancho Azusa de San José, a holding that receives no mention in any of the censuses. Antonio Avila, sindico in 1836, appears in the 1836 count (p. 698) as a ranchero. But in 1844 (p. 765) he is a labrador proprietario. Bancroft notes, though, that sometime around 1836 (*The History*, 3:765) Avila received title to Rancho Sausal Redondo, another holding not reflected in any of the censuses. Bernardo López, regidor in 1837 and 1839, is a ranchero at Rancho Santa Gertrudes in 1836 (p. 714), but in 1850 (p. 36), he is a farmer at San Gabriel. He does not appear in the 1844 count. (Juan) Cristomo Vejar, regidor in 1839, is a ranchero living in Los Angeles in 1836 (p. 696), but he is a labrador proprietario, still in Los Angeles, in 1844 (p. 750). Rafael Guirado, regidor in 1847, is a labrador proprietario in 1836 (p. 670). But, in 1844 (p. 754), he is a campista.

Here follow the five men who held title to their properties: Felipe Lugo, regidor in 1832, 1833, 1836, and 1844, was proprietor of Rancho de Antonio María Lugo (1836 census, p. 703). José Sepúlveda, alcalde in 1837, regidor in 1823, 1834, 1839, and 1847, was proprietor of Rancho San Joaquin. But in the 1836 census he lives in Los Angeles (1836 census, p. 700). Bancroft suggests, however, (*The History*, 5:716) that he may have lived on the rancho. José del Carmen Lugo, Felipe Lugo's brother, regidor in 1838 and 1839, is a labrador proprietario in 1836 (p. 680). In 1844 (p. 754), he lists his occupation as campista and lives at Rancho San Bernardino. Bancroft (*The History*, 4:720) says that José del Carmen received title to San Bernardino sometime around 1844, perhaps earlier. By 1850 (p. 102) he is a grazier. José Antonio Yorba, regidor in 1847, was proprietor of Rancho Santa Ana Abajo (1836 census, p. 705 and 1844 census, p. 769). Ignacio María Alvarado, regidor in 1832 and 1833, held title to Rancho San José (1844 census, p. 773).

96. In a way, these numbers, already meager, might be inflated. Sometimes a cattleman would sit as an alcalde and, at another time, serve as sindico, thus making the pool of ranchero officeholders a bit smaller because one man held two or more positions. In 1839, for instance, the cattleman Antonio Machado sat as sindico, but later, rose to alcalde when a colleague resigned. Machado was regidor in 1833 and 1838, and later served as sindico and alcalde in 1839.

97. Here follow the ranchos of Los Angeles. Please note that we present information as it appears in the censuses. When the name of the rancho appears in the census, we record the name of the person who, for all intents and purposes, should have been the proprietor. Our reading of the evidence may put us at odds with Bancroft's findings. One need only to read the information above in n. 95 to see how our findings do not necessarily square with Bancroft's. To muddle the picture even more, we make no attempt to solve any mysteries. For example in 1844, in the case of Rancho de la Merced, we see the name of Domingo Salgado. He might have been the proprietor as the 1844 count suggests, but as a ten-year-old boy identified as a *sirviente*, or servant,

he might have had difficulty getting the attention of his ranch hands. Nor do we find out why some ranchos appeared in 1836, but do not make the census eight years later. For example, Bayona, or La Ballona, which is the proper spelling, sits in the 1836 count, but is missing in 1844.

1836

	Proprietor	Rancho	Page in census
1.	Policarpio Higuera	Rincon de la Brea	701
2.	José Manuel Cota	Bayona	701
3.	Juan Feliz	San José	702
4.	Macis (?) Sánchez	Alamitos	703
5.	Felipe Lugo	Rancho de Anto. Lugo	703
6.	Teodosio Yorba	Santa Ana	704
7.	José Antonio Yorba	Santa Ana Abajo	705
8.	Joaquin Ruiz	Las Bolsas	706
9.	Bernardo Yorba	San Antonio	706
10.	Juan Pacifico Ontiveros	Rancho San José Pacifico	707
11.	Juan José Nieto	Rancho de los Coyotes	708
12.	Juan Perez	Rancho Santa Gertrudis	708
13.	José María Saens	Rancho de San Rafael	713
14.	Luciano Váldez	Rodeo de las Aguas	714
15.	Martín Ruiz	San Vicente	715
16.	Santiago Johnson	Rancho de San Pedro	718
17.	Julio Verdugo	Rancho de los Verdugos	718

1844

	Name	Rancho	Page in census
1.	Ramón Yorba	Santa Ana	769
2.	Catarina Ruiz	Bolsas	770
3.	Benito Wilson	Jurupa	772
4.	Francisca Uribes	Coyotes	772
5.	Andrés Duarte	Santo Domingo	773
6.	Ygnacio Alvarado	San José	773
7.	Diego Sepúlveda	Iucaipa (Yucaipa)	774
8.	David de Alejandro	Rincon	775
9.	Santiago Martinez	San Bernardino	775
10.	Juan Roland (Rowland)	Rancho de la Puente	777
11.	Julian Williams	Santa Ana del Chino	777
12.	Nasario Domínguez	San Pedro	778
13.	Pedro Perez	Santa Gertrudis	780
14.	José Sepúlveda	San Joaquin	780
15.	Julio Berduzco	San Rafael	784
16.	Domingo Salgado (?)	Rancho de la Merced	784

98. Bancroft claims that the angeleños held title to thirty-nine ranchos between 1831 and 1840, and then forty-seven for the next period between 1841 and 1845. Admittedly, Bancroft is not sure how many ranchos there were between 1841 and 1845. He counts thirty-seven, but when he adds the figures from other authorities, the number increases to forty-seven and perhaps fifty. We stick with forty-seven. See *The History,*

3:634n. 3, and then 4:634–35n. 13. For another view of ranchos in California, see Ogden Hoffman, *Report of Land Cases Determined in the United States District Court for the Northern District of California* (San Francisco: Numa Hubert, 1862).

99. Antonio Ríos-Bustamante, "Nineteenth Century Mexican Californians a Conquered Race: From Landowners to Laborers and 'Tenants at Will,'" in *Regions of La Raza: Varying Interpretations of Mexican California,* ed. Antonio Ríos-Bustamante, 237–65 (Encino, CA: Floricanto Press, 1993).

100. Benjamin Hayes, "Notes on California Affairs," 3, Bancroft Library, University of California, Berkeley.

101. Bancroft, *The History,* 4:785.

102. Antonio Coronel Collection, #455, no year provided, SCWH. Evidently, the creator of the calendar—was it Coronel?—copied the original from an almanac.

103. Coronel, *Cosas de California,* 79. As will be discussed, Coronel said that when it came time to pray the angeleños consulted the family clock.

104. Lugo, "Life of a Rancher," 215. Lugo says that families rose at "three o'clock in the morning" to perform their daily chores. Perhaps they used a clock or watch to know what time to get out of bed.

105. *Exposition Addressed to the Chamber of Deputies of the Congress of the Union by Señor Don Carlos Antonio Carrillo, Deputy for Alta California Concerning the Regulation and Administration of the Pious Fund, Mexico, 1831,* trans. and ed., Herbert Priestley (San Francisco: John Henry Nash, 1938), 14. Carrillo says that the town crier should spread the contents of his proposal. Perhaps as part of their other duties, the town criers also announced the time.

106. *Diaries and Accounts of the Romero Expedition in Arizona and California,* ed. Lowell John Bean and William Marvin, (Los Angeles: Ward Ritchie Press, 1962), 40–41.

107. Piña's service record is in Bancroft, *The History,* 4:780.

108. Piña diary in Cook, *Expeditions to the Interior of California, Central Valley, 1820–1840,* (Berkeley: University of California Press, 1962), 177.

109. Vallejo to the commandant at the Port of San Francisco, San José. June 4, 1829. Cook, *Expeditions to the Interior,* 176

110. Ibid.

111. LACA, vol. 2, January 5, 1833, 16; November 13, 1836, 196; January 8, 1838, 514–15, trans.

112. Los Angeles Ayuntamiento Archives, vol. 4, September 24, 1833, Sp., Bancroft Library.

113. Archives of the Prefecture, vol. 1, March 4, 1841, 349, trans. City Clerk's Office of Los Angeles. The prefect is Santiago Arguello.

114. Archives of the Prefecture, vol. 1, February 10, 1842, 603, trans. City Clerk's Office of Los Angeles.

115. The length of a vara may be cause for debate. Nonetheless, by our reckoning, to follow the thinking of some other scholars, a vara measures 32.99 inches. See Antonio María Osio, *The History of Alta California,* ed. and trans. Rose Marie Beebe and Robert M. Senkewicz, (Madison: University of Wisconsin Press, 1996), 347.

116. LACA, vol. 1, February 11, 1836, 126–27, Sp.

117. LACA, vol. 1, February 25, 1836, 59, Sp., and LACA, vol. 1, February 4, 1836, February 11, 1836, 255–66, Sp.

118. LACA, vol. 1, March 10 and May 9, 1836, 290–95, Sp.

119. The religion of Mexican California awaits its historian. Older studies abound, but a more modern approach would help sort out some of the period's complexities. Nonetheless, for a good review of religion in Mexican California, see Father Zephyrin Engelhardt, 4 vols., *The Missions and Missionaries of California* (San Francisco: James

K. Barry Co., 1908–1915); Hubert Howe Bancroft, *The History,* esp. 2:158–73 and 3:301–62; Sherburne Cook, "The Indian versus the Spanish Mission," in *The California Indian and White Civilization* (Berkeley: University of California Press, 1976), esp. 91–134; Gerald Geary, *The Secularization of the California Missions, 1810–1846* (Washington D.C.: Catholic University of America, 1934); David Weber, *The Mexican Frontier, 1821–1846, The American Southwest Under Mexico* (Albuquerque: University of New Mexico Press, 1982), esp. 15–68; and Lisbeth Haas, *Conquests and Historical Identities* (Berkeley: University of California Press, 1995).

120. *Oxford English Dictionary,* 4th ed. (Oxford: Oxford University Press, 1993). I am not the first person to speculate on the meaning of religion's etymology. Joseph Campbell and Mircea Eliade have discussed the idea in great detail.

121. 1841 Will of Don Vicente Ortega, Book A, 1077, Los Angeles Prefect Records, SCWH.

122. 1849 Will of José Gaspar Valenzuela, Book A, 695, Los Angeles Prefect Records, SCWH.

123. Will of Anastacio Avila, Book A, 303, Los Angeles Prefect Records, SCWH. I am indebted to my friend and colleague Miroslava Chávez for translating the wills of Ortega, Valenzuela, and Avila.

124. The priests, of course, as did the gente de razón, claimed, but did not govern, the entire territory. For the figures concerning California's depth and reach, see James D. Hart, ed., *A Companion to California* (Berkeley: University of California Press, 1987), 74.

125. The image of the benevolent and kindly priests is an enduring image. To see how the Franciscans have contributed to the myth and history of southern California, see Starr, *Inventing the Dream,* 56–57.

126. In 1836, the vigilantes wanted a priest from San Fernando to confess a pair of murderers. See Victor Prudon "The Los Angeles Vigilantes," 11, Bancroft Library.

127. Carlos Antonio Carrillo, *Exposition,* 8.

128. Zephyrin Engelhardt, O.F.M. *The Missions and Missionaries of California,* 3:315–16. Engelhardt also argues that some missionaries thought the californios greedy and inconsiderate.

129. For a spirited defense of the missionaries' treatment of the Indians, see Francis Guest O.F.M., "Cultural Perspectives on California Mission Life" *Southern California Quarterly* 65 (Spring 1983): 1–65.

130. Woodrow Hansen, *The Search for Authority in California* (Oakland: Biobooks, 1960), esp. 6–8. Also see Engelhardt, *Missions and Missionaries,* vol. 3, esp. 67, 162, 629–37. Bancroft helps out as well. Consult, *The History,* 2:415, 479, 487.

131. Engelhardt, *Missions and Missionaries,* 3:69–70. It is not clear if the sum is a record of transactions up to that date, or if it is the result of one year's worth of business. But however one arrives at the figure, the money owed still proved to be a substantial amount. It should be noted that Engelhardt is a passionate defender of the missionaries. He is so committed to the cause of the priests that he cannot resist the temptation to chastise Bancroft for daring to utter criticism. See, for instance, his footnote condemning Bancroft as a "materialist" who "failed to understand the missionaries." Ibid., 68n. 30.

132. *The Southwest Expedition of Jedediah Smith,* ed. George Brooks (Glendale, CA: The Arthur Clark Company, 1977), 103–8.

133. Ibid., 104–5.

134. Prudon, "The Los Angeles Vigilantes," 12. The priest who Prudon condemns is Father Pedro Cabot, a Spaniard. One reason why Cabot may have earned enmity is that he refused to pledge allegiance to the Mexican republic. Still, even if political differences gave some angeleños reason to condemn the priest, he may have had a taste for luxury that did nothing for his reputation. See Bancroft, *The History,* 3:645–46n. 11.

135. For a critique of the Church's excesses, see Jean Franco, "En espera de una burguesía: la formación de la intelligentsia mexicana en la época de la Independencia" *Actas del Congreso de la Asociacion Internacional de Hispanistas*" (Madrid: Comisión Editorial del VIII Congreso de la AIH, 1986), esp., 21–35.

136. Coronel, *Cosas de California*, 75–76. Coronel implies that Zalvidea did not lose his senses until the 1840s, well after secularization. But it could also be that the priest's peculiar habits had persisted for some time.

137. Angustias de la Ord, *Occurrences in Hispanic California*, trans. and ed. Francis Price and William H. Ellison, (Washington D. C.: Academy of American Franciscan History, 1956), 35.

138. Antonio María Osio, *The History of Alta California*, 53n. 26, 267, 343.

139. Bancroft, *The History*, 2:42–43; 2:411–13.

140. Ibid. In fairness, Bancroft blames the soldiers for the controversy. I read his account a different way.

141. Bancroft, *The History*, 2:659.

142. Ibid.

143. Ibid.

144. Los Angeles Ayuntamiento Archives, vol. 2, February 13, 1837, 86, Sp., Bancroft Library.

145. LACA, vol. 2, April 14, 1838, 199–20, Sp.

146. Prudon, "The Los Angeles Vigilantes," 11.

147. LACA, vol. 2, June 11, 1837, 425–26, Sp. As a curiosity, the translation, also in the City Clerk's Office of Los Angeles, says the event happened on October 6, 1837, 197, trans.

148. Bancroft, *The History*, 5:621–22.

149. We do not necessarily speak of scourging for punishment. Think more of the penitent on his knees, seeking divinity with each application of the whip. For an explanation on the matter of whipping in California and Mexico, see Francis Guest, O.F.M., "Cultural Perspectives on California Mission Life" esp. 1–17.

150. Ramón Gutiérrez, "Crucifixion, Slavery, and Death," in *Over the Edge, Remapping the American West,* ed. Valerie Matsumoto and Blake Allmendiger, 253–71 (Berkeley: University of California Press, 1999).

151. Madame Calderón de la Barca, *Life in Mexico* (London: Chapman and Hall, 1843), in Lorayne Ann Horka-Follick, *Los Hermanos Penitentes* (Los Angeles: Westernlore Press, 1969), 64.

152. Hugo Reid Collection, San Joaquin to Mr. Editor, n.d. SCWH. Of course, we might think that the *cofradias,* the religious brotherhoods of New Mexico, had arisen in California. Indeed, with so many people whipping themselves it seemed that only a brotherhood could conduct the exercise. But thus far there is no evidence of the cofradias in Los Angeles.

153. Sepúlveda/Mott Collection, Box #1, Items #747 a, b, *coplas* by Francisco Avila, SCWH.

154. Don Pancho Rangel, "Vida de un ranchero," Thomas Temple Collection, Box 2, File #22, 33, trans. SCWH.

155. Lugo, "Life of a Rancher," 215.

156. Coronel, *Tales of Mexican California*, 79. To learn more about religion, magic, and witchcraft in the modern American Southwest and imagine how the residents of Mexican California approached spirituality, see *Papa Jim's Book of Spells* (San Antonio, 1999). Papa Jim, a *brujo*, or witch, runs a shop in San Antonio where he sells many ingredients to cure a variety of ills. One can find a cure for a broken heart or a way to avenge a wrong by learning how to cast a spell and purchasing some of his potions.

Chapter Three

1. *Alcalde Court Records, 1830–1850, vols. 1–7,* Natural History Museum, County of Los Angeles, SCWH. The tabulation is my own. I thank my friend and colleague Miroslava Chávez for showing me this reference.

2. For a brief discussion on the indigenous terms used by the gente de razón, see Stephen Hackel, "Land, Labor, and Production, The Colonial Economy of Spanish and Mexican California," in *Contested Eden, California Before the Gold Rush,* ed. Ramón Gutiérrez and Richard Orsi, 111–46 (Berkeley: University of California Press, 1998).

3. Gabriel García Márquez, *The General in His Labyrinth,* trans. Edith Grossman (New York: Penguin Books, 1990).

4. The diligencias, the summaries entered by priests to describe the betrothed and those who witnessed the marriage, could provide clues about the identity of husband and wife. A diligencia often stated where one of the wedding partners was born—for instance if one came from an Indian village, the name appeared in the record—or the document simply declared that the husband or wife was an Indian. When Francisco López, to take an example, married María de Jésus on April 24, 1846, the diligencia identified the bride as a "neofita . . . [from] the mission of La Purísima. See Thomas Temple Collection, Box 5, File B, #1, 11, SCWH.

5. Thomas Temple Collection, Box 9, Folder #M2, #M3, 25, SCWH.

6. Ibid., 30.

7. Ibid., 86.

8. Other difficulties deserve mention. The marriage records could be filled with mistakes. San Fernando Mission, for instance, has no record of gente de razón marrying Indians between 1821 and 1848, an omission that strains credibility.

9. Thomas Temple Collection, Box 9, Folder #M2 and #M3, Vicente Lorenzana, "Indio" marries María Ana Verdugo, (25); Pascual Joseph "of the ranchería Topet" marries María de Los Angeles, Joseph Manuel (Rosas?) "de la mision" marries María Domingo Saez, and Manuel Antonio (Pérez), "indio viudo de Margarita" marries María Florentina Alvitre (30); José Miguel "neofito de la mision de la ex-mision de San Fernando" marries Rafaela Arriola, (45); Thomas Temple Collection, Box 5, Section B, File #1 Pedro Ramón "neofito" marries Antonia Pérez, (n.p.) SCWH.

10. Hugo Reid of Scotland marries Bartolomea Comicrabit, in September 1837, Thomas Temple Collection, Box 9, Folder #M-2, #M-3, (44), SCWH. Later in 1847, Felipe Lancia of Germany (?) marries Aniceta, "neofita de la mision," Box 5, File B, #1 (13), SCWH.

11. Thomas Temple Collection, Box 9, #M-2, #M-3, Antonio Matias Villa marries María de Jésus de Asubsabit "neofita de esta mision" and José Pantaleon (?) Guerrero marries María Dorotea "de Masima, india y de padre no conocido" (41); Thomas Temple Collection Box 5, File B, #1, SCWH, Francisco López marries "la neofita" María de Jésus (11); Felipe Valenzuela marries María Cesaria, "neofita de la mis[ion] de San Luis Rey" (13); Francisco Benites marries Fabiana "neofita de San José" and José María López marries Guadalupe Martínez "neofita"(14). Thomas Temple Collection, Box 5, Section B, File #1, n.p. (Note that Box 5, Section B, File #1 is different from Box 5, File B, #1.), SCWH, Estanislao Valenzuela marries María Manuela "neofita;" Juan Francisco Salazar marries María de Jésus, "neofita;" Manuel D'Oliveira marries Rufina "neofita;" José Dolores Gracia (?) Higuera marries Bibiana "viuda india;" Francisco Verdugo" marries Francisca "neofita de San Gabriel." We also include people mentioned in the death book from the Plaza Church. Thomas Temple Collection, Plaza Church Death Records, Box 5, Section A, File #2, n.p., SCWH. The deceased are

mentioned first. Pedro García was married to María Rafaela "Neophyte of San Diego;" Geronima Yupinisin was married to Juan José Villa (?); Potenciana Granario "neophyte of San Ignacio, Baja California" was married to José María Duarte.

12. Salvador Vallejo, "The Origin of the Californian Aborigines," 1874 (?), trans. 1–2, Bancroft Library, University of California, Berkeley.

13. "Memoirs of Diego Olivera," as told to Alexander Taylor, 1864, Thomas Temple collection, Box #2, File 19, 86, SCWH.

14. For more on how Indian women resisted and suffered the assaults of Spanish and Mexican troopers, see Antonia Castañeda "Engendering the History of Alta California, 1769–1848: Gender, Sexuality and the Family," in *Contested Eden, California Before the Gold Rush,* ed., Ramón Gutiérrez and Richard Orsi, 230–59 (Berkeley: University of California Press, 1998).

15. "Memoirs of Diego Olivera," 3–4.

16. Gerald Geary, A.M., *The Secularization of the California Missions* (Washington D.C.: The Catholic University of America, 1934), 172.

17. Zephyrin Engelhardt, O.F.M, 4 vols., *The Missions and Missionaries of California,* vol. 4, (San Francisco: James Barry and Company, 1913), 8–10.

18. LACA, vol. 1, February 19, 1846 and May 2, 1846, 527–35, Sp.

19. LACA, vol. 1, May 2, 1846, 527–35, Sp.

20. David Courtwright, *Violent Land* (Cambridge, MA: Harvard University Press, 1995).

21. See Michael Costeloe, *Centralism in Mexico, Santa Anna and the* Hombres de Bien, *1835–1846* (Cambridge, England: Cambridge University Press, 1990), esp. 10–22.

22. Hugo Reid Collection, "Anecdote of a Lawyer," n.p. (1850s?), SCWH.

23. Antonio María Osio, *The History of Alta California,* trans. and ed. Rose Marie Beebe and Robert Senkewicz, (Madison: University of Wisconsin Press, 1996), 151n. 36, 297.

24. For more on Coronel's life, see Bancroft, *The History,* (San Francisco: The History Company, 1883–1887), 2:768.

25. Coronel, *Tales of Mexican California,* 6.

26. Thomas Temple Collection, Baptismal Record, April 19, 1848, Box 5, File C (1–10), SCWH.

27. *Census of the County and City of Los Angeles, California for the year 1850,* ed. Maurice Newmark and Marco Newmark, (Los Angeles: The Times-Mirror Press, 1929), 41. Antonio María Osio says that it was not uncommon for gente de razón households to employ Indian women from the missions as domestic servants. See Osio, *The History of Alta California,* 134.

28. 1836 Census, *The Historical Society of Southern California Quarterly* 18, no. 3 (1936): 728.

29. Aldous Huxley, *The Devils of Loudon* (New York: Harper Colophon Books, 1965), 14–15.

30. Bancroft, *The History,* 3:641–42n. 8. For a passionate defense of Boscana, see Maynard Geiger, O.F.M., *Franciscan Missionaries in Hispanic California* (San Marino, CA: The Huntington Library, 1969), 31. Father Geiger explained that any charge against Boscana's morality was "confused and unsubstantiated." For more on Boscana, see Bancroft, *The History,* 3:641–42n. 8. In time, Boscana would write the scholarly study, *Chinigchinich.* Also consult, *As the Padres Saw Them, California Indian Life and Customs as Reported by the Franciscan Missionaries, 1813–1815,* ed. Maynard Geiger, O.F.M., (Santa Barbara: Santa Barbara Mission Archive Library, 1976), 105.

31. Bancroft, *The History,* 4:751. Ordaz was at La Purísima and Santa Barbara, two of the seven missions he served.

32. Travis Hudson, ed. *Breath of the Sun, Life in Early California As Told by a Chumash Indian, Fernando Librado to John Harrington,* (Ventura: Malki Museum Press, 1979), 52–53.

33. Ibid., 52.

34. Ibid., 52–53.

35. The priest who performed the ceremony could have bungled the names or birthplaces of the parents who presented their child for a christening. If he did err, we could count more children.

36. Thomas Temple Collection, Box 5, C (1–10), SCWH.

37. See esp. Box 5, Section #A, File #2m Plaza Church Death Records, SCWH.

38. For a discussion of war as a means of reproduction, see Edward Tabor Linenthal, "From Hero to Anti-Hero: The Transformation of the Warrior in Modern America," in *Religion and Politics in the Modern World,* ed. Peter Merkl and Ninian Smart (New York: New York University Press, 1983), 232–48. Also see James William Gibson, *Warrior Dreams, Violence and Manhood in Post-Vietnam America* (New York: Hill and Wang, 1990), esp., 17–32.

39. Linenthal, "From Hero to Anti-Hero," 232–33.

40. D. A. Brading, *The First America, The Spanish monarchy, Creole Patriots, and the Liberal state, 1492–1867* (Cambridge, England: Cambridge University Press, 1991), esp. 583–87, 601–2.

41. For the renaming of the province and the design of California's crest, see Bancroft, *The History,* 3:38.

42. C. Alan Hutchinson, "The Mexican Government and the Mission Indians of California," *The Americas* 21 (1965): 335–62.

43. For more on the liberal fear of racial equality, see Florencia Mallon, "Peasant and State Formation in Nineteenth Century Mexico," *Political Power and Social Theory,* vol. 7 (1988): 1–54.

44. Mallon, "Peasant and State Formation," esp. 5, 9. Also consult, Charles Hale, *Mexican Liberalism in the Age of Mora, 1821–1853* (New Haven: Yale University Press, 1968), esp. 234–39.

45. Toricuato S. Di Tella, "The Dangerous Classes in Early Nineteenth Mexico," *Journal of Latin American Studies,* 5, no. 1 (1973): 79–105. Consult as well, Silvia Arrom, "Popular Politics in Mexico City: The Parían Riot, 1828" *Hispanic American Historical Review* 68, no. 2 (1988): 245–68.

46. Lorenzo de Zavala, "La sociedad mexicana y despues de la independencia," in *Espejos de discordias, la sociedad mexicana vista por Lorenzo Zavala, José Luis Mora, y Lucas Alaman,* ed. Andrés Lira, 31–43 (Mexico D.F.: SEP Cultura).

47. Lucas Alaman, "La sociedad mexicana y la vida nacional," in Ibid., 168–95.

48. José Luis Mora, "Una vision de la sociedad mexicana," in Ibid., 72–140.

49. Population estimates come from two sources. For the gente de razón, see Leonard Pitt, *Decline of the Californios, A Social History of the Spanish-Speaking Californians, 1846–1890* (Berkeley: University of California Press, 1971), 4–5. Pitt, however, makes a rough guess. The figures for the Indians may be more exact. See Sherburne Cook, "The Indian Versus the Spanish Mission," in *The Conflict Between the Indian and White Civilization* (Berkeley: University of California Press, 1976), 1–194, (table 1, p. 4).

50. For more on the meaning of proletario, see J. Corominas, *Diccionario crítico etimológico de la lengua castellana* (Bern, Switzerland: Editorial Francke, 1954), 3:892. Corominas quotes a predecessor "Proletario . . . de proletarius 'que sólo importa al Estado como proceador de hijos: proletariado.'" Also see, Martín Alonso, *Enciclopedia*

del idioma (Madrid: Aguilar, 1958) 3:3409. Alonso provides one more interpretation. He writes, "En la antigua Roma, ciudadanos pobres que sólo con su prole [from the Latin, *proles*—lineage] podían servir al Estado."

51. LACA, vol. 2, May 2, 1846, 1082–84, Sp.
52. LACA, vol. 4, November 3, 1847 and November 20, 1847, 620–38, Sp.
53. LACA, vol. 4, August 11, 1849 and August 14, 1849, 722–24.
54. Both quotations on the Chumash rebellion and Estanislao's attacks come from Juan Bautista Alvarado, *Historia de california*, trans. and ed. Earl Hewitt, 2:42, 2:52, Bancroft Library.
55. Carlos Carrillo, *Exposition Addressed to the Chamber of Deputies of the Congress of the Union by Señor Don Carlos Antonio Carrillo, Deputy for Alta California Concerning the Regulation and Administration of the Pious Fund, 1831*, trans. and ed. Herbert Priestley, (San Francisco: John Henry Nash, 1938), 3. For more on Carrillo's career (he was also a soldier), see Bancroft, *The History*, 2:743.
56. In 1833, Carrillo received a grant to Rancho Sespe, an estate carved from lands once belonging to Missions San Buenaventura and San Fernando, *Exposition*, xvii.
57. Ibid., 4.
58. Ibid.
59. Ibid., 5.
60. Ibid., 7.
61. Ibid.
62. The controversy of 1834 involved the Híjar-Padrés expedition and the government's plan to secularize the missions. Figueroa suspected that the expedition and the national government conspired against him. He was wrong, but the dispute consumed a great amount of his energy and may have figured in his death a year later. For more information, see C. Alan Hutchinson, *Mexican Frontier Settlement: The Híjar-Padrés Colony and Its Origins* (New Haven: Yale University Press, 1969). Also see, *Manifesto to the Mexican Republic which Brigadier General José Figueroa, Commandant and Political Chief of Upper California, Presents on His Conduct and That of José María de Híjar and José María Padrés as Directors of Colonization in 1834 and 1835*, trans. and ed. C. Alan Hutchinson, (Berkeley: University of California Press, 1978).
63. Ibid., "unhinge society" remark is on 92. The "ominous sect" statement appears on 95.
64. Juan Bautista Alvarado was Figueroa's secretary. Ibid., 96.
65. Bancroft, *The History*, 4:68.
66. James Sandos, "Levantamiento!" *The Californians* 5, no. 1 (Jan–Feb., 1987): 8–20.
67. Osio, *The History of Alta California*, 62.
68. F. W. Beechey's translation of José Antonio Sánchez' diary, in Sherburne Cook, *Expeditions to the Interior of California, Central Valley, 1820–1840*, (Berkeley: University of California Press, 1961), 167–68.
69. Antonio María Osio, "Historia de California," Cook, *Expeditions*, 169–71. Here we use Cook's translation rather than the Beebe and Senkewicz version.
70. Ibid., Cook, *Expeditions*, 171.
71. "Journal of Sergeant Sánchez," in Cook, *Expeditions*, 168.
72. Bancroft, *The History*, 3:630–31n. 1.
73. Ibid.
74. Ibid., 4:208n. 6.
75. George Harwood Phillips, *Chiefs and Challengers* (Berkeley: University of California Press, 1980), 40.
76. LACA, vol. 2, May 31, 1837, 422–23, Sp.

77. Phillips, *Chiefs and Challengers*, 41–42.
78. Di Tella, "The Dangerous Classes in Early Nineteenth Century Mexico," esp. 81, 103–5. For another view, see Hale, *Mexican Liberalism in the Age of Mora*, esp. 239–47.
79. LACA, vol. 2, May 2, 1846, 1082–84, Sp.
80. See Zephyrin Engelhardt, O.F.M., *The Missions and Missionaries of California*, 3:416–17. Also consult Gerald Geary, A.M., *The Secularization of the California Mission*, 124–25.
81. See the *Manifesto*, 64–5nn. 120–21; also see the original text, 106–8.
82. Osio, 133–35.
83. For more on Figueroa's battles against Indians in Mexico, see Figueroa's *Manifesto*, 4.
84. Cook, *Expeditions*, 201.
85. Ibid., 201.
86. Ibid., 197.
87. Coronel, *Tales of Mexican California*, 44.
88. The Diary of Joaquin Piña in Cook, in *Expeditions* 177–80.
89. Jack Holtermann, "The Revolt of Estanislao," *The Indian Historian* 3, no. 1 (197): 43–44; also see Cook, *Expeditions*, 165–66.
90. Cook, *Expeditions*, 171.
91. José de Jésus Vallejo to Mariano Guadalupe Vallejo, San Jose, August 21, 1837, Cook, *Expeditions*, 190. Also see Bancroft, *The History*, 5:753. José de Jésus Vallejo, a relative of Mariano Vallejo, was the civil administrator of San José Mission.
92. Coronel, *Tales of Mexican California*, 44.
93. Juan Bernal, "Memoria," in Cook, *Expeditions*, 194–96.
94. Cook, *Expeditions*, 166.
95. The Pardo—the name means "brown" incidentally—biography appears in Bancroft, *The History*, 4:766–77.
96. Archives of the Prefecture of Los Angeles, vol. 1, June 30, 1842, 688, trans. City Clerk's Office of Los Angeles.
97. See the photographs in Pitt, *Decline of the Californios*.
98. A quick study of the name changuanoso, however, reveals origins beyond New Mexico. Bancroft says the word comes from "Shawnee." By the mid-nineteenth century in Sonora, a state in northern Mexico, the word evolved into changuano, a mercenary who fought the Apaches. In time the term rested on Indians and non-Indians who traveled the Santa Fe Trail, the route connecting New Mexico with southern California. Bancroft Research Notes, "Commerce, 1829–1838," Heading 1838. Also see Bancroft Research Notes, Heading 1837, *El Sonorense*, April 4, 1851.
99. See Bancroft Research Notes, "Commerce, 1841–1848," Heading 1841, Dept. State Papers, Angeles, 6, 77–78. Aug. 19, 1841; and Bancroft Research Notes "Commerce 1838–1870," Heading 1840, Dept. State Papers, Angeles, Prefect of Juzgados, 4, 55
100. Bancroft Research Notes, "Commerce, 1827–1838," Heading 1837, Botello "*Anales del Sur*," 37.
101. Bancroft Research Notes, "Commerce, 1829–1838," Heading 1838.
102. Bancroft Research Notes, "Commerce, 1839–1870," Heading 1840, Dept. State Papers, February 21, 1840, Prefect of Juzgado, 4, 43.
103. Description of raid and discussion of "white Indians" appears in Phillips, *Chiefs and Challengers, Indian Resistance and Cooperation in Southern California*, 42–43. For one more discussion on "white Indians," see Don Pancho Rangel, "La Vida de un vaquero" as told to Thomas Temple in 1934. The Thomas Temple Collection, Box #2, File 22, 2, SCWH. In the tradition of Bancroft, Temple hunted down old angeleños and recorded

their life histories. Pancho Rangel, one of Temple's subjects, was ninety-four-years-old when he recounted his life. Born in 1840 at Mission San Gabriel, Rangel never moved far from his birthplace and witnessed the transformation of Los Angeles and environs.

104. Juan Bautista Alvarado, "Historia de California," 2:150, trans. Earl Hewitt, typescript Bancroft Library.

105. Osio, *The History of Alta California*, 216.

106. Angustias de la Ord, *Occurrences in Hispanic California*, trans. and ed. Francis Price and William H. Ellison (Washington D.C.: Academy of American Franciscan History, 1951), 54. In the footnotes compiled by Price and Ellison, they quote Agustín Janssens who thought that hunger and poverty drove the cholos to commit depredations. Janssens, apparently, did not think the cholos bloodthirsty beasts. *Occurrences in Hispanic California*, 90n. 150.

107. Alvarado, *Historia de California*, trans. and ed. Earl Hewitt, 2:120, Bancroft Library.

108. As some might joke, González was upset about the meaning of his surname. One authority suggests that the name comes from "Gonzalo," German or Gothic for battle and/or elf, hence warrior dwarf, or warrior elf; see H. Amanda Robb and Andrew Chesler *Encyclopedia of American Family Names* (New York: HarperCollins Publishers, 1995), 252. One more source says that González, and other related names, is "[un] nombre personal germánico de tradición visigoda Gundislavus; éste, a su vez, es una forma latinizada compuesta del radical gótico *gunthis-*, 'lucha.'" Then, to disavow any mention of elves, the authority claims that the second part of the name is "not very clear." Nonetheless, the authority speculates that the second part could come from the Latin "albus," meaning white; Roberto Faure, María Asunción Ribes, and Antonio García, *Diccionario de appellidos españoles* (Madrid: Espasa, 2001), 392.

109. For more on Alvarado's attempts to consolidate his rule in California, see Bancroft, *The History*, esp. 3:481–84.

110. Bernal, "Memoria," in Cook, *Expedition*, 194–96.

111. Ibid., Cook, *Expedition*, 194, 198n. 20, 209.

112. José María Amador, "Memoria sobre la historia de California," in Cook, *Expedition*, 196–98.

Chapter Four

1. Copy of José Palomares' "Memoria," Thomas Temple Collection, Box #2, 28, in Spanish, SCWH. For the remark about Palomares' "psychopathic tendencies," see Sherburne Cook, *Expeditions to the Interior of California, Central Valley, 1820–1840* (Berkeley: University of California Press, 1961), 194. Palomares's treatment of the captured Indian deserves more mention. In a manner of speaking, he gelded the Indian as he did his roosters.

2. José María Amador, "Memorias sobre la historia de California," in Cook, *Expeditions*, 196–98.

3. Joaquin Piña, "Diario de la espedicion de San José," in Cook, *Expeditions*, 177–80.

4. Juan Bojórquez, "Recuerdos sobre la historia de California, in Cook, *Expeditions*, 171–72.

5. José Palomares, "Memoria," in Cook, *Expeditions*, 199–203.

6. For more on the Indian approach to war, see Kenneth Stewart, "Mohave Warfare," 431–44. Also consult Walter Goldschmidt, George Foster, and Walter Essene, "War Stories from Two Enemy Tribes," 445–58. Both appear in *The California Indians: A Source Book*, ed. R. F. Heizer and M. A. Whipple, (Berkeley: University of California Press, 1980).

7. The angeleños apparently went into battle well armed. A list of angeleño weaponry for 1836 suggests that many men possessed a great amount of firepower. Vicente Sánchez, for instance, owned a "double-barreled shotgun." Louis Bouchet had a "rifle, one ounce caliber." Luis Arenas, meanwhile, owned a "rifle, a quarter ounce caliber, a musket, a pair of pistols and a sword." See Archives for the Prefecture, Book "A," 1825–1850, May 24, 1836, 51–61, 67, trans. City Clerk's Office. In addition to guns, the angeleños rode into battle with other types of weapons. Pancho Rangel says that "we also carried knives in a scabbard on the outside of the right leg, thrust into the garter of our [boots]." At other times, men "usually carried swords secured to the right side of the saddle, underneath the leg." Pancho Rangel, "La vida de un vaquero," as told to Thomas Temple II, Temple Collection, Box 2, File 22, 23, SCWH.

8. Joaquin Piña, in Cook, *Expeditions to the Central Valley*, 177.

9. Ibid.

10. Ibid.

11. José Palomares, in Cook, *Expeditions to the Central Valley*, 202–3.

12. Ibid., 203.

13. José de Jésus Vallejo, "Reminicencias Historicas de California," 1874, 6, Sp., Bancroft Library.

14. Vallejo could have responded to Yankee taunts that the californios resembled Indians. During the Gold Rush, delegates at the constitutional convention argued that Indian blood made the Spanish-speaking populace as "bad as any free Negro in the North or the worse slaves of the South;" see J. Ross Brown, *Report of the Debates in the Convention of California on the Formation of the State Constitution in September and October, 1849*, (Washington D.C., 1850), 143. A bit later, Manuel Domínguez, a ranchero from Los Angeles, also endured Yankee taunts. Traveling to San Francisco to testify in a court case, opposing counsel protested that Domínguez had indigenous blood, and by state law no Indian could give evidence against a white man. The judge agreed and dismissed Domínguez. These incidents, no doubt known by Vallejo and other californios, cut deeply; see Pitt, *Decline of the Californios*, (Berkeley: University of California Press, 1965,) 202.

15. For more on mutilation during war, see Richard Trexler, *Sex and Conquest* (Ithaca: Cornell University Press, 1995), 12–37.

16. José María Amador, Cook, *Expeditions,* 196–97.

17. Jeremy Adelman and Stephen Aron, "From Borderlands to Borders: Empires, Nation-States, and the Peoples of North American History," *The American Historical Review* 2 (June 1999): 814–41.

18. José Palomares, "Memoria," Thomas Temple II, Box 2, File #28, 1–3, Sp. SCWH.

19. According to the historians William Mason and Lowell Bean, the Indians, save for collecting the sometime scalp, did not mutilate their foes until the arrival of Spanish-speaking settlers. *Diaries and Accounts of the Romero Expedition*, trans. and ed. Lowell John Bean and William Marvin Mason, (Los Angeles: Ward Ritchie Press, 1962), 84n. 6, 112.

20. For each incident of severing ears, see Mason and Bean, *Diaries and Accounts*, 84n. 6, 112.

21. Juan Bernal, "Memoria," in Cook, *Expeditions*, 194–96.

22. José del Carmen Lugo, "Life of a Rancher," trans. Helen Pruitt Beattie, *Historical Society of Southern California Quarterly* 32, no. 3 (1950): 185–236.

23. Jack Holtermann, "The Revolt of Yozcolo," *The Indian Historian* 3, no. 2 (1970): 19–23.

24. F. W. Beechey, "Voyages to the Pacific," in Cook, *Expeditions to the Interior of California*, 167–68. Cook says there are problems with Beechey's description. He was visiting San Francisco during the episodes he recorded in his memoir.

25. See chap. 1 for examples of non-Indians forced to work for gente de razón.

26. Alan Almquist and Robert Heizer, *The Other Californians, Prejudice, Discrimination under Spain, Mexico and the United States to 1920*, (Berkeley: University of California Press, 1977), 18–19.

27. Bancroft Research Notes, "Agriculture, 1841–1854," Heading 1842, n.p.

28. William Wilcox Robinson, "The Indians of Los Angeles," *Historical Society of Southern California Quarterly* 29, no. 4 (December 1938): 156–57. Also see, George Harwood Phillips, "Indians in Los Angeles, 1781–1875: Economic Integration, Social Disintegration," *Pacific Historical Review* 49, no. 3 (1980): 427–52. On other occasions, the angeleños practiced debt peonage. The master advanced the worker some form of pay. The Indian would have to work off the debt, but a few entered a trap they had difficulty escaping. The compensation often went quickly, and they asked for another advance. In time, the workers' burden increased, and they found themselves bound to the employer's service for an extended period. See Douglas Monroy, *Thrown Among Strangers* (Berkeley: University of California Press, 1990), 86,160–71. Also consult Lisbeth Haas, *Conquests and Historical Identities in California*, (Berkeley: University of California Press, 1995), 55–60.

29. Admittedly, it is difficult to determine the number of households. In most instances, Mexican surveyors did not distinguish one household from another.

30. For more on the 1844 census, see Bancroft, *The History*, 4:628n. 9.

31. For more on the capture of Indians, especially the men, see Cook, *Expeditions to the Interior of California*, 191, 193.

32. In the 1844 census for instance, Manuela, a twelve-year-old Indian, carried domestica next to her name. 1844 census, 776. In Mexico's northern reaches, residents also called their captive children, *criados*, a word meaning, "one being raised." The term could also describe a servant. However, the word criado rarely, if at all, appears in angeleño records.

33. Howard Lamar adds that in New Mexico and elsewhere, the gente de razón often identified an Indian captive as an orphan. See "From Bondage to Contract: Ethnic Labor in the West, 1821–1890," in *The Countryside in the Age of Capitalist Transformation* (Chapel Hill: University of North Carolina Press, 1985), 293–324.

34. Vicente Gomez, "Lo Que Sabes Sobre Cosas de California," 85–86, Sp. Bancroft Library.

35. Leland Creer, "Indian Slavery in the Great Basin," *New Mexico Historical Review* 25, no. 3: 171–83.

36. Ibid.

37. Ibid.

38. Creer, "Indian Slavery," 180–81.

39. "F. W. Beechey's translation of the journal kept by José Antonio Sanchéz," in Cook, *Expeditions*, 168.

40. Cook, *Expeditions*, 180, 189. For more on taking captives in the years before secularization, see Sherburne Cook, "The Physical and Demographic Reaction of the Non-Mission Indians in Colonial and Provincial California," in *The Conflict Between the California Indian and White Civilization*, 197–251 (Berkeley: University of California Press, 1976).

41. Coronel, *Tales of Mexican California*, 54.

42. Howard Lamar, "From Bondage to Contract," 296–98.
43. Excerpts from Beechey's "Voyage of the Pacific," in Cook, *Expeditions*, 167–68.
44. Ibid.,191.
45. Ibid., 193.
46. Bancroft, *The History,* 5:566.
47. Joaquin Piña "Diario," in Cook, *Expeditions,* 179.
48. Here follows are methodology for identifying captives: A name, for instance, always the first item entered in the censuses, could provide good clues. An Indian prisoner would earn a Christian first name upon baptism, with the master and mistress often standing as godparents. But, in most cases, the captive would not receive the family name. Hence, one would see a Juan or Toribio, but no surname. Yet, many gente de razón children, often following the mother and father in the census, would be no different. They, too, often lacked a family name. As a result, we must take care not to confuse an Indian captive with gente de razón children.

Sometimes, along with the name, the census taker entered other tidbits that identified captives. Age, for instance, offers some clues. A three-year-old child living with a gente de razón couple well up in years, some fifty or older, certainly demands another look. The little one may have been a captive being groomed to serve the household. An odd word here and there offers even more information. For example, in the 1836 census we see huerfano, and the feminine form huerfana, or orphan, squeezed into the census columns. A family, of course, could have adopted a nephew or niece, but in an era when the gente de razón often seized Indian children, the youngster could have been a captive torn from his parents.

The census column designating occupation can also help us identify captives. The method, though, does not always work for Indian adults. A mature captive forced to work for a master would bear the title "servant" or "laborer." However, the Indians who earned a salary, as did the gente de razón laboring for pay, often carried the same designations. Occupation, or any rank that compares, applies best to children. In many parts of Mexico's northern territories, settlers often called captive children, criados. To be honest, however, the term criado rarely appeared in angeleño records. Instead, a captive child often bore the title of domestic.

In the end, place of origin seems the best way to identify captives. Nevertheless, we need to exercise great care. When listing an Indian's birthplace, the surveyor sometimes wrote gentil, a vague term that could describe a Cahuilla or Serrano, Indian peoples close to Los Angeles, or refer to a Paiute from New Mexico. A Paiute, like any other Indian from far away, could qualify as a captive. But a Cahuilla, or another Indian from southern California, though sometimes mistreated by gente de razón employers, could have labored on his own volition and not count as a captive pressed into service.

We only consider Indians who the census taker specifically identified as coming from beyond the Los Angeles area. Mohaves, Paiutes, and Yumas, all peoples who inhabited the eastern deserts of California or the Great Basin, make our list. A tulareño, from tulares, the Spanish word for California's Central Valley, counts as well. Indians from the Mexican state of Sonora qualify too, but those from Baja California give us pause. In the seventeenth and eighteenth centuries, first the Jesuits, then the Franciscans constructed missions in Baja California. As a consequence, many Indians from Baja California who had converted, and acquired Spanish or Mexican habits, learned to live like the gente de razón. If they gained their freedom from the missions, some headed to Los Angeles or other settlements. No one, as far as we can tell, forced them to travel north. Still, in some cases, Indians from Baja California could have been captives. The trader described by Vicente Gómez sold Indian youths captured in Baja California. Therefore, to understand which Indian could, or could not, be a captive calls for patience. A name, a person's age, more likely an Indian's birthplace, each by itself, or, in combination, may reveal a captive's identity.

49. Here follows a list of Indians who may have been captives in Los Angeles. The names come from the 1836 and 1844 censuses. The 1836 census is in the *Historical Society of Southern California Quarterly* 18, no. 3 (1936): 667–730. The 1844 census is in the *Historical Society of Southern California Quarterly* 42, no. 4 (1960): 360–414. To compile an accurate Indian count for 1844, we also use the original census found in the Los Angeles City Archives, 3:732–84.

1836

	Name	Sex	Age	Origin	Page
1.	Manuel	male	5	Apache	673
2.	María de Jésus	female	12	Yuma	721
3.	Nicolas	male	30	Yuma	721
4.	Ygnacio	male	25	Yaqui	721
5.	Francisco Arenas*	male	7	Yuma	722
6.	Ventura	female	16	Yuma	722
7.	Catalina	female	12	Yuma	722
8.	Francisca	female	7	Yuma	722
9.	Gentil*	male	23	Gentil	722
10.	Francisco	male	12	Yuma	722
11.	Francisco	male	6	Baja Cal.	723
12.	Leguia	female	9	Baja Cal.	723
13.	Manuel Caniedo (?)	male	11	Yuma	723
14.	Cristobal Polica (?)*	male	27	Canieyo (?)	723
15.	Gentila*	female	20	Canieyo (?)	723
16.	Gentila*	female	20	Canieyo (?)	723
17.	Gentila*	female	12	Canieyo (?)	723
18.	Miguel	male	18	Yuma	723
19.	José Antonio	male	18	Yuma	723
20.	Gentil*	male	25	Gentil	723
21.	Isidro*	male	19	Cayego (?)	724
22.	Indio*	male	30	Tulares	724
23.	Indio*	male	30	Tulares	724
24.	Indio*	male	29	Tulares	724
25.	Indio*	male	31	Tulares	724
26.	Gentil*	male	33	Tulares	724
27.	Gentil*	male	31	Tulares	724

Explanation of asterisks: Francisco Arenas seemed to be the adopted son of Luis Arenas. The titles "Gentil," "Gentila," and "Indio" went to Indians who had not converted. Manuel Caniedo and Cristobal Polica retained part of their indigenous names. Finally, Canieyo and Cayego are the names of regions or Indian groups that have yet to be identified.

The Indians for the 1844 census come from the Los Angeles City Archives, vol. 3. The reproduction that appears in the Historical Society for Southern California Quarterly failed to include the Indians.

1844

	Name	Sex	Age	Origin	Page
1.	Viviana	female	20	Los Angeles	737
2.	María Antonia	female	24	New Mexico	775
3.	Guadalupe*	female	18	New Mexico	775
4.	Pablo	female	12	New Mexico	775
5.	Carolina	female	16	Payuche	785
6.	Gertrudes	female	10	Yuma	785
7.	Peladito*	male	20	Gentil	786
8.	Concepción	female	11	Yuma	786
9.	Adelaida	female	11	Yuma	786
10.	Valero	male	11	Payuche	786
11.	Aucencia	female	10	Payuche	786
12.	Dario	male	3	Payuche	786
13.	Brigida	female	13	Baja Cal.	787
14.	Dolores	female	12	Yuma	787
15.	Angel*	male	30	Fulareño	790
16.	María Antonia	female	10	Payuche	790
17.	Narciso	male	6	Yuma	790
18.	Manuel	male	25	Yuma	791
19.	Domingo	male	28	Yuma	791
20.	Juan Miguel	male	11	Payuche	791
21.	Juan Nepomuceno	male	9	Payuche	791
22.	José María	male	11	Yuma	791
23.	Agustín	male	16	Yuma	791
24.	Griselda	male	18	Yuma	791
25.	José	male	12	Baja Cal.	791
26.	Luis	male	16	Yuma	792
27.	José Antonio	male	14	Palluche	793
28.	Antonio	male	12	Palluche	793
29.	María Antonia	female	13	Palluche	793
30.	José Leon	male	10	Palluche	793
31.	Soleda[d]	female	12	Yuta	793
32.	José Manuel	male	9	Yuta	793
33.	José Antonio	male	12	Yuta	793
34.	Guadalupe*	female (?)	10	Yuta	793
35.	Miguel	male	25	Yuma	794
36.	Domingo	male	12	Baja Cal.	794
37.	Mateo	male	3	Sonora	795

Explanation of asterisks: "Peladito" means "fool." The census taker identifies Angel as a "fulareño," or "stranger." The word "fulano" usually describes someone who lives far away. Guadalupe, meanwhile, could go to a male or female.

For good measure we add possible captives from the 1850 census (*Census of the County and City of Los Angeles California for the year 1850*, ed. Maurice Newmark and

Marco Newmark (Los Angeles: Times Mirror Press, 1929). 29–121. All captives come from within the Los Angeles city limits. We do not add captives who lived in the county portion of Los Angeles. The area covered by the Los Angeles municipality during the Mexican era differed from the territory administered by the city after the United States assumed control of California. Therefore, as the only accurate point of comparison, we stick with the city portion of the Mexican and American censuses.

	Name	Sex	Age	Origin	Page
1.	Martina	female	12	California	29
2.	Dolores	female	6	California	29
3.	María Carmel	female	16	California	30
4.	Tomás	male	14	California	30
5.	Estéban	male	15	California	30
6.	Bernarda	female	14	California	30
7.	Rafael	male	10	California	31
8.	Antonio	male	15	California	31
9.	José	male	45	California	31
10.	María Antonia	female	15	California	32
11.	Carlota	female	18	California	34
12.	Barsilo	male	18	California	34
13.	Benito	male	64	California	37
14.	Feliciana	female	13	California	40
15.	José Antonio	male	7	California	41
16.	Gabriela	female	11	California	41
17.	Adelaida	female	18	California	41
18.	María Antonia	female	16	California	43
19.	Celedonia	female	13	California	43
20.	Jésus	male	7	California	44
21.	Francisca	female	10	California	46
22.	Tomás	male	10	California	47
23.	Refugio	male	8	California	47
24.	Ramon[a]	female	18	California	49
25.	María Dolores	female	14	California	49
26.	Augustin [sic]	male	75	California	53
27.	Antonio	male	16	California	61
28.	Isidro	male	16	California	61
29.	Concepción	female	5	California	65
30.	María	female	3	California	65
31.	Marcos	male	14	California	66
32.	María	female	11	California	66

50. We have combined non-californio and Mexican households. People like Henry Dalton (40) and John Domingo (49) in the census had lived in Los Angeles for some time. They had become Mexican citizens and participated in city affairs. As for the Indians we count as captives, several selections may raise eyebrows because they seem a bit old and may be employees. However, after careful consideration, they could be captives. Two examples explain our reasoning. Basilio Váldez, for instance, (37) has Benito, a sixty-four-year-old Indian, working in the family home. Benito, no doubt old and tired probably could not do much around the family property. Perhaps he was

a captive who had been in the family for some time. But if he had a place in the family home, it was not his ability as a wage laborer that kept him on. Thus, any other Indian male who was forty and above, makes the list. John Domingo, a German or Dutch "ship-carpenter" who had come to Los Angeles in 1830—see Bancroft, *The History*, 2:782—employed Ramón[a], an eighteen-year-old woman. She could have been a domestic who hired herself out, but given the local passion for taking Indian women and children, chances are that she was a captive. Any other Indian woman who fits a similar profile figures in our calculations.

We give the names of the twenty dueños:

Master or Mistress	Possible Captives and their Age	Page
1. Eulogio Celis	Martina, 12	29
	Dolores, 6	
2. Carmen Johnson	María del Carmel, 16	30
	Tomás, 14	
3. Pio Pico	Estéban, 15	30
	Bernarda, 14	
	Jacinta, 25	
4. Antonio María Váldez	Rafael, 10	31
	Antonio, 15	
5. Isidro Alvarado	José, 45	31
6. Casildo Aguilar	María Antonia, 15	32
7. Julian Váldez	Carlota, 18	34
	Barsilo, 18	
8. Basillo (sic) Váldez	Benito, 64	37
9. Henry Dalton	Feliciana, 13	40
10. Ignacio Coronel	José Antonio, 7	41
	Gabriela, 11	
11. Francisco Figueroa	Adelaida, 18	41
12. Isabel Botella Guirado	María Antonia, 43	43
	Celedonia, 13	
13. Manuel Castillo	Jésus, 7	44
14. María Ignacia Amador	Francisca, 10	46
15. María Clara Reyes	Tomás, 10	
	Refugio, 8	47
16. John Domingo	Ramon[a], 18	49
17. Juan Sepúlveda	María Dolores, 14	49
18. Juan Sánchez	Augustin (sic), 75	53
19. Julian Chavis (sic)	Isidro, 16	61
20. Barsillo [sic] Jurado	Concepción, 5	65
	María, 3	
	Marcos, 14	66
	María, 11	

51. Of the thirty-two Indians we count as captives in 1850, another twenty-six could also qualify. Nonetheless, we cannot confirm the status of this latter group. Because each of the twenty-six is over eighteen and had learned some sort of trade—the census taker often identified them as laborers, suggesting they worked for a wage—they could

have come to the master on their own free will. If we add the extra Indians to our total, twenty-nine families, nearly fifteen percent of all angeleño households in Los Angeles (14.94 percent), may have had a captive. But we remain with the lower figure of ten percent. Moreover, we emphasize that we count households *within* Los Angeles. The 1850 census included communities, or ranchos, that sat nearly seventy miles to the south, a sweep of territory that did not sit within the jurisdiction of Los Angeles during the Mexican era.

52. 1836 census, 7.

53. 1836 census, 39.

54. 1844 census, 755.

55. 1844 census, 743.

56. At times, to give due credit, the surveyor made appropriate distinctions. In 1836, for example, the census taker met Francisco Arenas, a seven-year-old Yuma, and put him in the "Indio" section. See the 1836 census, 13, 56. Or, when the surveyor identified each person who lived in the home of Manuel Requena, he noted that Manuel Montezuma was an Apache. 1836 census, 8.

57. 1836 census, 9.

58. Archives of the Prefecture, Book A, May 11, 1832, Thomas Temple Collection, SCWH.

59. María Ruperta Martínez composed her will in 1849. Thomas Temple Collection Box 5, C-8, 6, Book Two, La Placita Records, SCWH.

60. Avila Family Papers, Juana Ballesteros will, Item A #5746–34, 1850, SCWH.

61. Bancroft, *The History*, 2:693.

62. 1850 census, Amador, (46); Reyes, (47); Ballesteros, (49). The evidence suggests that Isabel Guirado was Carmen's mother. See Bancroft, *The History*, 4:693.

63. 1850 census, 43.

64. Bancroft, *The History*, 4:693.

65. In a community where the grammar books and primers for children warned "God sees all . . . iniquity," some gente de razón who had read the admonition when young thought it was their duty to aid the meanest of heaven's creatures. For the quotation see the Coronel Collection, Grammar book #714, n.p, SCWH.

66. *A Manifesto to the Mexican Republic which Brigadier General José Figueroa, Commandant and Political Chief of Upper California presents on his conduct and that of José María de Híjar and José María Padrés as Directors of Colonization in 1834 and 1835*, ed. and trans. C. Alan Hutchinson, (Berkeley: University of California Press, 1978), 96.

67. Palomares, "Memoria," in Cook *Expeditions*, 201.

68. James Oakes, *The Ruling Race* (New York: Vintage Books, 1983), 153–91. Oakes modifies his views in a later work. See James Oakes, *Slavery and Freedom: An Interpretation of the Old South* (New York: Knopf, 1990). For more on the ideology of white slave owners, consult Edmund Morgan, *American Slavery, American Freedom* (New York: W.W. Norton, 1975). Also see, George Frederickson, *The Black Image in the White Mind* (New York: Harper Torchbooks, 1971).

69. Stanley Green *The Mexican Republic: The First Decade, 1823–1832* (Pittsburgh: University of Pittsburgh Press, 1981), 117–18.

70. 1836 census: Wilson was 36, p. 35; Africano, 71, p. 5.

71. Bancroft, *The History*, 5:778.

72. Lucia, the widow of Africano, married Gaspar Chávez on September 5, 1836. Africano lived long enough to see his name recorded in the 1836 census, but apparently died soon thereafter. Thomas Temple Collection, San Fernando Mission Records, Box 8, File I, p. 7.

73. Archives of the Prefecture, vol. 1, March 9, 1842, 618, Los Angeles City Clerk's Office.

74. *Alcalde Court Records, 1830–1850,* vol. 3, March 30, 1842, 686–89, SCWH.

75. LACA, vol. 2, May 6, 1844, 400, Sp.

76. Bancroft, *The History,* 5:624n. 2.

77. Pio Pico, "Historical Narrative," trans. Earl Hewitt, (Los Angeles: Dawson's Book Shop, 1960), 151–53.

78. Bancroft, *The History,* 4:68.

79. Bancroft, *The History,* 3:594n. 34.

80. Gerald Smith and Clifford Walker, *The Indian Slave Trade Along the Mohave Trail* (San Bernardino County Museum of Natural History, 1965), 10–11. The attack apparently was in 1844.

81. The *Romero Expedition,* Bean and Mason, 85.

82. In an aside, the first expedition retreated with Soto, the commander, dead with an arrow to the eye. Jack Holtermann, "The Revolt of Estanislao," *Indian Historian* 3, no. 1 (1970): 43–54.

83. Ibid.

84. Victor Prudon, "The Los Angeles Vigilantes," trans. Earl Hewitt, Bancroft Library, 9.

85. Bancroft, *The History,* 3:479–81n. 27.

86. Bancroft, *The History,* 5:310n. 22.

87. For a tabulation of captives, see note 49 above.

88. See Trexler, *Sex and Conquest,* esp., 12–63.

Chapter Five

1. For the "hombre nuevo," see Jean Franco, "En espera de una burguesía, la formación de la inteligencia mexicana en la epoca de la independencia," in *Actas VIII Congreso de la Asociacion Internacional de Hispanistas, Agosto 1983,* 21–36 (Madrid: Ediciones Ismo, 1986); For the "hombre positivo," see Charles Hale, *Mexican Liberalism in the Age of Mora, 1821–1853* (New Haven: Yale University Press, 1998), 337, 340. The discussion of the "hombre digno" appears in Anne Staples, "Alfabeto y catecismo, salvación del nuevo pais," *Historia Mexicana* 29, no. 1 (1979): 35–58. For a broader perspective, consult Stanley Green, *The Mexican Republic: First Decade 1821–1832* (Pittsburgh: University of Pittsburgh Press), 89–91.

2. Charles Hale, *Mexican Liberalism,* 13.

3. Simon Schama, *Citizens* (New York: Vintage Books, 1989), 186–286, 582–84.

4. For more on the development of the Mexican man during the independence era, see Jean Franco, "En espera de una burguesía,"33.

5. Ibid.

6. The question of French influence in Latin America is receiving more comment. See J. H. Elliot, "A Pan-American Flight," *New York Review of Books* (February 26, 2004): 38–40.

7. Michael Costeloe, *Church and State in Independent Mexico* (London: Royal Historical Society, 1978), 10–12.

8. To choose one of many examples, the list of men who won seats to the ayuntamiento in 1838 shows that each officeholder bears the title of "C" for "ciudadano" or "citizen." See LACA, vol. 3, December 30, 1837, 500, Sp.

9. Remember that Victor Prudon, a Frenchman once attached to the Híjar–Padrés expedition, wrote the vigilante appeal. Vignes, our friend from the 1846 petition, and two

French merchants, Luis Bouchet and Juan D. Meyer—each hispanicized his first name—signed the document penned by Prudon, their countryman. Save for Prudon, the vigilante secretary, Bouchet and Meyer held no political office, but perhaps they reminded the angeleño vigilantes of a grander revolutionary purpose. See Prudon's appeal, "Death to the Homicides," in Bancroft, *The History*, 2:186–90. For the original, see LACA, vol. 2, April 7, 1836, 86, Sp. For the Committees on Public Safety, see Simon Schama, *Citizens*, 753–60.

10. "God and Liberty," or in Spanish "Dios y Libertad," seemed most prevalent in the late 1820s and early 1830s. Zephyrin Engelhardt, the Franciscan priest who wrote several histories in the early twentieth century to defend California's missionaries from criticism, quotes Lucas Alamán to show the depth of French influence. Alamán, a prominent statesman, scholar, and conservative thinker in Mexico City, says that liberals in Mexico "endeavored to adopt the dating, style of address, and other usages after the manner introduced during the French Revolution." Such influences, we say, made their way north to California. For more, see Zephyrin Engelhardt, O.F.M., *The Missions and Missionaries of California* 4 vols., (San Francisco: James F. Barry Company, 1913), 3:208–9. Engelhardt adds that the legacy of the French Revolution sometimes addled the minds of the californios. Quoting Fray Narciso Durán, the Father President of the Missions in the 1830s, Engelhardt says that in the early years of Mexico's independence, "Jacobinism," the term describing the more radical elements of the Revolution, "dominated . . . the Mexican Republic," and as a consequence, California. See Engelhardt, *The Missions and Missionaries of California*, 4:107.

11. For more on the meaning of the French Revolution, one may read Isaiah Berlin, *The Crooked Timber of Humanity: Chapters in the History of Ideas*, ed. Henry Hardy (New York: Knopf, 1991). I am indebted to my colleague Molly McClain for bringing this point to my attention.

12. See Schama, *Citizens*, 162–73, for more on how some French revolutionaries venerated the ancients. Also, consult Hugh Honour, *Neo-Classicism* (Harmondsworth, England: Penguin, 1968).

13. For more on how classical images influenced Mexican culture after independence from Spain, see Justino Fernández, *El Arte del Siglo XIX en México* (México: Imprenta Universitaria, 1967), esp. 5–12. Also see D. A. Brading, *The First America, The Spanish Monarchy, Creole Patriots, and the Liberal State, 1492–1867* (Cambridge, England: Cambridge University Press, 1991), esp. 561–602. For a more thorough discussion on Aztecs and their appeal, see John Leddy Phelan, "Neo-Aztecism in the eighteenth century and the genesis of Mexican nationalism," in *Culture in History: Essays in Honour of Paul Radin*, ed. Stanley Diamond, 760–70 (New York: New York University Press, 1960). Also, consult D. A. Brading, *Myth and Prophecy in Mexican History* (Cambridge, England: Cambridge University Press, 1984), 41.

14. Lucas Alamán, "La sociedad mexicana," in *Espejos de discordias, la sociedad mexicana vista por Lorenzo de Zavala, José Luis Mora, y Lucas Alamán*, ed. Andrés Lira, 168–95 (Mexico, D.F.: SEP Cultura, 1984).

15. José Luis Mora, "Una vision de la sociedad mexicana," in *Espejos de discordias, la sociedad mexicana vista por Lorenzo de Zavala, José Luis Mora, y Lucas Alamán*, ed. Andrés Lira, 72–140 (Mexico, D.F.: SEP Cultura, 1984). .

16. Michael Costeloe, *The Central Republic in Mexico, 1835–1846, Hombres de Bien in the Age of Santa Anna* (Cambridge, England: Cambridge University Press, 1993), 56.

17. For more on Mexican art in the early nineteenth century, see Fausto Ramírez, "The Nineteenth Century" in *Mexico, Splendors of Thirty Centuries*, ed. Phillipe de

Montebello, 499–538 (New York: The Metropolitan Museum of Art and Boston: Bulfinch Press, 1990). As an example of a Mexican Indian appearing in a neo-classical guise, see the photograph of Manuel Vilar's sculpture of "The Tlaxcalan General Tlahuicole Doing Battle on the Gladiator's Stone of Sacrifice," in *Mexico, Splendors of Thirty Centuries*, 504.

18. Or more simply, "I know the ways of men." Antonio Coronel #510B, Agustin Zamorano primer, 5. SCWH.

19. Del Valle Collection, Box 13, Item #679, 5, 7. SCWH.

20. Antonio Coronel Collection, #510B, 6. SCWH.

21. José María Figueroa, *Manifesto to the Mexican Republic which Brigadier General José Figueroa, Commandant and Political Chief of Upper California presents on his conduct and on that of José María de Híjar and José María Padrés as Directors of Colonization in 1834 and 1835*, trans. and ed. C. Alan Hutchinson, 94, for translation; and in Spanish, 174 (Berkeley: University of California Press, 1978).

22. Los Angeles Ayuntamiento Archives, vol. 5, July 24, 1845, 145–46, Bancroft Library. The word comes from the Latin *hecatombe*, meaning a sacrifice of hundred or more living things. Thus says the *Diccionario de la Lengua Española* (Madrid: Real Academia Española, 1992), "Sacrificio de cien reses vacunas u otras víctimas, que hacían los antiguos a sus dioses." The word, rare in Spanish, seems to reflect classical learning, and for Cota to use it would suggest that he had read his share of the ancients.

23. Bancroft, *The History*, 5:138–39n. 21.

24. Michael Costeloe, *The Central Republic*, 12, 26.

25. "Register of citizens [vecindario] who can vote for the renewal of the ayuntamiento for the year of 1848," LACA, vol. 4, December 5, 1847, 970–79, Sp.

26. Anne Staples, "La lectura y los lectores en los primeros años de vida independiente," in *Historia de la lectura en Mexico* ed. Josefina Vásquez, 94–125 (Mexico, D.F.: Colegio de Mexico, 1986).

27. *Doctrina Cristiana con una exposicion por el maestro Hieronymo de Ripalda de la compania de Jesus*, ed. José Bravo Ugarte, S.J., (Mexico, D.F.: Buena Prensa, 1950), 29–31.

28. José Luis Mora, *Catecismo politico de la federación mexicana 1831*, Nettie Lee Benson Library, University of Texas, Austin.

29. Mora, *Catecismo*, 7. In 1833, José Gómez de la Cortina produced another, somewhat simpler catechism. Nine chapters, containing a total of sixty pages, spanned the pamphlet. In the first chapter, "On Society and the Government Which Results Therefrom," a question wonders, "What is a civil society?" The response intones: "It is the union of many people, who, though expressed in tacit agreement, pursues security and tranquility." In chapter three, "On Popular Juntas," a question asks how citizens vote. The response explains that, on the appointed day, people assemble "in good order to participate in national votes, or decide local matters." José Gomez de la Cortina, *Cartilla social o breve instrución sobre los derechos y obligaciones de la sociedad civil*, (Mexico, 1831), 3, 21. Nettie Lee Benson, University of Texas, Austin.

30. Antonio Coronel Collection, *Cartilla sobre cria de gusanos de seda*, n.p. 1831, #678, SCWH.

31. Ibid.

32. For all information on theater in California prior to 1846, see Nicolás Kanellos, *Mexican-American Theater: Legacy and Reality* (Pittsburgh: Latin American Literary Review Press, 1987), 89–94.

33. See the "Pastorela," in the Antonio Coronel Collection, Item #288A, SCWH.

34. LACA, vol. 3, "Fondo Municipal," September 27, 1836, 68, Sp.

35. LACA, vol. 3, "Fondo Municipal," October 4, 1836, 46, Sp. Antonio María Osio says that the "maromeros" (his spelling of the word), were a popular attraction. See Antonio María Osio, *The History of Alta California,* trans. and ed. Rose Marie Beebe and Robert M. Senkewicz, (Madison: University of Wisconsin Press, 1996), 142–43.

36. LACA, vol. 3, "Fondo Municipal," February 20, 1840, 127, Sp.

37. Antonio Magaña-Esquivel, 5 vols., *Teatro mexicano del siglo XIX* (México: Fondo de Cultura Economica, 1972),1:7–9, 17.

38. Ibid., 17–29.

39. Ibid., 8–9.

40. Ibid., 33.

41. Ibid., 17.

42. For more on women in Spanish-Mexican California and in the Mexican interior, see Antonia Castañeda, "Engendering the History of Alta California, 1769–1848: Gender, Sexuality and the Family," in *Contested Eden: California Before the Gold Rush,* ed. Ramón A. Gutiérrez and Richard Orsi, 230–59 (Berkeley: University of California Press, 1998); Antonia Castañeda, "Presidarias and Pobladoras: The Journey North and Life in Frontier California," *Renato Rosaldo Lecture Series Monograph 8* (Stanford: Stanford University Press, 1990–1991); Gloria Miranda, "Gente de Razón Marriage Patterns in Spanish and Mexican California: A Case Study of Santa Barbara and Los Angeles, *Southern California Quarterly,* 63, no. 1 (1981): 1–21; Mark A. Burkholder, "Honor and Honors in Colonial Latin America," in *The Faces of Honor: Sex, Shame and Violence in Colonial Latin America,* ed. Lyman L. Johnson and Sonya Lipsett-Rivera, 18–44 (Albuquerque: University of New Mexico Press, 1998); Silvia Arrom, *The Women of Mexico City, 1790–1857* (Stanford: Stanford University Press, 1985); Steve J. Stern, *The Secret History of Gender: Women, Men, and Power in Late Colonial Mexico* (Chapel Hill: University of North Carolina Press, 1995); Jean Franco, *Plotting Women: Gender and Representation in Mexico* (New York: Columbia University Press, 1989); Doris Summer, *Foundational Fictions: The National Romances of Latin America* (Berkeley: University of California Press, 1991); Francine Masiello, *Between Civilization and Barbarism* (Lincoln: University of Nebraska Press, 1992).

43. See, for example, Angustias de la Ord, *Occurrences in Hispanic California,* trans. and ed. Francis Price and William H. Ellison, (Washington D.C.: Academy of American Franciscan History, 1956). For more about the woman's voice in Mexican California, see Rosaura Sánchez, *Telling Identities, Californio Testimonios* (Minneapolis: University of Minnesota Press, 1995). Bancroft explains that he collected eleven recuerdos from californio women. He says de la Ord's reminiscence compares "with the best in [his] collection." See Bancroft, *The History,* 1:55.

44. Bancroft, *The History,* 3:495–96n. 26.

45. Bancroft, *The History,* 3: 486–87n. 10. Bancroft reproduces part of Luis Castillo Negrete's appeal to the Los Angeles ayuntamiento. Castillo Negrete, a Spaniard by birth who served the Mexican government as a judge in Monterey before heading south to Los Angeles, admittedly does not mention Alvarado by name, but there is no doubt about who he is describing. He says that, "foreign smugglers . . . have set up in Monterey the throne of anarchy." For more on Castillo Negrete's life, see Bancroft, *The History,* 3:466n. 24.

46. Bancroft, *The History,* 3:470–71n. 28.

47. Osio, *The History of Alta California,* 160.

48. Ibid.

49. Ibid., 162.

50. Ibid.

51. Ibid., 163.
52. Ibid.
53. Ibid., 160.
54. See Ramón Gutiérrez, *When Jesus Came the Corn Mothers Went Away,* (Stanford: Stanford University Press, 1992), 227–35, for more about the politics of marriage.
55. Ibid.
56. Some couples took their vows in the Plaza Church in Los Angeles, while others went to San Gabriel or San Fernando mission. See the tabulations in the Thomas Temple II Collection, Box #9, Files M-2, M-3. SCWH.
57. The following list features weddings with men who were at least ten years older than their wives. The information comes from the Thomas Temple II Collection, Box 9, Files M-2, M-3:

Couples	Date
1. Juan Pollorena, 32, marries María Joaquina Sepúlveda, 18	July 14, 1824
2. George Rice, 29, marries Catalina López, 16	November, 9, 1829
3. Manuel d'Oliviera, 31, marries Micaela Poyorena (Pollerena?)	January, 18, 1831
4. Casciano Carreon, 37, marries, María Josefa López, 22	January 21, 1831
5. Ramón de la Trinidad Orduño, 38, marries María Felíz, 15	May 2, 1833
6. Francisco Marquez, 36, marries María Roque Valenzuela, 19	July (?), 1834
7. Francisco Figueroa, 30, marries María Jésus Palomares, 16	November 11, 1834
8. Jordan Pacheco, 53, marries María de Jésus López, 30	May 15, 1835
9. Luis Arenas, 45, marries María Josefa Palomares, 20	January (?), 1837
10. Miguel Pryor, 32, marries María Teresa Sepúlveda, 14	October 24, 1837
11. Juan Domingo, 40, marries María Raymunda Felíz, 18	January 10, 1839
12. Francisco Castillo, (?), marries María del Carmen Peña, 15	August 29, 1839
13. Guillermo Stenner, 34, marries Andrea Duarte, 18	June 25, 1839
14. Joaquin López, 26, marries Mariana de Jésus Lara, 14	June 27, 1840

The following marriages come from the Thomas Temple II Collection, Box 5, Section B, File #1:

Couples	Date
15. Abel Stearns, 40, marries Arcadia Bandini, 14	June 22, 1841
16. Joaquin de los Rios y Ruíz, 36, marries Narcisa Alvarado, 15	October 15, 1841
17. Santiago Carpenter 32, marries María Domínguez, 18	June 28, 1844
18. Eduardo Callaghan, 30, marries María Antonia Silvas, 16	May 1, 1845
19. Santiago Boyle, 29 marries Joaquina Gallardo, 14	July 6, 1845
20. Francisco Plineo Temple, 25, marries Antonia Workman, 15	September 2, 1845

Here follow married couples where the wives were in their teens, but not necessarily ten years younger than their husbands. The first set come from Thomas Temple II Collection, Box, #9, Files M-2, M-3:

Couples	Date
1. Juan José Duarte, 22, marries María de los Angeles Serrano, 15	(?)
2. Antonio Acebedo, 21, marries María Soledad Reyes, 16	September 8, 1821
3. Miguel María Blanco, 21, marries María Rosario Guillen, 17	May 24, 1831

The next group comes from Thomas Temple II Collection, Box 5, Section B, File #1:

Couples	Date
4. Francisco Aranda, 24, marries María Jacinta Sánchez, 15	February 19, 1843
5. Julian Perdue, 25, marries María Luz Martínez, 17	May 3, 1845
6. Santiago Barton, 23, marries Margarita Roland, 17	May 3, 1845

58. Adrian Forsyth, *A Natural History of Sex: The Ecology and Evolution of Mating Behavior* (New York: Houghton-Mifflin, 1996), 92–94.

59. For more insight about the life of women in California before 1846, see Kathy Hughart, "The Women of Spanish and Mexican California," (master's thesis, University of San Diego, 1999).

60. Bancroft, *The History,* 5:732, and 3:631–32n. 1.

61. For a more thorough study on women's property rights in Los Angeles and environs, see Miroslava Chávez, "Mexican Women and the American Conquest in Los Angeles, From the Mexican Era to American Ascendance," (Ph.D. diss., University of California, Los Angeles, 1998), 51–53.

62. Ibid., 63. The number of women does not square with our count listing the proprietors of a rancho. But the point remains that women still managed a rancho during the Mexican period.

63. Thomas Temple II Collection, Pancho Rangel, "La vida de un ranchero." Box 2, File 22, 18, trans., SCWH. Rangel was ninety-five-years-old in 1935.

64. Coronel, *Tales of Mexican California,* 78.

65. "List of owners of agricultural land in the city of Los Angeles interested in the water of the community," LACA, vol. 4, 1848, 665, Sp. Here are the women:

First Section
Juana Alvarado
Dolores Sepúlveda
Luisa Avila
Ysabel Avila
Rosalia Pollorena

Third Section
Benancia Sotelo
Josefa Alvarado

Fourth Section
Josefa López
Josefa Cota
Dolores Urquidez
María del Rosario

In Spanish, a section would be a "manzana." Apparently no woman who owned property, and had to pay a fee to maintain the zanja, lived in section two.

66. LACA, vol. 3, "Fondo Municipal," from January 1 to June 30, 1836, 75–83, Sp.

67. In the account books for 1836, there is no record of Luisa Cota serving alcohol. Prudon, "The Los Angeles Vigilantes," trans. Earl Hewitt 1-12. Bancroft Library, University of California, Berkeley.

68. See the 1836 census, *The Historical Society of Southern California Quarterly,* 18, no. 3 (September–December, 1936): 667–730.

69. See the 1844 census, *The Historical Society of Southern California Quarterly* 42, no. 4 (December 1960): 360–414.

70. Figures tabulated from the 1850 census, *Census of the County and City of Los Angeles, California for the year 1850*, ed. Maurice Newmark and Marco Newmark (Los Angeles: The Times-Mirror Press, 1929).

71. Archives of the Prefecture (hereafter AP), Book "A," 1825–1850, May 25, 1840, 481–87. The case, though first heard in 1840, comes up for review five years later.

72. AP, vol. 1, May 6, 1842, 150–56. As a sidenote, the Bishop in Monterey protests the decision and says that only an ecclesiastical court can grant a divorce. He says that "higher authorities" need to revisit the case.

73. AP, Book "B" May 10, 1842, 632, June 7, 1842, 635, and Book "A" May 6, 1842, 651, and May 7, 1842, 685, trans. Incredibly, the case of Casilda Aguilar and Casilda Sepúlveda involve the same man, Teodoro Trujillo. It is possible that the person who recorded the information mixed up the names and that Casilda Aguilar is the same as Casilda Sepúlveda. But to look at the particulars of each case—Casilda Aguilar wants a divorce; Casilda Sepúlveda wants an annulment because she was forced into marriage—suggests that each woman is different. But why is Teodoro Trujillo present in both situations? Did the clerk make an error about the man's name? Or were there two Trujillos in Los Angeles? Bancroft says that in 1846 that there were a half a dozen men in Los Angeles with the name Trujillo. Perhaps in 1842—four years earlier—there were two Teodoro Trujillos. Bancroft, *The History*, 5:752.

74. AP, Book "A," May 6–16, 1842 631–"B," June 10–17, 1842, 632–35, trans.

75. Marie Northrop, 2 vols., *Spanish–Mexican Families of Early California: 1769–1850*, (New Orleans: Polyanthos, 1976) 1:289.

76. For incest, see Alcalde Court Cases, vol. 3, May 21, 1842, 729–42, "Sumaria contra Vicente Lorenzana por incesto." For abduction, see vol. 5, November 22, 1845, 1–20, "Criminal contra Anto. Reina por María Navarro." Seven cases featured men beating their spouses or female companions, see vol. 1, February 8, 1843, 890–917, "Criminal Esteban Lopez, esposa Doña Petra Varela"; vol. 2, July 5, 1841, 659–78, "Sumaria contra Acencio Alipas por golpes a Vitalicia"; vol. 3, March 31, 1842, "Sumaria contra Tomas Urquides por su mujer"; vol. 4, May 22, 1843, 142–44, "Resumen de Enrique Sepulveda con su esposa"; vol. 4, April 12, 1844, 870–91, "Criminal contra Mariano Silvas por golpes a su mujer"; vol. 4, May 14, 1845, 332–55, "Criminal contra Felis Gallardo por golpes a una india; and vol. 7, July 9, 1847, 465–92, "Causa instruida contra Juan Piera por tropelias a su esposa." Two other cases involved men accused of rape, see vol. 1, March 20, 1840, 506–62, "Criminal contra Cornelio Lopez por violencia a una mujer"; and vol. 4, December 31, 1844, 1179, "Criminal contra Domingo Olivas y Ygnacio Varelas por forzadores de una mujer casada." One dispute, which did not make the Alcalde court cases, saw Mariano Dominguez and Blanca Sotelo accuse each other of "incestuous conduct." See AP, vol. 1, September 4, 1841, 112–15, trans.

77. In the ayuntamiento proceedings, a register that would not usually contain a legal hearing, we see María Elizalde accuse her brother-in-law of "immoral" intentions, a case that does not appear in court records. LACA, vol. 1, August 13, August 24, August 27, 1840, 383–85, trans.

78. In other circumstances, when a marriage foundered or love went sour, the authorities often punished the woman. In 1836, for example, María del Rosario Villa left her husband to live with her lover, Gervasio Alipas. It could be that her husband, Domingo Felix was a tyrant, and she ran off with someone who promised her better treatment.

When city authorities forced Villa to return home and live with her husband, she plotted her escape. She helped kill her husband—Alipas the lover committed the murder—and the adulterous pair rode off. Angleño vigilantes, some calling the wife a "monster," eventually captured the pair. Angry that the ayuntamiento moved too slowly to make the two stand trial, the avengers organized again, and broke into the jail cell where sat Villa and her lover. The vigilantes shot the man first, and after making Villa wait a half-hour, they forced her to gaze upon her lover's bleeding form before cutting her down with a volley. See Prudon, "The Los Angeles Vigilantes," 14–15. Also see Bancroft, *The History,* 3:417–18.

79. AP, vol. 1, November 6, 1840, 237, trans.

80. AP, vol. 1, September 4, 1841, 112–15, trans. Admittedly, it is not quite clear what the prefect intends to do. Does he want the petitioner, Doña Benancia Sotelo, to submit the petition again? Or does he reject the petition altogether?

81. Many women, not just a prostitute of course, would bear a child out of wedlock. Some could have submitted to a lover, or even suffered rape. María Cañedo, for instance, gave birth to a girl in April 1826. She lists no father; perhaps María thought it was not worth it to bring the man to account. Eight months later, Ricarda Valenzuela had a boy, but she, too, decided not to name the father. For both examples, see Thomas Temple II Collection, Baptismal Records, Box 5, C(1–10). SCWH.

82. Other than Apolonaria Varelas, Dolores Varelas, Pilar Almenarez, Encarnación Navarro, Concepción Navarro, and Ricarda Valenzuela, the other possible prostitutes in Los Angeles between 1826 and 1849 could be: María del Rosario Urquidez (three children by separate fathers); Vibiana Lara (three children); and Dolores Valenzuela (two children). See Temple II Collection, Baptismal Records, Los Angeles Plaza Church, Box 5, C (1–10), in English. SCWH.

83. AP, vol. 1, January 31, 1842, 615, trans.

84. Dolores had another daughter, Juana, born on March 20, 1849, Temple II Collection, Box 5, Baptismal Records, C (1–10). SCWH.

85. For more on the woman's role in marriage, see Asunción Lavrin, "Sexuality in Colonial Mexico; A Church Dilemma," *Sexuality and Marriage in Colonial Latin America,* ed. Asunción Lavrin, 47–95 (Lincoln: University of Nebraska Press, 1989).

86. See Miroslava Chávez, "Mexican Women and the American Conquest in Los Angeles: From the Mexican Era to American Ascendancy," esp. 26–88.

87. For a quick study on the "powers of the weak," see Victor Turner, *The Ritual Process: Structure and Anti-Structure* (Ithaca: Cornell University Press, 1969), 94–130.

88. See Franco *Plotting Women,* 179–80.

89. For a more thorough discussion about women inculcating virtue in their children, see Franco, "En espera de una burguesía."

90. Mora, "Una vision de la sociedad mexicana," 112.

91. Franco, *Plotting Women,* 179–80.

92. Ibid., 283.

93. "Plana—work sheet—of Doña Francisca Sepúlveda, presented to her on the occasion of her fifty-second birthday on April 11, 1878," Sepúlveda/Mott Collection, Box #2, no file number, SCWH.

94. The family's lessons could continue into the years beyond. In the 1870s, Ascensión Sepúlveda wrote her aunt "Amada Tía" that, "I believe you will commend me to the Almighty so that I receive a good education and afterward, I will be able to provide counsel to my parents." See, the Sepúlveda/Mott Collection "Amada Tía," n.d.

95. Age calculated from Marie Northrop, *Spanish-Mexican Families of Early California*, 2 vols. (New Orleans: Polyanthos Press, 1976), 1:279.
96. Antonio Coronel Collection #679, *Panoramas de las señoritas* 10 (October 20, 1842), and 13 (November 10, 1842).
97. Jane Herrick, "Periodicals for Women during the Nineteenth Century," *The Americas* 14, no. 2 (1951): 135–44.
98. *Panoramas de las señoritas* 13 (November 10, 1842).
99. Ibid.
100. The letter could be some sort of facsimile in which a nineteenth-century writer wrote in the voice of a woman from antiquity. But the letter seems to be an authentic translation.
101. Ibid. All references to the Theana letter come from *Panoramas* 13 (November 10, 1842): 321.
102. Ibid., 322–23.
103. Herrick, "Periodicals for Women," 137.
104. Bancroft, *The History*, 2:429.
105. Marie Northrop, *Spanish-Mexican Families*, 279.
106. Osio, *History of Alta California*, 94.
107. Hale, *Mexican Liberalism in the Age of Mora*, 173. Also consult, Franco, *Plotting Women*, 179–80, and Anne Staples "Panorama educativo al comienzo de la vida independiente," in *Ensayos sobre la historia de la educacion en Mexico*, ed. Josefina Vasquez, 117–69 (Mexico: El Colegio de Mexico, 1981).
108. Staples, "Panorama educativo," 118–19.
109. Ibid.
110. Eight years earlier, according to the 1836 census, 1, Cayetano was eleven.
111. California Archives Department State Papers, vol. 33 *Juzgados y Naturalizacion*, July 18, 1844, 133, Bancroft Library, University of California, Berkeley.
112. Cayetano Arenas was the son of Luis Arenas, a Mexican emigrant from Sonora.
113. California Archives Department State Papers, vol. 33 January 11, 1844, 121–22, Bancroft Library, University of California, Berkeley.
114. See "Introduction" to *Al Bello Secso*, ed. Henry Wagner (Los Angeles: Zamorano Club, 1953).
115. Antonio Coronel Collection Primers printed by Agustín Zamorano, seven pages, n.d. #510b.
116. Bancroft, *The History*, 3:638.
117. Narciso Botello, "Anales del Sur," 178–79, Bancroft Library.
118. List of teachers possibly retained by the Los Angeles ayuntamiento:

1821: Doña María Ygnacia Amador taught at San Gabriel Mission (Doña Eulalia Pérez' "Memoria," Temple II Collection, Box #2, File 21, 3, trans.). Apparently, the priests at San Gabriel, not the ayuntamiento would have requested the services of Señora Amador.

1829: Enrique Sepúlveda earns mention as a "tutor" in the ayuntamiento records (LACA, vol. 3, November 18, 1829, 302–3, Sp.). Admittedly, "tutor" in Spanish could also mean "guardian."

1830: "Father-Teacher" (Padre-Maestro) Francisco González y Ybarra appears in Los Angeles (LACA, vol. 3, August 2, 1830, 361, Sp.)

1832: Vicente Moraga, chosen by the ayuntamiento to begin "the civilizing and moral training of the children," becomes a teacher in Los Angeles (LACA, vol. 2, January 19, 1832, 1, trans.).

1833:   Vicente Moraga teaches in February with Francisco Pantoja assuming respon-
        sibilities from April to September (LACA, "Fondo Municipal," vol. 3, January 1
        through September 30, 1833, 1).

1834:   Vicente Moraga teaches from February to May. Cristobal Aguilar takes over
        from May to August. In September, Francisco Grijalva assumes the teaching
        position (LACA, "Fondo Municipal," vol. 3, February 1 through December 31,
        1834, 8–10).

1835:   Vicente Moraga teaches until at least April (LACA, "Fondo Municipal," vol. 3,
        1835, 37). However, according to the LACA, vol. 2, January 31, 1835, 80–82, Sp.,
        Francisco Pantoja began the year as teacher only to resign on January 2, 1835. By
        the end of the month, on January 31, 1835, Cristobal Aguilar begins teaching.
        When Moraga begins as teacher is not clear.

1838:   Ygnacio Coronel agrees, at the request of the ayuntamiento, to teach until
        October 30, 1838. He will teach in the home of Father Alejo Bachelot. Bachelot,
        perhaps, lent Coronel a hand. In September José Zenon Fernández agrees to
        teach. The evidence does not say if Fernández helped Coronel or replaced
        Coronel (LACA, vol. 2, July 3, 1838, 575–76, Sp, and LACA "Fondo Municipal,"
        vol. 3, 1838, 118–19).

1839:   Ygnacio Coronel once again agrees to teach (LACA, vol. 2, February 16, 1839,
        615–16, Sp.)

1844:   "Señor Medina," the man we know as Lieutenant Guadalupe Medina teaches in
        Los Angeles (LACA, vol. 2, November 29–December 2, 1844, 647–51, Sp., and
        Bancroft, *The History*, 4:631n. 11).

1845:   Doña Luisa Arguello receives an invitation to teach in Los Angeles (LACA, vol.
        2, January 7, 1845, 1153, Sp.)

119. LACA, vol. 3, "Fondo Municipal," January 1, 1833 and November 30, 1833, 1–2, Sp.
120. LACA, vol. 3, "Fondo Municipal," 1834, 18, Sp.
121. California Archives, Department State Papers, vol. 33, January 1, 1844, 121–22, Sp.,
      Bancroft Library, University of California, Berkeley.
122. The school year in Los Angeles could vary.
123. Bancroft reports that Governor José María Echeandía, a lieutenant colonel, tutored
      his share of pupils in liberal thought. Bancroft, *The History*, 2:788. Captain Zamorano,
      meanwhile, the man who printed the primers, probably espoused liberal convictions,
      maybe even the radical notions of the yorkinos. Admittedly, we do not know for sure,
      but Zamorano's interest in education would suggest an enlightened, and maybe a lib-
      eral philosophy. However, sharing the same liberal ideas did not stop Zamorano from
      contesting Echeandía for the governor's seat in 1832.
124. LACA, vol. 3, July 13, 1838, 575–76, Sp.
125. Coronel, *Tales of Mexican California*, 7.
126. Narciso Botello, "Anales del Sur," 178–79.
127. California Archives, Department State Papers, vol. 33, February 29, 1844, 126, Sp.,
      Bancroft Library, University of California, Berkeley.
128. Ibid.
129. California Archives, Department State Papers, vol. 33, June 4, 1844, 131, Sp., Bancroft
      Library, University of California, Berkeley.
130. LACA, vol. 4, June 9, 1844, 705–6. The priests were Sebastian Bongiovanni, Juan
      Crisotomo, and Antonio Jimeno del Recio.

131. California Archives Department State Papers, vol. 33, July 18, 1844, 133, Bancroft Library, University of California, Berkeley.

132. Dorothy T. Estrada, "Las escuelas lancasterianas en la ciudad de Mexico, 1822–1842," *Historia Mexicana* 22, no. 4 (1973): 494–513.

133. By 1842, La compania lancasteriana supervised public instruction for the government and proposed to establish the mutual learning regimen throughout the nation. See Mary Kay Vaughan, "Primary Education and Literacy in Nineteenth Century Mexico, Research Trends" *Latin American Research Review* 25, no. 1 (1990): 31–66. Also see Estrada, "Las escuelas lancasterianas," 494–500.

134. LACA, vol. 3, February 1–2, 1844, and January 17, 1845, 394–95, Sp.

135. California Archives, Department State Papers, vol. 33, July 18, 1844, 133. Bancroft Library, University of California, Berkeley.

136. For more on the purpose of the Lancaster method see David Hogan, "The Market Revolution and Disciplinary Power: Joseph Lancaster and the Psychology of the Early Classroom System," *History of Education Quarterly* 29, no. 3 (Fall 1989): 381–417. Also see Estrada, "Las escuelas lancasterianas," for more on how Mexican reformers used the system in the early nineteenth century.

137. For a discussion on the spectacle—which we alter a bit—see Michel Foucault, *Discipline and Punish*, trans. Alan Sheridan, (New York: Vintage Books, 1995), 32–69, and 195–252.

138. For more on the conscience and its relation to authority, see Ibid., 135–69.

139. The substance of the recitations only supported the teacher's intent to drill good habits, and, it was hoped, responsible conduct into his charges. See Anne Staples, "Alfabeto y catecismo, salvación del nuevo pais," *Historia Mexicana* 29, no. 1 (Julio 1979): 35–58. Also examine Anne Staples, "La lectura y los lectores en los primeros años de vida independiente." For more on the logic of the Lancaster system, see Hogan, "The Market Revolution and Disciplinary Power."

140. According to the 1844 inventory of a Lancaster school, the instructor, no doubt Lieutenant Medina, had thirty-six primers, eleven "second readers" (possibly material for what we call now second grade), and fourteen Ripalda catechisms.

141. Antonio Coronel Collection, #714, primer from between 1840–1850, no title, n.p. SCWH.

142. See the *Panoramas de las señoritas* magazines mentioned above for comment on the human body's relation to proper conduct and behavior.

143. Coronel primer #714.

144. Ibid.

145. Ibid.

146. Ripalda's *Doctrina* could also serve as a way to remind children of their moral and religious obligations.

147. Del Valle Collection Box 13, #679, no title, SCWH.

148. Ibid.

149. Ibid.

150. *La Estrella*, March 13, 1852, Benjamin Hayes Scrapbooks, vol. 43, 219, Bancroft Library, University of California, Berkeley.

151. Osio, *The History of Alta California*, 256n. 48.

152. See Andrew Rolle, *California, A History* (Wheeling, Illinois: Harlan Davidson, 2003), 61–67.

153. Osio, *History of Alta California*, 246.

Bibliography

A Word on Sources

For secondary sources, interested scholars can scan the notes to find the titles for books and articles. As for the primary sources, I list items of interest and show where they can be found.

PUBLISHED WORKS

Bandini, Juan. *Noticia estadística de la alta California, 1831.* Documentos oficiales para la historia de Mexico, vol. 4. Mexico: Archivo General de la Nación.

Blanco, Miguel (Michael White). *California All the Way Back to 1828.* Los Angeles: Dawson's Book Shop, 1956.

Carrillo, Carlos. *Exposition Addressed to the Chamber of Deputies of the Congress of the Union by Señor Don Carlos Antonio Carrillo, Deputy for Alta California Concerning the Regulation and Administration of the Pious Fund.* Translated and edited by Herbert Ingram Priestley. San Francisco: John Henry Nash, 1938.

Cook, Sherburne. *Expeditions to the Interior of California, Central Valley, 1820–1840.* Berkeley: University of California Press, 1961.

Coronel, Antonio. *Tales of Mexican California.* Translated by Diane de Avalle-Arce. Edited by Doyce Nunis. Santa Barbara: Bellerophon Books, 1994.

Engelhardt, Zephyrin, O. F. M. *The Missions and Missionaries of California.* 4 vols. San Francisco: James F. Barry Co., 1913.

Figueroa, José María. *Manifesto to the Mexican Republic which Brigadier General José Figueroa, Commandant and Political Chief of Upper California presents on his conduct and on that of José María de Híjar and José María Padrés as Directors of Colonization in 1834 and 1835.* Translated and edited by C. Alan Hutchinson. Berkeley: University of California Press, 1978.

Geiger, Maynard, O.F.M. *As the Padres Saw Them: California Indian Life and Customs as Reported by the Franciscan Missionaries.* Santa Barbara: Santa Barbara Mission Archive Library, 1976.

Hammond, George P. *The Larkin Papers: Personal, Business, and Officia Correspondence of Thomas Oliver Larkin, Merchant and U.S. Consul in California*. 10 vols. Berkeley: University of California Press, 1951–1968.

Hoffman, Ogden. *Report of Land Cases Determined in the United States District Court for the Northern District of California*. San Francisco: Numa Hubert, 1862.

Layne, J. Gregg. "The First Census of the Los Angeles District, Padrón de la ciudad de Los Angeles y su jurisdicción, Año 1836." *Historical Society of Southern California Quarterly* 18, no. 3 (1936): 667–730.

Librado, Fernando. *Breath of the Sun, Life in Early California as Told by a Chumash Indian, Fernando Librado to John Harrington*. Edited by Travis Hudson. Ventura: Malki Museum Press, 1979.

Lira, Andrés. *Espejos de discordias, la sociedad mexicana vista por Lorenzo Zavala, José Luis Mora y Lucás Aláman*. Mexico: SEP Cultura, 1984.

Lugo, José del Carmen. "Life of a Rancher." Translated and edited by Helen Pruitt Beattie. *Historical Society of Southern California Quarterly* 32, no. 3 (1950): 185–236.

Newmark, Marco and Maurice Newmark. *Census of the County and City of Los Angeles, California for the year 1850*. Los Angeles: The Times-Mirror Press, 1929.

Northrop, Marie. "The Los Angeles Padrón of 1844." *Historical Society of Southern California Quarterly* 42, no. 4 (1960): 360–414.

Northrop, Marie. *Spanish-Mexican Families of Early California: 1769–1850*. 2 vols. New Orleans: Polyanthos, 1976.

Osio, Antonio María. *The History of Alta California, A Memoir of Mexican California*. Translated and edited by Rose Marie Beebe and Robert Senkewicz. Madison: University of Wisconsin Press, 1996.

Pico, Pio. *Historical Narrative*. Translated by Earl Hewitt. Los Angeles: Dawson's Book Shop, 1960.

Reid, Hugo. *The Indians of Los Angeles County, Hugo Reid's Letters of 1852*. Edited by Robert Heizer. Los Angeles: The Southwest Museum.

Ripalda, Hieronymo. *Doctrina cristiana con una exposicion por el maestro Hieronymo Ripalda de la compania de Jésus*. Edited by José Bravo Ugarte, S.J. Mexico, D.F.: Buena Prensa, 1950.

Romero, José. *Diaries and Accounts of the Romero Expedition in Arizona and California*. Translated and Edited by Lowell John Bean and William Mason. Los Angeles: Ward Richie Press, 1962.

Russell, Kell. "Regulations for the Cosmopolitan Company." *Historical Society of Southern California Quarterly* 28, no. 1 (1946): 143–75.

Ord, Angustias de la. *Occurrences in Hispanic California*. Translated and edited by Francis Price and William H. Ellison. Washington D.C.: Academy of American Franciscan History, 1956.

UNPUBLISHED OR RARE MATERIALS

BANCROFT LIBRARY, UNIVERSITY OF CALIFORNIA, BERKELEY

Alvarado, Juan Bautista. *History of California*. 5 vols. Translated by Earl Hewitt. 1876. MS.

Bancroft Research Notes. MS.

Botello, Narciso. "Anales del sur." 1870 (?) MS.

Bojórquez, Juan. "Recuerdos sobre la historia de California." 1877. MS.

Gómez, Vicente. "Lo que sabes sobre cosas de California." 1876. MS.

Hayes, Benjamin. "Scrapbooks." 138 vols. MS.
Hayes, Benjamin. "Notes on California Affairs."
Los Angeles Ayuntamiento Archives. 5 vols. MS.
    Padrón, Los Angeles, [1818?]. De la Guerra Documents.
San Diego Ayuntamiento Archives. 2 vols. MS.
Sepúlveda, Ygnacio. "Historical Memorandum to Hubert Howe Bancroft."
    Translated by Earl Hewitt. 1874. MS.
Prudon, Victor. "Los Angeles Vigilantes." Translated by Earl Hewitt. MS.
Vallejo, José de Jésus. "Reminicencias historicas de California." 1875. MS.
Vallejo, Salvador. "The Origin of the Californian Aborigines." Translated by Earl
    Hewitt. 1870 (?) MS.

CHICANO STUDIES LIBRARY, UNIVERSITY OF CALIFORNIA, BERKELEY
    El Clamor Público (1855–1859). Microfilm.

LOS ANGELES CITY CLERK'S OFFICE
    Los Angeles City Archives (Ayuntamiento records in Spanish)
        El Fondo Municipal, vol. 3. 1–114.
        Invitation to honor the Virgin of Guadalupe in 1838, vol. 3, 390.
        Mass meeting to debate political question in 1838, vol. 2, 552–55.
        Padrones of voters for 1835 and 1838, vol. 3, 526–669.
        Padrones for 1836 and 1844 (censuses), vol. 3 1/2.
        Padrón of Vigilantes in 1836, vol. 2, 188–90.
        Padrón of voters in 1848 and their ability to read and write, vol. 4, 970–79.
        Padrón of Proprietors and their *peones* in 1848, vol. 4, 665.
    Los Angeles Archives of the Prefecture
    Abel Stearns Records
        Miscellaneous Documents. 1850s.

NETTIE LEE BENSON LIBRARY, UNIVERSITY OF TEXAS, AUSTIN
    *Colección de los principales trabajos en que se ha ocupado la junta nombrado
        para meditar y proponer al supremo gobierno los medios mas necesarios para
        promover el progreso de la cultura y civilización de la Alta y Baja California.*
        Mexico, 1827.
    Cortina, José Gómez de la. *Cartilla social o breve instrución sobre los derechos y
        obligaciones de la sociedad civil.* Mexico, 1831.
    Mora, José Luis. *Catecismo politico de la federación mexicana.* 1831.
    Zavala, Lorenzo. *Juicio imparcial sobre los acontecimientos de México en 1828 y
        1829.*
    Valentín Gómez Farías Papers.
        Anonymous. *Canción sobre el amor del trabajo.* n.d.
        Fernández, José to Francisco Elorriaga. October 13, 1833. MS.
        Gómez, Valentín Farías to Don Manuel González Cosio. February 25, 1848.
            MS.
        Híjar, José María to José Figueroa. October 23, 1834.

Seaver Center for Western History, Los Angeles County Museum for Natural History

Los Angeles Prefect Records (or Archives of the Prefecture).

Alcalde Court Records, 1830–1850. 7 vols. MS.

Avila Family Papers

Anonymous. "Love Poem." Item A. #5796–55, #38j.

Anonymous. "Poem." Item A. 5796, # 38g.

The Will of Juana Ballesteros. Item A. #5746–34.

Antonio Coronel Collection

Ayuntamiento miscellanea. Files 16 and 17.

"Pastorela." #288A.

Panoramas de las señoritas. October 20 and November 10, 1842. #679.

School Primer. #714.

School lesson. #663-A 5.

Yllanes, Tomás. *Cartilla sobre cria de gusanos.* Mexico: 1831. #678.

Agustín Zamorano Primer. #510B.

Del Valle Collection

Anonymous. "Poem to Mother." Item #441. n.d.

School Primer. Box 13. Item #679. 1840s (?)

Hugo Reid Collection

"Dissertation on Cockroaches." n.d.

"Anecdote of a Lawyer." n.d.

San Joaquin to Mr. Editor. n.d.

Sepúlveda/Mott Collection

"Amada Tia." Letter from Asención Sepúlveda to María Serrano. n.d.

Francisco Avila. "Coplas." Box #1, #747 a, b.

Marriage dispensation for José Antonio Carrillo and Francisca Sepúlveda. Box #2. n.d.

Plana of Doña Francisca Sepúlveda. 1878. Box #2.

Thomas Temple II Collection

Avila, Juan. "Historia de california," as told to Thomas Savage. Box 2, File #8.

Baptismal Record. Box 5, C (1–10).

Diligencias. Box 9. Files M-2, M-3.

García y Lugo, Felipe Santiago. "Memoirs of Don Felipe Santiago García y Lugo as told to Alexander Taylor in 1854." Box #2, File 1.

Maitorena, José Joaquin to Padre [Tomás] Sánchez, September 25, 1828. Box 2, File #25.

Olivera, Diego. "Memoirs of Diego Olivera" as told to Alexander Taylor. 1864. Box #2, File 19.

Palomares, José Francisco. "Memorias de Don José Francisco Palomares," as told to Thomas Savage. Box 2, File #28.

Plaza Church Death Records. Box 5, C (1–10).

Vejar, Pablo. "Recuerdo de un viejo" as told to Thomas Savage. Box 2, File #30.

Rangel, Pablo, "La vida de un ranchero." (Also "La vida de un vaquero.") Box 2, File #27.

Index

Angeles of, 30, 36; ranchos and, 71; skin color and, 55–59, 92, 112; troopers, 120, 121, 123–24; war and, 100–117, 121, 222n. 7. *See also Angeleños; californios*

Gente de razón and identification with Indians: class and, 102–3; crime and, 90; equality and, 104; mixed race marriages and, 92, 95; race and, 100–101, 112, 122, 222n. 14; "sameness" and, 89–90; sex and, 90–91, 92–94, 96–99; war and, 100–117, 143

Gente de razón relations with Indians, 19–26; children of, 98–99; cooperation between, 108–11, 115–16, 200n. 76; dislike between, 48, 89, 141; distinctions between, 89; domestics and, 96–97, 142; extermination and, 147; fear and, 61–64, 135–36; fiestas and, 32, 35, 54, 90; mistreatment and, 38–40, 119–21; segregation and, 20, 59–60; sexual, 20, 32, 90, 92–99, 109, 136; social status and, 92; violence and, 119–21; war and rebellion and, 100–117, 119. *See also Angeleños' relations with Indians*

Gente de razón women, 91; Indian captives and, 133–34, 137, 142, 228n. 50, 229n. 62. *See also Angeleño women*

Gómez, Vincent (*El Capador*), 44, 225n. 48

Gómez Farías, Valentín, 44, 205n. 46

González, Captain Miguel (*el macaco*), 114–15, 221n. 108

Guirado, Isabel, 133–34, 229n. 62

Guirado, Rafael, 80, 197n. 50, 211n. 95

Gutiérrez, Governor Nicolas, 95–96, 98, 141; Alvarado and, 163

Hale, Charles, 148

Hernández, Cornelio, 116

Herrick, Jane, 175

Hidalgo, Father Miguel, 101; army of, 101–2, 103, 106–8, 115

Higuera, Bernardo, 131–32

Híjar, José, 7, 108–9, 154

Híjar-Padrés colony, 7, 154; education and, 181, 183

Híjar-Padrés expedition: Governor Figueroa and, 153–54, 160, 219n. 62; José Zenon Fernández and, 209n. 76; Valentín Gómez Farías and, 44; Victor Prudon and, 230n. 9

hijos naturales, 98–99

hombre digno, 148

hombre nuevo: Angeleño children and, 177; *Angeleño* men and, 149–61; *Angeleño* women and, 161, 176; classicism and, 156–57, 160; education and, 156–57, 160, 187; French Revolution and, 149–52; genesis of, 149–52; importance of parents to, 149–50, 173; liberals and, 148, 156–57, 174–75, 176; Mexican liberalism and, 148–50; Mexican theater and, 159–60

hombre positivo, 148

huerfanos/as (orphans): Indian, 127, 131, 132–33, 143, 222n. 33, 224n. 48. *See also* Indian children; Indian children captives

Huxley, Aldous, 98

Ibarra, Juan, 123

Ignacio de Jerúsalem, 37

Indian captives, 124–44, 225n. 49; Apache, 130, 225n. 49, 229n. 56; benefits of taking, 134–44; Canieyo, 50, 225n. 49; Cayego, 50, 225n. 49; and censuses (*see* censuses); children (*see* Indian children captives); demand for, 139; *gente de razón* women and (*see gente de razón* women); girl, 129, 134; local, 137; men, 131; New Mexican raiders and, 127–28, 137; origins of, 137, 224n. 48; Paiute, 127–28, 137, 138, 142; *tulareño*, 127, 130, 224n. 48, 225n. 49; Ute, 128; women, 129, 131–32, 136, 142–43, 228n. 50; Yaqui, 225n. 49; Yuma, 130, 142, 224n. 48, 225n. 49; Yuta, 130

Indian children: domestics, 127, 131–32, 143; mixed race, 98–99; orphans, 127, 131, 132–33, 143, 222n. 33, 224n. 48; selling of, 127–28; servants, 129–30, 132, 134, 136, 142–43; soldiers and, 128

Indian children captives: censuses and, 223n. 33, 224n. 48, 228n. 50; Mohave, 128; New Mexican traders and, 127–28, 129; Paiute, 127–28; passing as *gente de razón*, 131–33; as servants, 129–30, 132, 134, 136, 142–43; soldiers and, 128; Yuma, 130. *See also* Indian captives

Indian converts (neophytes): *Angeleños* and, 36–37, 40, 41; censuses and, 30–31; control of, 103–4, 121; disease and, 61–62; domestics, 137, 217n. 27;

Mexico: 1824 Constitution of, 37, 92, 101; education in, 178; equality and, 39, 58; instability in, 13–14; liberalism in (see Mexican liberalism); northern territories of, 8; relations with Angeleños and (see Angeleños); theater troupes from, 157–62, 176; work ethic in, 43–48

Mexico City, 68

Mexico Libre, 158, 160

Meyer, Juan D., 231n. 9

Micheltorena, Manuel, 114

Missionaries, 214n. 131, 224n. 48, 231n. 10; Indians and, 103; provincial government and, 82

Missions: colonization and, 5; Indian converts and, 5, 37, 39; Mexican independence and, 5–6; secularization of (see secularization of California missions); Spain and, 5–6

Mohave Indians, 106, 128, 140, 224n. 48

Monterey, California, 2, 3; as capital, 67; governors in, 11–12; penal colony in, 44; U.S. takeover of, 12

Montesquieu, 3, 192n. 8

Mora, José Luis, 73, 102, 152, 156, 173

Morillo, Justo, 169

Navarro, Concepcíon, 171, 237n. 82

Negrete, Luis Castillo, 197n. 53, 233n. 45

New Mexico: raiders from, 113; settlers from, 7; traders, 127–28, 137

Northrop, Marie, 169, 199n. 75

Oakes, James, 136, 138–39, 142

Olivera, Diego, 93

oraciones, 86

Ord, E. O. C., 64

Ortega, Francisco Luis, 158

Ortega, Ignacio, 139

Ortega, Vincente, 81

Osio, Antonio María: *cholos* and, 114; Estanislao and, 105; Indians in war and, 110; as officeholder, 195n. 38, 196n. 50; *recuerdos* of, 10, 41, 95, 109, 188, 233n. 35; women and, 162–65, 173–74, 176–77

Pacheco, Pablo, 141, 196n. 40

Pacheco, Romualdo, 10, 141

Padrés, José María, 45, 154

Padrés, María, 7

padrónes, 21, 200n. 84; 1835, 22, 200n. 84; 1838, 22, 200n. 84; 1847, 155; 1848, 125–26, 133

Paiutes, 31, 40; captives, 127–28, 137, 138, 224n. 48

Palomares, Ignacio, 211n. 95

Palomares, José Francisco, 54, 109; Indian captives and, 135, 221n. 1; Indian raiders and, 120–23

Panoramas de las señoritas, 174–75, 240n. 142

Pantoja, Francisco, 63, 180, 197n. 50

Pardo, Roberto, 112

Pastorelas, 158

Payeras, Father Mariano, 105

Paz, Octavio, 194n. 28

Peña, Cosme, 65, 140

Peninsulares, 43

peones, 125; captive, 133–34

Pico, Pio, 112, 140, 154, 161

Piña, Joaquin, 78, 110, 121, 129

Poblanos, 10

Pollorena, Juan, 91

Pollorena, María Antonia, 22, 200n. 75, 85

Pollerena, María Gabriella, 66, 133, 168

Presidios, 6–7

Priests: control of Indians by, 103; excess and restraint and, 81–85; flagellation and, 85–86, 152, 215n. 149; Franciscan, 84, 85–86; in Los Angeles, 84; Indian women and girls and, 97–98; power of, 5; as teachers, 180, 181

proletarios: Indians as, 102–3

Property ownership: *Angeleños and*, 23–25; censuses and, 25, 75; *gente de razón* and, 34

Prudon, Victor, 24, 214n. 134, 231n. 9; Híjar-Padrés expedition and, 230n. 9; as teacher, 68, 181; vigilantes and, 23, 141, 168, 230n. 9

Pryor, Miguel, 167, 199n. 75; time and, 77

pueblitos, 20

Race: *Angeleños* and, 53–60. See also skin color; whiteness

Racial equality: liberalism and, 39, 42, 100–101; problems of, 101

Racial segregation: Indian fiestas and, 59–62

Ramírez, Bernardo, 91

Ramírez, Francisco, 47

2816